# CHRISTIAN APOLOGETICS

# Christian Apologetics

by

## J. K. S. REID

T.D., M.A., D.D.

Professor of Christian Dogmatics
in the University of Aberdeen

D. Edmond Hiebert
Collection

WILLIAM B. EERDMANS PUBLISHING COMPANY
GRAND RAPIDS, MICHIGAN

This U. S. edition is published
by special arrangement with
Hodder and Stoughton Limited

Library of Congress Catalog Card Number: 71-127632

First U.S. edition, July 1970

Printed in the United States of America

# CONTENTS

# CHRISTIAN APOLOGETICS

# INTRODUCTION: What is Apologetics?

What on earth is Apologetics? Everyone understands the meaning of the word apology. It means variously the admission of an offence committed, a declaration that no offence was intended, and also an explanation or vindication. The last sense is less usual than the others but makes closer contact with the root meaning of the Greek from which the word comes. This suggests simply a "saying away" of something. Though we may find it hard to bring ourselves to make an apology we have no dislike of the thing itself. However, it is rather different with the cognate word apologetic. Turned into adjectival form the idea is weighted distastefully. It can keep its place high up the slope, but at the lower end it keeps company with the contemptible humbleness of Uriah Heep. When the adjectival form is used as a noun and we talk of an apologetic, the more pejorative sense is often read into it: if there is need for apologetic, there must be some flaw, fault or weakness to be excused.

At the very beginning of this study we must divest ourselves entirely of all such prejudice. If usage has tended to load the words unattractively, it has not extinguished other and more purely original meanings, and these we ought to rescue, restore and employ. Essentially apology means a defence. More precisely it carries the meaning of a speech made in defence. This is important, for it indicates that the context implied is not in the first instance military but judicial. In what follows military metaphors will occur frequently. But it must be remembered that they are no more than metaphors. No doubt both on the battlefield and in court the objective is victory over the opponent. But the victory is quite different in each case. In the one it means destroy, in the other convince. A host of other differences are immediately implied: clearly weapons, tactics and means will all differ greatly, though no doubt basic human qualities like courage, resolution, and nerve will be equally valuable in both cases.

A fairly obvious distinction exists between apology and apologetics. An apology is the defence offered in reply to a specific attack, accusation or charge. Justin Martyr writes his *1st and 2nd Apologies* to counter the accusations of immorality that pagans were passing round against Christians. Origen in his *contra Celsum* undertakes to repel the charges Celsus had made in writing against Christianity. In a much later age Bishop Butler in his *Analogy* embarks on a famous defence of Christianity against those who disparaged revelation. On the other hand Apologetics (hereafter with a capital initial letter) ought strictly to be the science of apology. Properly speaking it would then be the study of no more than the principles underlying the correct defence of the Christian faith, the "defence of Christianity reduced to a system". It is doubtful whether such a science in any pure sense would be possible or useful or interesting. Apologetics has something to do with defence. But defence is always defence against something that attacks or accuses; and this can and must be done in specific ways. The principles of Christian defence can be distilled only from or in view of actual situations in which defence is offered. Hence there are two ways in which the skeleton principles of Apologetics can be clothed in decent flesh and blood and given life and usefulness. One could address himself resolutely to the contemporary situation and, summoning as much of the past story of the defence of Christianity as seems useful, outline the way in which Christianity may be appropriately defended in the present day. This is the path followed by two well-known apologetic works in English—and there have not been so many all told: A. B. Bruce's *Apologetics*—Edinburgh, 1892, and A. Richardson's *Christian Apologetics*—London, 1947. The other method is historical: the attempt would be made to outline the actual ways in which Christianity, faced with particular situations which called for defence, responded to the challenge and with what results. In such a study at least some of the principles of apology ought to become clear; and from such an account at least some help may be derived for the defence of Christianity today, facing as it does rather different charges and attacks. At all events it is this method that has been asked for and is adopted here.

If Apologetics consists essentially of defence, some questions arise that should be given some preliminary attention. The first question is: what does Apologetics defend? The simple answer is given in words from Scripture where Jude refers with some precision to an apologetic situation and appeals to his correspondents "to join the struggle in defence of the faith, the faith which God entrusted to his people once and for all" (Jude 3). This is not a formula that settles everything. If it were, faith would not be a living thing: the faith would be simply a number of propositions, and the faith that believed them would dwindle into mere assent. Since it is not, areas of perplexity emerge where it is difficult to say what should or should not be regarded as belonging to the faith, and we have the whole vexed question of development of the faith upon our hands, together with the intriguing question about the relationship between substance of doctrine and its formulation. This continuing discussion must be short-circuited here. There is a central core of matter witnessed to in Scripture which fans out as its implications are discerned under the impact of circumstances. Both core and periphery are important, but not equally important. It has been the office of the Church faithfully to transmit the core; in order to do so it has constructed the periphery. Without the periphery the core would not be understood; and without the core the periphery would have no purpose. The situation is not dissimilar to the relationship between Shakespeare's text and Shakespearean commentary. Two things follow. The first is that those who practise Apologetics should be on their guard against diverting attention and energy to defending peripheral at the expense of central matters. The other is that in defending the centre and repelling attacks upon it the significance of the central core unfolds. Apologetics is rarely purely negative in character: its encounter with unbelief pays handsome dividends of richer understanding of Christian faith. It must also be remembered that faith points away from itself—as indeed the Bible also does—to Jesus Christ. The Christian faith is worthwhile defending or commending only because it indicates Jesus Christ.

A second question: can Apologetics be faithful to the faith? *Tradittori traduttori*, says the Italian proverb—transmission is inseparable from treason. At least it indicates the presence of a tension and the need for alertness. St. Paul is conscious of the tension: "if I still sought men's favour, I should be no servant of Christ . . . the gospel you heard me preach is no human invention" (Gal. 1. 10f); but again: "I have become everything in turn to men of every sort . . . this I do for the sake of the gospel" (1 Cor. 9.22f). And he is also on the alert: the Gospel preached cannot be "at variance" with the Gospel received (Gal. 1.9). At many turnings of the road ahead we shall find ourselves asking: was the Gospel at this point transmitted intact?

The third question is: against what or whom is the defence conducted? Obviously different answers must be given at different points in the story, and the distinction already made between apology and Apologetics is involved. Origen had a specific opponent in mind when writing his *contra Celsum*, and accordingly particular misunderstandings and slanders. But what is to be said of St. Thomas Aquinas' *Summa contra Gentiles*? This work is not directed against any clearly specified opponent, but is designed rather to clarify the general and fundamental certainties of the Christian faith, so that Christian faith may better understand itself. Here and in other similar instances Apologetics addresses itself not specifically to those who have declared hostility to Christianity but to men in general, in the hope that they will be induced to give Christianity "a fair hearing."[1] We must simply recognize the fact that Apologetics has been practised in both senses. A related question arises, whether Apologetics has as its selected audience believers, or enquirers, or confessed unbelievers. Precisely *cui bono*? Here the answers differ again. There is general agreement that Apologetics as such and alone does not do the work of converting the confessed unbeliever. Apologetics is after all argument, and "it does not please God to convert men by argument." At the same time the systematic dismantling of the reasons upon which unbelief is founded cannot but do something to prepare the passage into belief for those who do not deliberately entrench themselves in dogmatic unbelief.[2] Apologetics in this sense is a *praeparatio evangelii*. If the unbeliever is in any sense an enquirer, then Apologetics has something to offer him. At the other extreme Apologetics can hardly be purely an exercise for the benefit of Christians as such and alone, "by Christians for Christians."[3] This would be theological narcissism. Apologetics must allow itself to be taught by the doubts and difficulties arising from whatever source. In any case the distinction that divides belief from unbelief very rigidly is unrealistic. It is a singular Christian who does not have the seeds of doubt within himself. If these are answered the answer holds good for unbelief that entertains similar doubts. In this area Apologetics is not very different from Dogmatics: the clear systematic statement of what faith holds (which is Dogmatics) cannot but fortify faith already held, and at the same time dissipate the fringe of doubts with which it may find itself edged; but in doing so it is doing the work of Apologetics.

A fourth question similarly complex concerns how the defence is to be conducted. It has just been said that there is no absolute distinction between Apologetics and Dogmatics. Even Karl Barth, despite frequent misunderstanding by some who refer to him, can be cited in agreement with this view. "Dogmatics too," he says,[4] "has to speak all along the line as faith opposing unbelief, and to that extent all along the line its language must be apologetic." What he is critical of is "intended apologetic" (*gewollte Apologetik*); and by this he evidently means a theological activity which, for the sake of getting to grips with unbelief, loosens or even loses its hold upon essential Christianity. At the other extreme Barth points out that Christian faith is not engaged in a mere "game with unbelief",[5] taking neither itself nor unbelief seriously.[6] The lesson to be learned from Barth's writings is that only a confident faith can engage properly in Apologetics, and that in being confident such a faith cannot but do so. Emil Brunner carries clarification of the relationship between the two further when he suggests[7] that dogmatics is *Sach-bezogen* and Apologetics *Hörer-bezogen*—the one is bound or, better, orientated to the thing proclaimed, the other to the hearer of the proclamation.

We draw the conclusion that Apologetics and Dogmatics cannot be understood in isolation from one another. At most they are distinguished by a difference of style. As John Macquarrie says,[8] "Apologetics is not a branch of theology, but rather a style of theology, namely that style which defends faith against attacks." Apologetics operates from a position of strength combined with humility: strength because it is conscious of possessing a Gospel that the whole world needs; humility because the Gospel discloses further riches as it is applied to the world and its difficulties. It consists of the positive declaration of this Gospel in the face of the facts and circumstances with which it is confronted and by which it is often opposed. Apologetics engages with confessed enemies of Christianity outside, defending it against the ignorance, misunderstanding and defamation of unbelief. It engages with the wreckers from within, defending the Gospel against heresy that would ruin or disable it. And it engages more generally in expounding the faith so that it may secure a fair hearing, knowing that it is equally important to emphasize that reason is not the whole of faith and that faith is not tenable in utter defiance of reason.[9] Apologetics not only defends but also commends the faith.

# CHAPTER ONE

# APOLOGETIC ELEMENTS
# IN THE NEW TESTAMENT

IF there were no apologetic elements in the New Testament, the activity known as Apologetics might still be valid and useful, but it would be unable to appeal to Scripture for justification. On the other hand, the presence of apologetic elements in the New Testament would not alone demonstrate conclusively that Apologetics ought to be practised outside the New Testament, but only provide a *prima facie* argument in its favour. The best way of settling these issues is simply to ask whether such elements are to be found in the New Testament, and if so what is their nature. If these two enquiries can be pursued till they yield answers, we shall know more about both the justification and the continued validity of Apologetics. To this enquiry the present chapter is devoted.

There is in fact no difficulty in identifying apologetic elements in the New Testament. They appear both early and prominently. Apologetic activity is built into the foundations of the apostolic witness. In **Acts** we find it embedded in the first address ever to be delivered by a Christian believer in the name of Christ following the first Whitsunday and the pentecostal gift of the Holy Spirit. The story is told in Acts 2, and its importance in the history of faith is crucial.

The narrative falls into three parts. There is first the record of certain unusual events which have caught the attention of great crowds. The centre and core of these events the narrator defines when he says: "they were all filled with the Holy Spirit" (Acts 2.4); and round this a number of other remarkable manifestations occur. The second part of the narrative consists of an account of various reactions to this constellation of events on the part of bystanders. Three distinguishable types of reaction are noted. There was amazement, expressed in the exclamation: "How is it that each of us hears these Galileans speaking to us in our own language?" There was perplexity, and some said: "What does this mean?" And according to the record there was also scorn, and the contemptuous judgment: These men have been drinking. While the facts were there for all to see, those present were already making their own assessment: different interpretations were being formulated and expressed.

The third part of the narrative opens with the simple words: "But Peter"; and unceremoniously precipitated on to the stage Peter begins the first Christian sermon. We need not stay to consider how differently the course of world history would have run if, instead of "but" the narrator had been obliged by the facts to say "and"—*and* Peter was equally mystified; *and* Peter rather agreed with what was being said; *and* Peter, seeing the size of the crowd, lost his nerve and observed a discreet silence. If this had happened, Christian faith would have died at birth. There would have been no alternative to the hasty response of the insensitive crowd; their precipitate interpretations would have precluded all attempts at fairer appreciation. Instead, Peter did two things. He demolished the interpretation that had been offered, by pointing out that it was not yet opening time; and he replaced that interpretation, and the amazement and perplexity that accompanied it, by his own construction of what was happening. What he said contains three elements. He presented his audience with a fact, an explanation, and an implication. The fact is the risen Jesus, once crucified and now made Lord and Christ. The premise is prophetic statements which found their endorsement in what is now going on. That all this has an implication is instantly recognized by those who listen, and they break out spontaneously asking what they are to do about it. Peter's reply is: "Repent and be baptized." The demolition of false interpretation, and the positive statement of the Christian faith including explanation and implication—here at this early point in Christian history the landmarks that indicate the scope of all apologetic activity have emerged with suprising clarity. What Peter rose to do was to defend the faith, and from that time on the defence of faith has unceasingly been undertaken and faithfully discharged.

Within the New Testament, the task Peter finds himself almost involuntarily obliged to undertake is discharged in varying circumstances, and at different levels of deliberation. To begin with, the word apology and its cognate Apologetics are of Greek origin. *Apologia* (in general, meaning defence) and its verbal form *apologoumai* (make a defence) are words used in classical Greek, in New Testament Greek, and also in the Patristic writings. Their meaning in these three linguistic forms does not differ significantly. But it is with their employment in the New Testament that we are here concerned. The words appear with some frequency. The lexicons show that *apologia* occurs about eight times and the verbal form about eleven. This is evidence enough to show pretty accurately what their meaning is. It appears that the verbal form always, and the nominal form usually, denote an answer given in reply to a charge levelled against an individual, or an argument justifying a claim advanced by an individual. This is the invariable meaning when the terms are used in Acts, where in fact about half the total number of occurrences are found.

It needs little imagination to see why this should be so. Christianity was no sooner launched than it ran into trouble of various kinds and for various reasons. The Book of the Acts is full of incidents in which Christians, and especially Paul, figure as the storm-centre of contention and altercation. Sometimes it is the hostility of the Jews that the adherents of Christianity have to face. As early as Acts 4 we are told how "the Jewish rulers, elders and doctors of the law" instigated proceedings against Peter and John, arrested them, and arraigned them before the court and later before the Council (Acts 5). Before long the Roman authorities become involved. Acts 21 shows how "all Jerusalem was in an uproar" (21.31), precipitated by Jewish opposition to Paul and his companions; the Roman commandant calls out troops to quell the riot; Paul is arrested, and making his defence eventually appeals to Caesar (25.11); and accordingly the case passes out of Jewish hands and is transferred to Rome for judgment. Sometimes again the bother is adventitious, as when (Acts 16) the residents of Philippi, outraged by Lydia's defection to Christianity and their consequent financial loss, denounce Paul and Silas to the magistrates who order them to be imprisoned in the local gaol. In such circumstances there is frequent need to reply to charges. Peter is the first to defend not so much Christianity as such, but himself (Acts 5.29), though the Greek words in which we are interested are not used in the narrative.

By way of contrast, Paul is frequently represented as replying against charges laid against him. For example he is invited by Agrippa to speak for himself. The narrative tells us that he "began his defence", reporting that his first words are of gratitude that it is in the presence of Agrippa "that I am to make my defence today upon all the charges brought against me by the Jews". In both quotations the word used is *apologoumai*; and in these later chapters of Acts it recurs in the same connection.

Obviously in these examples no technical meaning can be read into the word used. It is in the service of the Gospel that Paul incurs the charges made, and it is to the Gospel that he appeals in making his defence. But the word might equally well be used in the case of any one accused of breach of the peace and attempting to justify himself. Its use in a Christian connection is adventitious. The same may be said of other occasions of the use of both the nominal and the verbal forms. It is not Christianity or the Christian faith that is at stake when Alexander tries to clear himself and the other Jews from complicity with Paul's propaganda against the making of silver shrines to Diana in Ephesus (Acts 19.33). And when Paul defends himself against those "who put me in the dock" for his exercise of freedom in eating and drinking what has been consecrated to heathen deities, the dispute is not over Christianity as such, but over differing views of what is permissible within Christianity (1 Cor. 9.3f.). The context in which these events occur and these words are used is a Christian context. But it is not Christianity itself that is being defended.

But there are other occasions when Christianity is the immediate object defended. When Paul, in prison in Rome or elsewhere, writes to his fellow Christians in Philippi, he twice refers to his plight as the consequence of his defence of the Gospel. His correspondents know, he says (Phil. 1.17), that it is because of his apologia of the Gospel that he suffers imprisonment. Indeed (1.7) they share in the privilege that is his when lying in prison or appearing in the dock to make apologia for the truth of the Gospel. Paul takes his stand as representative of the Gospel and the Christian faith. He engages not in individual and personal exculpation and justification, but in explicit defence of Christianity. The words lose their neutral colouring. Christian Apologetics becomes a specific activity. Those who adhere to the Christian faith may at any time be similarly involved: the privilege of "vouching for the truth of the Gospel" (Phil. 1.7) may without warning fall on their shoulders.

There is close similarity between what Paul says here and the thought of Peter at 1 Pet. 3.15–16, where he gives a realistic assessment of the reception Christians may expect to encounter. Devoted to what is good, it might be thought, they would expect no hostility or opposition. But this is too sanguine an appreciation of the situation. They are likely to be called on to suffer for their virtues, and they are to count themselves happy if this is so. But, at the same time, if the opportunity occurs they are not to neglect it: "Be always ready with your defence whenever you are called to account for the hope that is in you, making that defence with modesty and respect." Evidently a more sophisticated stage has been reached in the advance of Christianity. If rosy hopes were ever entertained that the whole world would fall into the lap of Christianity without hesitation or reluctance, this optimism is here resolutely set aside. Opposition is certain; and Christians are to regard the prospect not with dismay but with alacrity as an occasion for proclaiming and substantiating the faith they hold. Hence they should have their apologia of the faith in readiness for instant use: they are to be ready to offer a *logos*, an intelligible account, of the hope that sustains them.

Here the contrast with Luke's injunction (Luke 12.11, 21.14) is to be noted. According to Luke, Jesus tells his disciples not to meditate in advance what reply they are to make to their accusers. When Peter writes his letter, this disingenuous approach has become inadequate and must be replaced by something more formal and prepared. For Apologetics the development here implied is momentous. For the first time apparently there is being advocated a deliberate and sustained effort to work out a defence of the Christian faith in anticipation of the situations that might call for it. The dominical injunction to rely on moment to moment inspiration in the face of opposition is supplemented by the requirement to prepare defence works in advance. The transition is being made to the science of Christian defence. The beginnings of the reflective discipline of Apologetics are here apparent in New Testament times and built into Holy Scripture.

Apologetic activity occurs in the New Testament beyond the

occasions where the formal words are used. Here attention focuses naturally upon the Apostle **Paul**. After all he is the most prolific contributor to the New Testament, and comes nearest of all the New Testament writers to offering a systematic statement and account of Christianity. Thirty years ago C. H. Dodd pointed out the need to recognize two aspects distinguishable within the central tradition of Christianity.[1] There is the " 'preaching' or 'proclamation' (*kerygma*) about God's action for the salvation of men, by which the Church was called into existence, and which it announces to all men everywhere as the ground of faith and hope"; and there is too what Dodd calls "an ethical ideal for corporate and individual life", and for this the most general term is "teaching" (*didache*).[2] Dodd goes on to say: "Several of the Pauline epistles fall naturally into two parts, one of which is theological in character and the other ethical ... The theological sections represent the development of ideas contained or implied in the 'preaching', the ethical sections enforce what Paul calls 'the type of teaching to which you are committed' (Rom. 6.17). The 'preaching' is described as 'the Gospel of Christ' (Rom. 15.19). The 'teaching' is given as representing 'the law of Christ', or 'the commandment of Christ' (Gal. 6.2; 1 Cor. 7.25)." It has to be remembered who the recipients of these letters for the most part were. "The epistles were in no case written to give instruction in the fundamentals of Christianity to people who previously knew nothing about it. They are all addressed to a public already Christian."[3]

Clearly both aspects have a proper place in writings designed for such recipients. *Kerygma* is necessary, for the Gospel has always to be sounded in the ears of believers to nourish their understanding of the faith and quicken their adherence to it. And *didache* is a "paraenetic" necessity (from *paraineo*, to admonish, as Acts 27.9, of Paul himself), a drawing out of the practical implications of the faith to which they had committed themselves. But, as the look we have taken at the Greek terms from which the English word derives has shown, Apologetics presupposes some other party not so committed and at least potentially hostile to or dubious about Christianity. Hence it is to be expected that the apologetic aspect is not to be so readily identified in Paul's writings. But as even Dodd himself allows, and as others have urged more persistently, the aspects of *kerygma* and *didache* do not exhaustively represent Paul's work, and to them an apologetic element has to be added, even if it is less obtrusive than the others.

A clear example of this further element is to be found at 2 Cor. 10.4f.: "The weapons we wield are not merely human, but divinely potent to demolish strongholds; we demolish sophistries and all that rears its proud head against the knowledge of God; we compel every human thought to surrender in obedience to Christ; and we are prepared to punish all rebellion when once you have put yourselves in our hands." Evidently Paul's attention here is turned not so much on already fully committed Christians as on some kind of opposition, whether external to his correspondents or resident in them. In either case, as he says in the preceding verse, there are battles to be fought. When the Christian engages in such battles he undertakes apologetic activity. Accordingly he does well to note the two elements Paul discerns in such activity. There is the demolition of the citadels from which opposition is conducted—the overturning of hostile modes or systems of thought; and there is the logically subsequent positive task of the winning over by persuasion of all thinking to Christian obedience. Paul adds no doubt in a third and less important place the need for what we should now call discipline, the retention of that to which one has been persuaded within the context of obedience. Here the salient and perpetual features of the apologetic task are clearly defined: the negative objective, to destroy what opposes the Christian faith; and the positive objective, to win over from opposition to acceptance. This is the aim of Apologetics whenever practised.

The opening chapters of Romans and of 1 Corinthians show Paul putting these apologetic principles into practice. On Dodd's classification, 1 Cor. 1 and 2 could be placed with the kerygmatic passages. But clearly the chapters are not bare proclamation uncoloured by other interests. They are addressed to those that are sensitive as to how the Gospel is to be related to other modes of thought; and this is essentially an apologetic enterprise. Paul says (1 Cor. 2.2): "I resolved that while I was with you I would think of nothing but Jesus Christ—Christ nailed to the cross." If he had left it at that, the discourse would be simply kerygmatic. But he is better than his word and goes farther. He thinks not only of Jesus Christ but also round him, considering his relation to what is other than Jesus Christ. The course of the argument is as follows. In addressing his correspondents Paul repudiates all "display of fine words or wisdom" (1 Cor. 2.1); and in this he merely repeats what he has already stated earlier (1.17), that he will not rely "on the language of worldly wisdom." Yet after all his business is with wisdom, though of another kind: not human wisdom, "yet I do speak words of wisdom" (2.6), a wisdom not "belonging to this passing age." This other wisdom of which he talks is of "things beyond our seeing, things beyond our hearing, things beyond our imagining" (2.9). But this has nothing to do with the obscurantism of Plotinus, or the contrived hocus-pocus of the mystery religions. It comes by revelation of God to those who are ready for it (2.10). This wisdom is possessed not by those who work hard (it is not "natural" or "unspiritual"), and not imparted by teachers in the schools. It is mediated by the Spirit and comes to the man who is "spiritual" or "gifted by the Spirit". For "only the Spirit of God knows what God is."

It is of great significance that in this first extended example of Apologetics in action there should appear a clear distinction of this kind, between two kinds of "wisdom". In different forms this is an issue that recurs throughout the whole course of theology, and presses with particular urgency upon apologetic theology. The solution Paul proposes is sober and restrained. He does not pit man's wisdom against Christianity in stark contrast; nor does he minimize the radical difference between them. Christianity itself is possessed of wisdom—a wisdom characteristic of itself, that can hold up its head without shame in the presence of other wisdom. Christianity must indeed set aside that other wisdom and put it in its proper place. But from neither side may the contrast be seen in terms of sense against nonsense, of cleverness against credulity. The spiritual man is characterized by wisdom—by a spiritual insight to which the natural man has no access. The Gospel is "superior to human wisdom, nobility and plausibility; yet it has a wisdom, nobility, and persuasiveness of its own, which it derives from God."[4] The two sides of the issue can be thus stated; and here is the apologetic bridge between them. It is not that faith is contrary to reason. Rather, "human reasonings in Paul's day as in ours failed to take sufficient cognisance of spiritual things."[5]

Paul's letter to the Romans opens up a quite different range of questions. Everyone knows some of the problems that have bothered the commentators and for which no unanimous judgement has been reached. But whether addressed to a quite particular group of Christians or designed as a more general statement of the Christian faith, Romans evidently includes strongly emphasized apologetic elements. The Jews of Israel occupy Paul's thoughts as he writes the letter: their plight, he says (Rom. 9.2), causes him "great grief and unceasing sorrow." A good deal of the exposition of the Gospel is directly addressed to their situation. First he shows that the rightness with God that constitutes what is meant by God's righteousness is not achieved by means of the law (2.1–3.20). There follows a more precise disquisition on the character of this righteousness (3.21–31). None the less righteousness of this kind is witnessed to by the law and the prophets (4.1–25); and by a supreme *tour de force* Paul shows that Abraham, the patriarch to whom the Jews themselves appeal, is a witness to the very point Paul is making over against them. The long section (5.1–8.39) reverts to statement—a detailed account of the life of freedom which those enjoy who by faith are righteous. Then once again Paul's attention turns to the case of his own people. The righteousness of faith which stands at the heart of the Christian Gospel, so far from being the contradiction of what has gone before, is in fact the fulfilment of the promise of God given long ago to the Jews. From this, two conclusions follow: the first, that Israel's exclusion from the benefits of the Gospel is traceable to Israel's own failure in obedience; and the second, that Israel's consequent rejection is not the last word, in as much as the Gospel has thereby been made available to those outside the chosen people, and Israel's very rejection on the ground of present disbelief will in the end lead to their inclusion within the true Israel that is based on the work of Jesus Christ. A final section of the letter deals with practical matters that arise parenetically from the exposition of the Gospel just outlined.

Here then is apologetic argument, powerful, penetrating, and persuasive. Paul the apologist submits to the rubric he himself lays down for Apologetics, that every thought is to be brought into subjection to Jesus Christ. His hold on the substance of the Gospel is tenacious. Application of it to the particular case is made not by concession or compromise, but by penetrating through the contrast that superficially marks the relation between Gospel and Judaism to presuppositions commonly held by both believer and unbeliever. In the course of its history apologetic theology has always had to be making up its mind how to reconcile these two interests. It has here an early object lesson in how this may be done.

The other front on which Paul engages in his letter is constituted by the Gentiles (Rom. 2.14) or as he sometimes calls them the Greeks (1.14). The apologetic argument which he unfolds for their benefit has given rise to some misunderstanding. It is not a full-scale apologetic that he deploys against the Gentiles (1.18–32). He does little to "demolish" their system of thought; and he does not at any length try to persuade them in terms of their own belief that Christianity is a faith they should embrace. Paul's objective is limited: to show that the Gentiles, under the wrathful aspect of the righteousness of God as they are, must be regarded as "blame-worthy"; the aim is not to provide a general apologetic for the Christian faith but to show that the Gentiles are *anapologetoi*, without excuse (1.20). It follows that the attempt to extract from what Paul says an answer to the inflamed question of "natural theology" is wrong-headed. Paul is not directly concerned to affirm that God reveals himself only in and through Jesus Christ, nor to deny that he does reveal himself in his works. The point he wishes to make is simply that, "however God has revealed himself in his mighty works, man does not honour him and thank him as God"[6]—he fails to pick up and appreciate the scattered evidence. The god that man finds by scrutinizing things around him is no more than an empty and vain idea—"they have bartered away the true God for a false one, and have offered reverence and worship to created things instead of to the Creator, who is blessed for ever" (Rom. 1.25). In so doing they have put themselves in the wrong with God, and hence stand under his wrath.

Paul here does not seem to encourage the idea that the dogmatic and apologetic activities should be held apart, so that the theologian must change gear in passing from one to the other. Nor does he think in terms of an element intact in unbelieving man to which a distinct apologetic appeal can be addressed. If these ideas appear in the later story of theological thinking, their justification is to be found elsewhere than in Scripture.

The distinctive features which the Epistle to the **Hebrews** manifests are illuminated when the Epistle is regarded as apologetic in intention. To read it thus does not indeed solve all the problems to which it has given rise: it remains doubtful how we ought to answer the questions by whom, to what destination, and for what particular people the Epistle is written. Evidently addressed to specific people in a specific situation, Hebrews offers not an altered Gospel but the Gospel in a form designed to commend it to the special circumstances. The title "To the Hebrews" is of course an addition to the document as it left the writer's hands. But its early acceptance and continued use by the Church, whether based on traditional evidence not now available or simply on appreciation of the character of the writing itself, is essentially sound. Even if the community addressed did not consist wholly of Jewish Christians, it seems certainly to have included Jews. The evidence for this is found in small indications, rather than the obvious interest shown in the Old Testament dispensation. At 6.6f. and elsewhere, for example, the writer regards the possibility that his correspondents may be adhering to a Jewish outlook and understanding as a relapse. In such a case the appeal to the Old Testament is certainly apposite. But it is equally appropriate for all other cases. The Scriptures of the Old Testament were for a century after its beginnings the source from which the early Church derived divine guidance, inspiration and knowledge of God's revelation and purpose. To base an interpretation of the Gospel on them was accordingly to attract the instant attention of all Christians from whatever background they came, and indeed of all enquirers concerning Christianity.[7] The particularity of the apologetic expounded in Hebrews in no way disables it from discharging a function for all times and places, as indeed ordinary readers have always discovered for themselves.

It is not possible to identify the author of the Epistle. However, inspection of the contents reveals a good deal of information about him. The Epistle displays a vocabulary that shows its author as a man of education; a rhetorical skill that could come only from an expert in the methods of the schools; a style of argument that implies a philosophic temperament and training. These features added together compose the picture of a Jew, perhaps of Alexandria, versed in the philosophical thinking of the day, and able not only to unfold the truths of Christianity but to set them in a world-wide intellectual context (cf. 1.1f.). If so, a new kind of Christian advocacy is making its appearance. The effort is being made to relate Christianity to the results of philosophical thinking and so attract men of education with their characteristic problems and doubts. "This new era in the development of our religion begins with the Epistle to the Hebrews," writes E. F. Scott.[8] "Its author may be regarded, in some respects, as the first of the theological doctors, the precursor of Justin and Irenaeus and the great Alexandrians." The correspondents he addresses display several characteristics. They are Christians of some standing, but they had become rather jaded in their profession (12.12). They entertained doubts and were ready to fall for strange doctrines (13.9). They had successfully resisted the pressure of persecution in the past (10.32f.), but were apparently threatened by a further instalment (12.3ff.) which their relaxed moral fibre did not equip them to withstand. In a word, it is a situation of frequent occurrence in the history of Christianity which stands in urgent need of a fortifying apologetic message.

The character of the reply offered is of exceptional and unique interest. It consists of a detailed comparison of the Old Testament dispensation with that inaugurated and effected by Jesus Christ, a comparison that discerns a certain point to point correspondence between the two and suggests a certain definite superiority enjoyed by the latter. The pivot used by Hebrews to explicate the relation is drawn from the Alexandrian doctrine in which its writer was trained and the Platonic thought upon which that doctrine was based. There is a visible world, and distinct from it an invisible world, the first phenomenal and the second alone finally real and eternal. This categorization the writer applies to the situation precipitated by the advent of Christ. The Old Testament dispensation belongs to what is seen and temporal, while the dispensation inaugurated by Christ belongs to the unseen and eternal. It follows that the first can be expected to be evanescent and the second lasting. But he is far from regarding the one as therefore cut off from the other: a relation is established between them. The Old Testament dispensation has been superseded by that of the New. But this does not rob the Old Testament of significance: supersession does not mean obliteration. The Old Testament constituted a step preliminary to the New: the Levitical cult and apparatus prepared the way for the divine salvation planned and executed by means of Jesus Christ. The way in which this is effected is suggested by what is apparently a cardinal verse, 10.1, where it is stated that the Old Testament contained a dim outline or "shadow" of the "good things to come", but not a full representation or "true image".

The distinction here deliberately made is rendered into modern terms by the contrast between symbol and type. A symbol refers to what is outside and beyond itself and is real without including the suggestion that anything more than itself will be given; a type on the other hand is anticipatory of what may be expected to realize itself and so is promissory of what is to be. The writer to the Hebrews suggests that the Old Testament dispensation is for those who know it alone a real sign of what lies beyond, while for those who have appreciated what the New Testament offers it is anticipatory of what they now enjoy. Here then is a careful analysis of how the Old Testament is prognostic of what is to come even if those who wrote cannot be credited with full advance knowledge of it. The apologetic offered is that Christianity fits into a framework already constructed in the Old Testament. Here is an early form of the argument from prophecy that constitutes so important an element in later Apologetics.

In the argument of Hebrews this pattern repeats itself in different contexts. The sacrificial cult of the Old Testament is thus related to the sacrifice of Jesus Christ, the function of the prophets to the role Jesus plays, the place of Old Testament faith to that of New Testament hope. But the author is particularly interested in the way in which Jesus Christ in person and function supersedes Aaron, and in 8.1–10.18 the relation is expounded in some detail. The argument turns on the Levitical principle that without the shedding of blood there is no forgiveness of sin (Lev. 17.11, Heb. 9.22). All the several imperfections adhering to the Old Testament realization of this principle are made good in its implementation by Jesus Christ. The Old Testament realization is characterized by the need for repetition, for application to the officiant himself, and the intervention of the blood of a third party, the victim; the realization in Jesus Christ on the other hand is a once-for-all sacrifice of a perfect victim who himself needs no benefit from the sacrifice, which accordingly is totally applicable to the needs of others. If objection is taken to the irregularity of this one's intervention in the office vested in the Levitical genealogy, the Old Testament itself provides a parallel in Melchizedek who on scriptural authority was reckoned greater than Aaron himself (Gen. 14.18 *et al*; Heb. 7.4–10).

The apologetic thus offered applies to all Christians, and especially to those who as Jews could not relinquish their faith in the Old

Testament Scriptures and those who as converts to Christianity were constrained to find in the Old Testament Scriptures their rule of faith and life. Of all the documents later recognized as canonically belonging to a New Testament and so set alongside the Hebrew Scriptures, the Epistle to the Hebrews is the clearest example of sustained apology for the Christian faith.

A special complication confronts the reader who turns to the **Gospels.** Clearly a distinction can be drawn between the *ipsissima verba* of Jesus and for that matter the events in which he plays a part on the one hand, and on the other the editorial elements (as we may call them) with which the Gospels are invested. Once the so-called Form Critical school of New Testament scholars had drawn the distinction it is impossible to ignore it, though this is no reason to exaggerate its importance. Hence it is convenient to ask what place Apologetics can be said to have in Jesus' teaching and work; and then enquire whether there are detectable apologetic elements in the way in which the Gospel writers present their material. A third enquiry will address itself to the rather special case of the fourth Gospel.

Jesus himself shows almost no signs of practising anything like a self-conscious Apologetics. Of course there are frequent occasions on which he defended himself and what he did against different sections of the community. When asked by John's disciples why they and the Pharisees fasted but Jesus' own disciples did not, (Matt. 9.14; the parallel Mark 2.18 credits "some people" with asking the question), Jesus' reply not only gives a reason but clearly a justifying reason for the practice of his disciples. In face of the Pharisees and scribes he gives justifying reasons for two violations of the laws governing Sabbath observance, plucking corn, rubbing and eating it, and healing the man with the withered arm (Luke 6.1–5, 6–11). The answers Jesus makes to "the Jews" immediately following the cure of the cripple at Bethesda, and subsequently to the accusation that he was claiming equality with God (John 5.2ff., 18f.), have so evidently the character of justifying his actions that the New English Bible translates: "defended himself", and "to this charge Jesus replied". It is on the occasion of trivial ritualistic breaches of the law that these examples of self-defence occur. To them must be added the more significant incident when his right to forgive sins is challenged

(Mark 2.3–12). Here Jesus' response is more than verbal: he deliberately effects the healing of the paralysed man in order, as he says, "to convince you that the Son of Man has the right on earth to forgive sins." Other examples could be given. Jesus does not disdain to give apologetic explanation for many of his individual actions.

But this willingness hardly extends to wider matters such as his plan of campaign, or the pattern underlying the mission which he conducted and the movement on which he engaged during his public career. The absence of express strategy is noticeable also in Jesus' handling of the disciples. "He gave them, so far as our records tell, no programme and no body of teaching to propagate. All they were to do was to heal the sick, to cast out demons, and to say: 'The Kingdom of God is at hand' (Matt. 10.7–8; Luke 10.9–11). It is not a programme for human action, but the proclamation of an act of God," writes C. H. Dodd.[9] Much the same could be said of Jesus himself. On the Markan account he moves straight from baptism at the hands of John the Baptist into the desert where he was tempted, and then launches himself instantly upon his public career: "Jesus came into Galilee, proclaiming the Gospel of God" (Mark 1.14). Proclamation is his constant preoccupation. E. Brunner says[10] that "the task of Jesus was not to teach the Christ but to *be* the Christ." He directs comparatively little interest towards himself, and he conducts little in the nature of direct self-defence or apologetic.

A certain qualification needs to be noted almost immediately. Before this is done another aspect calls for attention that tends in the same sense. Jesus steadily refused to perform miracles in order to attract interest, win conviction or overcome doubt. Asked to show a sign (Matt. 12.38f. *et par*), Jesus replies that "it is a wicked, godless generation that asks for a sign." This sentiment characterizes his handling of the matter of miracles throughout, and we are no doubt right in finding its basis in the searing experience of the temptations at the outset of his career. A scrutiny of the records shows that Jesus worked miracles where need was present, along with faith, not in order to create faith. They represented power present and active—the Kingdom of God in operation for the overthrow of what impeded or opposed it. They do not appear as tokens of his authority, but as evidence of the presence of the Kingdom. The healing of the paralysed man (Mark 2.3ff.) is here again instructive.

Here Jesus effected the healing "to convince" onlookers. But the convincing effect of the miracle is not the reason for its being done. Rather the miracle, being required in the situation, may in this case have this side effect.

This refusal to use miracles as apologetic evidence is important in view of the later exploitation of miracles along apologetic lines, and also of the reassumed reluctance of more modern days. A. B. Bruce tells us[11] that "it must be confessed that miracles cannot be offered as evidences of Christianity now with the confidence with which they were employed for this purpose by the apologists of a past age. Men do not now believe in Christ because of his miracles: they rather believe in miracles because they have first believed in Christ. For such believers Christ is his own witness, who accredits everything connected with him: Scripture, prophecy, miracle." This is well said and expresses at an early date the typically modern attitude. The past age to which reference is made is of course not the age of the New Testament and the incarnation, but an era long subsequent to that time whose story will come before us in the proper place. To turn away from such a view of miracle means reversion to the situation in which the Gospel was first proclaimed by dominical testimony. Then too Christ was his own witness.

The most considerable apologetic element in our Lord's witness is both indirect and ambivalent. It consists in the appeal repeatedly made by Jesus to the Old Testament. This is so marked a feature that the conclusion cannot be avoided that the Old Testament contains the key to an understanding of our Lord's life.[12] Oscar Cullmann has this to say:[13] "The first Christians were at pains to constitute a connection with the Old Testament. This was more than mere Scripture erudition; and it was certainly not, as Nietzsche said, a 'ridiculous philological farce with the Old Testament'. It was the consequence of a joyous consciousness that they belonged to the same history as the Old Testament." There are numerous examples. There are passages where a simple reference is made to the Scriptures of the Old Testament, as Matt. 12.38f. already cited, where the only "sign" Jesus will concede to the Pharisees' demand is "the sign of the prophet Jonah." There is evidence too of parallelisms between Old Testament writing and himself which are deliberately contrived. Of these the most evident example is the entry into Jerusalem, where Jesus imitates the Old Testament precedent of Zech. 9.9. But even more significant are the references where Jesus declares himself to be the fulfilment of what is written in the Old Testament. For example, in Luke he arrogates to himself the words of Isa. 61.1ff.; and again in the same Gospel (Luke 24.13ff.), "beginning at Moses and all the prophets, he expounded" to the disciples on the road to Emmaus "in all the scriptures the things concerning himself". To these must also be added the more constant refrain that enters his teaching especially after the critical confession by Peter at Caesarea Philippi, that what he does, he does under a certain compulsion. He has a role to discharge, a cup to drink, a necessity to obey; and all these are traceable to what is already witnessed to in the Old Testament. In other words Jesus links what he is doing quite explicitly with the Old Testament witness.

The apologetic value of this is indirect. That Jesus is, and in this explicit way declares himself to be, the fulfilment of the Old Testament is a fact which has apologetic overtones for those who care to hear them. It commended him and the cause in which he engaged by appeal to a court of highest instance. If this appeal were valid no further argument was needed to evoke unconditional acceptance. But was the appeal to be allowed? Did the Old Testament really sustain the claim that was being made? As an apologetic the claim proves ambiguous, for the issue it raises critically divided his contemporaries. In the record of the Fourth Gospel Jesus is presented precisely as the one predicted in the Old Testament Scriptures, and the response is immediate: "Can anything good come from Nazareth?" (John 1.45f.). The speaker is Nathanial who does not indeed abide by the rejection implicit in his words; but he spoke for countless others who did. On the other hand it is again in explicitly Old Testament terms that the choice is presented and in this case accepted, when at Caesarea Philippi Peter acknowledges Jesus as the Messiah (Matt. 16.13ff.). Jesus deliberately meshes himself and his career with the pattern of the Old Testament. But the apologetic value of what he thus does is ambivalent. His appeal to what was most sacred in Judaism won him both acknowledgement as Messiah and execration as a blasphemer.

The second issue to be considered here concerns the degree to which the Evangelists were moved by apologetic factors in compiling the Gospels which stand in their names. That there were such apologetic (and other) factors cannot now be doubted; but, since

Harald Riesenfeld's study on the subject,[14] the suggestion may be dismissed that they are so extensive and pervasive that little in the Gospel narratives survives their distorting influence. We should remember that one of the interests with which the Evangelists can most reliably be credited is simple faithful adherence to the facts of which they had had the privilege of being eyewitnesses. If they could not be absolute proof against the influence of subsequent and subsidiary factors, they were at least not unarmed against them. The Gospel according to Mark least of all manifests particular apologetic traits. Matthew's Gospel displays a special interest in his own Jewish contemporaries. It is suggested that his narrative is divisible into five books in correspondence with the Five Books of Moses constituting the law of the old covenant. He lays supreme emphasis upon Jesus as the fulfilment of the hopes and promises of the Old Testament. To this end, the Gospel he writes is more interspersed by "editorial comment" than either of the other two synoptics. An example occurs in the first chapter (Matt. 1.22f.), where the circumstances of Jesus' birth are recorded and the comment added: "All this happened in order to fulfil what the Lord declared through the prophet" (Isa. 7.14). In fact this apologetic element seems to have been effective, and the Gospel was almost at once accorded a pre-eminence of which its position as first of the four is a residual sign, superseding Mark and being often referred to in the early Church simply as "the Gospel".

The Gospel according to Luke is as distinctively directed in another direction: it is addressed to the Gentile world. This characteristic shows itself in the expansiveness with which the Gospel depicts the wideness of the divine mercy. Luke pays particular attention to the Gentiles who fall within the range of Christ's activity, e.g. the centurion of Capernaum and his sick servant, a story narrated in much greater detail than in Matthew. But there is perhaps a more polemical edge also to this mild apologetic. W. G. Kümmel thinks[15] that a subsidiary aim of the Gospel is to demonstrate the guilt of the Jews in connection with the death of Jesus and the innocence of the Roman authorities. Thus "there is no doubt that there is a political apologetic here which fully absolves the Romans of guilt in Jesus' crucifixion (Pilate does not condemn Jesus, 23.25, against Mark 15.15 et par Matt. 27.26)." Kümmel further thinks that Luke here "prepares the defence of the Christian against political accusation in Acts (e.g. Acts 17.7)." This special interest of Luke has been inflated to form the ground for supposing that the entire Book of Acts was written for submission as a defence of Paul when on trial at Rome. The idea is not tenable. As C. K. Barrett comments:[16] "No Roman official would ever have filtered out so much of what to him would be theological and ecclesiastical rubbish in order to reach so tiny a grain of relevant apology."

The Fourth Gospel merits special attention. This Gospel is more reflective in character than the other three, though this makes it less fundamentally different than is sometimes made out. The writer is so closely involved in the things he records, e.g. in the lengthy discourses that compose so much of the writing, that the reported words of Jesus merge into editorial contextual matter and are indistinguishable from it, both in style and content. "If the synoptic Gospels are rather like an art gallery through which one is allowed to wander at will, the Fourth Gospel is like a gallery through which one is taken on a conducted tour."[17] In these circumstances the apologetic note could readily be infused into the Gospel. The writer states the purpose of his writing in 20.31, but textual discrepancies make it difficult to know with precision what he had in mind. The A.V. translates: "These are written, that ye may believe that Jesus is the Christ, the Son of God", based on the Greek *pisteusete*; the N.E.B. on the other hand translates: "These (things) here written have been recorded in order that you may hold the faith that Jesus is the Christ, the Son of God," based on a Greek variant text *pisteuete*. The respective presence and absence of a single letter makes all the difference in the address to which this apologetic is being sent. It is designed either that people may come to believe, or that people already believing may continue in the faith.[18]

We may take it as proven that the Fourth Gospel is apologetically slanted against the Jews. It is doubtful only whether this purpose is to be regarded as a major or a minor theme. Some New Testament scholars have seen as a dominating objective "the refutation of Jewish charges against Christianity"—Kümmel[19] names several. Others think it to be only a secondary purpose, and the suggestion has been worked out that, so small is the antagonism shown against Judaism, that Jesus' sermons are given within the context of the Jewish ecclesiastical year. Perhaps it may suffice to quote Kümmel's judgment. "There can," he says,[20] "be no doubt that John polemizes especially sharply against 'the Jews', who from the beginning wanted to destroy Jesus (cf. 5.16, 18, 37f.; 7.1, 19; 8.22–24, 37–59; 10.31–39; 19.7). And this opposition is so sharp that Jesus can speak to the Jews of 'your law' (8.17; 10.34; see also 'the Word that is written in their law' [15.25] in the mouth of Jesus!)." It may be surmised that the writer of the Fourth Gospel is impelled along these lines by the violence of the enmity shown by the Jews towards Christianity in the time when he wrote; and we have a reflection of this when (16.2f.) Jesus predicts the expulsion of those that follow him from the synagogues.

What the Fourth Gospel reveals then is a situation in which Jewish opposition was increasing. While the precise form of this opposition is not made clear (it was to be made explicit soon enough in Christian writings belonging to the second century), the Gospel indicates Christianity already defending itself against attacks. Nor is this hostility regarded as contingent. Jewish "polemic is taken up into the fundamentally dualistic representation of the opposition between the *archon tou kosmou toutou* (the powers of this world) and the Christ who has overcome the kosmos."[21]

The most notable single apologetic element in the Fourth Gospel is the conception of Logos or Word that appears in the Prologue. The conception of Logos has a long history before it ever came to be employed in the Fourth Gospel.[22] Found in the Old Testament early on, as simply "the Word of the Lord", it came to be hypostatized and personalized in the Wisdom literature where it was assimilated to the idea of Sophia, Wisdom itself. In Greek thought, it appears as the eternal principle of order and as connected with the universe as mind is connected with body. For Philo, in the first half of the first century A. D., "Logos is the meaning, plan and purpose of the universe, conceived as transcendent as well as immanent, as the thought of God formed within the Eternal Mind and projected into objectivity."[23] Straddling the two halves into which the ancient world divided itself, the Jew and the Gentile, and employed by the two dominating intellectual hemispheres, the concept of Logos was of evident value as an apologetic means for commending the Gospel.

However, the use made of the concept in the Fourth Gospel is discriminating and cautious. It is used, but it does not dominate; it occurs in the opening verses of the Gospel and not explicitly at any other point. Its employment is finely sensitive: it is used to express the sublimity of Jesus Christ to whom it is referred, not to control him. "The author of the Fourth Gospel chose the Logos idea as the best available to say what, for him, was the meaning of Jesus Christ."[24] The wide currency of the term faced the Christian user with evident perils. In the Qumran literature, as William Albright points out,[25] it occurs in an at least similar usage, and the phrase "without it was nothing made that was made" occurs almost word for word. Yet Albright's conclusion is that "there is nothing in the Prologue to suggest that anything other than Hebrew teachings is here referred to." That is, the writer of the Fourth Gospel is little influenced in his understanding and use of Logos by contemporary peripheral Jewish writing. It is even clearer that an absolute difference separates the Logos in the Fourth Gospel from its use in current philosophical thinking. As has often been said, the simple statement: "the Word became flesh" (John 1.14) forms the impassable barrier between the Christian understanding of the concept, and the philosophical.

Using then this important and multi-coloured term, this late canonical writing offers a constructive lesson for all Apologetics. The recurrent peril confronting Apologetics in every age is so to engage with unbelief on its own terms as to be unable to transmit the faith with fidelity. Within the New Testament canon there is included this shining example of discriminatory engagment. There is always need for a very firm hold upon the object of faith and a very nice judgment of how this object can and how it cannot be commended.

# CHAPTER TWO

# THE APOLOGISTS AND OTHERS

CHRISTIANITY has had a long history. Whether it be regarded as starting with the events recorded in the New Testament, or, as some would hold, must be traced back in some real though preliminary sense into the Old Testament, it has been going on for a long time. Yet in the long course of its existence it has remained fundamentally and centrally the same. It has preserved its identity throughout, and its adherents and exponents, both the ordinary Christian and the most advanced Christian theologian, have wished to maintain this identity. This common end has been attempted by different means and with varying success.

Two factors are distinguishable in the attempt that has been and is still going on. Christians have felt obliged to hand on or transmit the Gospel. This factor may be called tradition. Alongside this Christians have recognized also a point from which the tradition takes its rise and to which it must show itself faithful. This point is Scripture. The nature of the relation between these two factors is a divisive and contentious issue among Christians. When Vatican Council II, in its opening session in 1962, was known to be deliberating a schema on "the two sources of revelation", i.e. Scripture and tradition, the Protestant world feared the worst: it appeared that the gulf dividing Rome and Reformation would only be dug deeper. But the Council rejected the schema, and in the dogmatic constitution on Divine Revelation (*Dei Verbum*) a substantially different view emerged as the expression of the mind of the Council. On the other hand Protestantism has often thought that its essential principle is adequately stated as *sola scriptura* (Scripture alone). But it has to be recognized that there is an element of tradition securely seated in Scripture itself, as the words of the Pauline warrant for Holy Communion (1 Cor. 11.23) suffice to show. The mutual examination of age-long slogans is both a conciliatory and a sensible undertaking.

Different people will no doubt continue to construe differently the relation between Scripture and tradition. But no one can fail to see the crucial importance of that period in time and history during which the Apostles diminish in number, finally die out, and are succeeded by other Christians. It is the time when first-generation Christians are being replaced by second-generation Christians, and the Apostolic age is followed by a post-Apostolic age. Not that one era ends abruptly to give place to the next. They overlap. But as in the relay race at an athletic meeting there comes a time when those who first carry the baton hand it on to others who must then be responsible for carrying it further, so it is here. To vary the metaphor, if we of twentieth century Christianity are bound to those of the first by an unbroken chain, those links in the chain that make contact with the all-important beginnings have themselves a unique importance. If a break occurs there, then all is lost; if on the other hand the hold with the beginnings is firm, then at least the chain has some chance of uncoiling itself intact. It is then a role of the utmost significance that devolves upon those who write in sub-apostolic times. To them has been assigned the name of the **Apostolic Fathers.** They take up what has been handed on to them from those that went before, and they in turn hand it on to those who come after, right up to the present day.

The reader who turns to the writings these men have left behind them instantly discovers that he is in the company of lesser men than those who composed the writings of the New Testament. "When the student of early Christian literature passes from the New Testament to the post-canonical writers, he becomes aware of a loss of both literary and spiritual power." So writes H. B. Swete.[1] He continues: "There is no immediate change in the form of the writings; the earliest remains of the sub-Apostolic age consist of letters addressed to churches or individuals after the model of the Apostolic Epistles. But the note of authority which is heard in the Epistles of St. Peter, St. Paul, and St. John has no place in those of Clement of Rome and Ignatius of Antioch; and there is little evidence in the latter of the originality or the inspiration by which the leaders of the first generation were distinguished. The spiritual giants of the Apostolic age are succeeded by men of lower stature and poorer capacity." The judgment cannot be disputed. Indeed it is endorsed with disarming and rather touching candour by one of them: "I do not, as Peter and Paul, issue commandments unto you. They were apostles" (Ignatius: *Romans* 4). After the exaltation the slump, as seems to happen so often in history. Nevertheless the debt of gratitude we owe these lesser men is incalculably great. Their abilities are meagre, but their love and loyalty to the Christian faith evidently far exceeded their power to express or defend their faith. There is martyr blood to prove it. While few can have been brought over to the Christian faith by the persuasive power of their writings alone, their witness triumphantly carried the burden of transmitting the Gospel. This is what Tertullian refers to when a century later he declares: "The more you cut us down, the more we increase: for the seed is the blood of Christians" (*Apologeticum* 50, commonly translated "the blood of the martyrs is the seed of the Church").

It might seem possible for the purpose here to skip the Apostolic Fathers and pass straight on to the Apologists in whom the apologetic thread being traced becomes unmistakably evident. But the Apologists ride on the shoulders of those that precede them; the situation they are called on to answer emerges only gradually in its salient features; the classes and periods into which it is convenient to divide things overlap and interlock with each other; and in any case there are apologetic elements discernible in the writers that precede those that won the name of Apologists for themselves. There is a sag in the line of transmission as the Apostles loosen their hold upon it. But where it sags the apologetic strand can be here and there detected. Besides, the period has certain features of special interest. Apologetics implies an opposition to be engaged and if possible overcome. This opposition may take many forms. At one extreme there is the residual doubt in the heart of the believer that ought to be confronted and removed; at the other there is the declared foe, sometimes armed with the instruments of persecution, who is likely to be past the stage of listening to the account of even the bare facts which would at least dissipate ignorance. In New Testament times it became clear that opposition of this kind was going to be offered to Christianity by the Jews and also by the adherents of the heathen religions. As this period merges into the sub-Apostolic age, Christianity had still to contend with these two different fronts offering an increasingly strong opposition. Yet in the writings that have come down to us, and of course they are only fragmentary, there is little evidence either of accurate appreciation of this opposition or of energetic or systematic measures taken to reply to it. The reason for this is evident. The lesser abilities of those who have taken it upon themselves to write about Christianity are fully stretched in coping with the many various problems arising within the Church of the day. Their interest is chiefly devoted to domestic concerns and the will to undertake a serious practice of Apologetics is languid. The earliest of the writings usually included in any collection of the Apostolic Fathers is the **Didache**, (dated early second century or earlier), which carries the manuscript title "The Teaching of the Lord to the Gentiles through the Twelve Apostles." The document hardly lives up to the expectations this longer title arouses. Essentially it is a manual of Church discipline, including moral instruction and Church order. As such it is of the greatest value and interest in helping us to see how the Church of the day lived. But it is preoccupied with domestic matters. When the Jews are mentioned, for example, it is to explain that they fast on Mondays and Thursdays; but the Christian community is commanded to fast instead on Wednesdays and Fridays.

**Clement of Rome** (Bishop of Rome in the last years of the first century) in his *Epistle to the Corinthians* is chiefly concerned to plead for an increase in the spirit of humility and forgiveness in general; and when he turns to more particular matters it is to deal in greater detail with the divisions with which the Church at Corinth was afflicted. To **Ignatius** (*c.*35—*c.*107), Bishop of Antioch, is to be credited the first use of the term Catholic Church. The seven letters that have survived are eloquent of an intense personal faith; and the well-known emphasis he lays on the three-fold Church order and especially the episcopal office in a congregation show him to be apprehensive of disturbing and disrupting influences by which the Church is menaced. But there is no singling out of those hostile factors and no confrontation of them. **Hermas** (probably second century), the author of the *Shepherd*, concentrates for the most part on the need for repentance and the problem of the possibility of forgiveness for post-baptismal sin. In general it is issues of this limited kind that occupy the attention of the Apostolic Fathers.

Yet there are to be found references, fleeting and insubstantial, to the unconvinced world lying outside and around the Christian community. The **Epistle of Barnabas** (probably end of first century) pays a good deal of attention to the Jews, pointing out their false understanding of the Scriptures which they had been the first to receive. But the references are marked more by hostility than by persuasiveness, and the symbolic interpretation by which the writer tries to appropriate them for Christian use is ingenious rather than convincing. It could conceivably be edifying or illuminating for believers to be told that Abraham, circumcising his 318 servants (see Gen. 14.14 and 17.26f.), is witnessing the cross of Christ, since the Greek T ($=300$) is in the form of a cross and IE ($=10+8$) are the first letters of **Iesous**, the Greek form of Jesus (*Epistle* 9). But it is hard to think that such argumentation would do much to dissolve unbelief. Perhaps the nearest systematic attempt to answer the Jews and the heathen is to be found in the moving little **Epistle to Diognetus** (probably second century). The writer seriously tries to show the superiority of the Christian way of life, deliberately contrasting it with the foolish worship of idols which the heathen practise and the arid legalism which is the hall-mark of the Judaic code.

In its earliest appearance, then, the Apologetics of the primitive Church was occasional and sporadic in character. Before Christianity could develop a strong defensive front against Jewish and heathen opposition, it came under the influence of another factor which powerfully affected the development of its thought especially during the second century and for most of the third. This factor is **Gnosticism**. The name derives from *gnosis*, the Greek word for knowledge, understood generally in the sense of saving knowledge. The contemporary Hellenistic world was intensely interested in religion. In the classical age of Plato and Aristotle it was reason that was held to be the key to the secrets of the universe. Now in a later age, and no doubt making a wider popular appeal, religion had displaced philosophy and religiosity rational enquiry. St. Paul testifies to this in the sermon he delivered on Mars' Hill (Acts 17.22ff.); and whether his words charge the Athenians with being "too superstitious" (as A.V.) or (as N.E.B.) with being "in everything that concerns religion uncommonly scrupulous," it is a designation equally applicable to the whole world of his day. In this situation the saving knowledge purveyed by Gnosticism both evoked and answered questions of deep contemporary concern.

But Gnosticism remains an extraordinarily complex phenomenon eluding a simple definition. The denotation of the term is variously conceived. Sometimes it is extended to include all Hellenistic thinking and teaching in which *gnosis* plays a role; sometimes it is restricted to systems in which Christian elements are present and whose intention at least, with whatever success, is Christian. Connected with this is the question of the limits to be put upon the period of Gnostic activity. It is now generally understood that elements of Gnostic provenance are detectable in Judaism; and this means that Gnosticism has to be allotted a pre-Christian origin. The Fathers tend to think of Gnosticism as a heretical variant of Christianity, and they trace its beginnings to Simon Magus who makes a brief and inconclusive appearance in the scriptural narrative at Acts 8. At the other end Gnostic activity is held to run on into the 8th or 9th century; but at least Christian involvement with it came to an end long before this. The literature produced by Gnosticism was immense. In its Christian variety it gave rise to apocryphal gospels imitative of those eventually included in the canon of Scripture, as well as other treatises. Of all this labour little has survived. The world is little the poorer for this; but the consequence is that we are for the most part dependent on those who made reply to the Gnostics for our knowledge of what they in fact said. However, since the notice given to their writings and the quotations made from them are generous, we probably have as much material as we need for forming a reliable estimate. It is impossible to think of Gnosticism as a school of thought. It can be described no more precisely than as an unorganized group of sects. It is not so much a movement as a tendency of thought. For the purpose here we may characterize Gnosticism as an ambient and pervasive atmosphere whose chief ingredients are pagan philosophy, astrology and Greek mystery religion, which seeped into later Judaism in a mild way and into Christianity with more lasting effects.[2]

The apologetic consequences will occupy attention for the remainder of this chapter. Only slowly did appreciation of the situation emerge.

The answers supplied by Christian writers at the beginning hardly keep pace with the growth of Gnostic influence and effect upon Christianity. It is only later that the Christian reply begins to overhaul the advance of Gnostic influence, and in the end destroys it as a serious danger. It is inappropriate to divide up the action between Gnosticism and Christianity into strict stages and watertight levels. The danger signals are already posted in the canonical New Testament books; the peril is intuited and warnings are issued. The **Apologists** are occupied with more than one concern. But they are aware of Gnostic pressures, though they resist them with little resolution. When in the middle of the second century Gnosticism emerges into the open and displays all its strength, it needed time for Christianity to realize what the issues at stake really were, and also much more resolute defenders than had done duty earlier. The second surge of Gnostic pressure is met by Christian theologians far tougher and more perceptive. It is just as well that Christianity could for the occasion summon thinkers of such calibre as Irenaeus, Clement of Alexandria, Tertullian, and Origen.

Gnosticism comprises an astonishing and bewildering array of speculative ideas, myths and fantasies, presented sometimes as emanating from the Apostles and conveyed by secret tradition, sometimes as direct revelations imparted to individual writers. Its character is syncretistic, and the widest hospitality is shown to ideas of all kinds from many sources. Its range is vast: at one extreme there is genuinely philosophical speculation; at the other it degenerates into wild and extravagant mythology. It can hardly be said to have a method. The books of the Old and New Testaments are sometimes used, though the interpretation offered differs widely from orthodox Christian usage. It does, however, manifest a general common intention: it seeks to give an account of things as they are, of man's place in the universe, of evil and of man's destiny. The role of *gnosis*, the knowledge of God supplied in revelation, is fundamentally important, for by means of it the spiritual element in man achieves redemption. At this point some kind of contact is made with Christianity, and Jesus is given a place of honour. But the contact is slight. Little attempt is made to show that Jesus is in any real sense unique. He is no more than the bringer of *gnosis:* it is the effective agent in salvation. In general, Christian elements are incorporated, but in no more than a diluted form.

The world is conceived by Gnosticism as the handiwork of a Demiurge or creator god. This Demiurge is quite distinguishable from the supreme Deity who is a being remote and unknowable; but he is derived from the divine being through a series of emanations or aeons. The world he made is radically imperfect, for its maker has himself been involved in a fall.

Gnosticism thinks of man as part of the created world and hence as characterized by imperfection and what is called sin. But men fall into three classes. Some men have incorporated within them a seed or spark of the divine, and rank as *pneumatikoi* or spiritual. In virtue of this they possess an element that is savable; and it is the *gnosis* offered that enables this element to gain release from the unworthy matter in which it is imprisoned. The other classes are less fortunate. Of the *psychikoi* (psychic) few if any have a chance of redemption; while for the *hylikoi* or *sarkikoi* (material or fleshly) there is no hope whatever.

Of the Gnostics, the best-known are Valentinus and Marcion (who, however, is distinguished by a practical bent of mind which largely disregarded the cosmological speculations that constituted so engrossing an interest for most Gnostics). It has to be repeated that most of the writings of the Gnostics have perished, and we are indebted mainly to those who contested their views for long, and, we may reliably suppose, quoted accurately from what they had to say. In the case of **Valentinus** (at Rome *c.*136—*c.*165, when he separated from the Catholic Church) we have a valuable additional source of information in the recently discovered Nag Hammadi texts, themselves dating from the fourth century but credibly regarded as an accurate translation of originals of the second century. Speculation is given free rein and results in bizarre imaginings. It is sufficient here to say that for Valentinus' intricate system of pairs of aeons emanating from the supreme Father and linking him with the birth of matter and the production of the particularly important pair of aeons, Christ and the Holy Spirit, there is not a trace of evidence in Scripture. Such biblical entities as *Aletheia* (truth), *Logos* (word), *Ecclesia* (Church), *Nous* (mind) and *Sophia* (wisdom) are named and expounded. But they are caught up into a system in which all similarity to their biblical counterparts is completely obliterated.

**Marcion** (excommunicated in July 144 at Rome) emphasizes an element common enough in other Gnostics when, prompted by violent antagonism to Judaism, he regards law and the Old Testament as proclaiming a quite different God from him to whom Gospel and New Testament witness. That the God of the Old Testament is evil is, according to him, demonstrated by Adam being allowed to sin, and even by such *trivia* as his ordering the observance of Sabbath rest and requiring the ark to be carried round Jericho on eight successive days. In contrast, the good God of the New Testament is proclaimed by Jesus Christ, and his character is made apparent in the teaching that only a good tree can bring forth good fruit and by his fruit we shall know him. Marcion not only rejected the Old Testament but compiled a highly selective version of the books now included in the New Testament. In this he included only a version of Luke in mutilated form, and ten of the Pauline Epistles, carefully excluding the Pastorals and Hebrews; and this Evangelium and Apostolicum form for him the Bible of Christians. This original method of replying to the opposition offered by the Jews was swiftly repudiated by the Church as a whole. The Jews no doubt had to be answered; but this was not the way to do it.

Today we may regard with some astonishment such views masquerading as Christian. But we have the advantage not only of hindsight but also of the critical work of those who at the time were obliged to assess them. Some of the Gnostic teachers sincerely claimed to be Christians. It is easy for us now to disallow the claim: clearly they were not succeeding in transmitting the Christian Gospel intact and unimpaired. But so far as the transmission of the Gospel was their sincere intention, it is not outrageous to regard the enterprise on which they embarked as an early exercise in Apologetics. What they were doing was to try to restate the Gospel in the terms current among their contemporaries. These terms were philosophical in character. It is evident now that they were unfitted to convey the Gospel faithfully and without diminution. But it was not so clear then. It is the achievement of the Apologists and of the greater figures who later come upon the stage, that the Church did not fall for this primitive and undoubtedly inadequate version of the faith.

The prevalent syncretism of the contemporary pagan intellectual climate could quite easily have stripped Christianity of its distinctive features and assimilated it into the vastly hospitable amalgam of beliefs to which it had given rise. Resistance to this development could be effectively offered not by the pagan intellectual but the alert believer. Yet this resistance was slow to manifest itself. It was in the sphere of practice that the issue began to clarify itself. For in contrast to the adherents of other religions, Christians found themselves obliged to play a non-conformist role. They refused to offer sacrifice at the command of the state; they declined civic and state office; and they found increasing difficulty in fulfilling military duties. Such deviationist tendencies were new in the world of the day. Naturally they incurred suspicion. Almost inevitably suspicion hardened into misunderstanding and gave rise to a lively crop of misrepresentation and slander. Those who defied the civil laws and customs could easily be thought capable of repudiating the moral law itself. The **Apologists** undertook the double task of showing that Christianity was politically innocuous and of refuting the ignorant charges of immorality brought against it.

Besides this there was a more intellectual duty to discharge. Pagans and Jews alike were possessed of intellectual systems that were different enough from Christianity to demand consideration. Judaism declared its opposition from the start: reconciliation was impossible between Christianity and a system that had not only rejected the claims of Jesus constituting the centre of the Christian faith, but had done all it could to get rid of him and destroy his influence. Contemporary philosophy was, as has been said, less disposed to dispute the new system of belief and much rather inclined to accept it on terms of assimilation. The procedure of the Apologists as they faced these two different fronts has a recognizable similarity. In answer to the Jews they developed their own thought about Old Testament prophecy, to show that in Christianity what the Old Testament had presaged had been fulfilled, and Christian doctrine was accordingly the legitimate descendant and heir of Old Testament thinking. In the case of pagan philosophy, the attempt was made to show the compatibility of Christian belief with what was highest and best in the ethical and philosophical affirmations of the non-Christian world. The strategy of the Apologists is in both cases to avoid, if possible, head-on conflict and, with the notable exception of Tatian, to emphasize in a mild and eirenic way that Christianity was the proper extension of the truest and best of the alternative systems.

Charges of immorality are the object of such serious examination and careful repudiation on the part of the Apologists that we must suppose them to have had an extensive currency and been widely believed. **Justin Martyr** (*c*.100–*c*.165), of whose work a *First Apology* and a *Second Apology* have survived, as has also a *Dialogue with Trypho*, declares his aim to be "to lay before the public a faithful memorial of our life and doctrine, that we may not thank ourselves for our sufferings, which for want of due information you may inflict upon us" (*First Apology* 3). The work, addressed to the Emperor Antonius Pius, begins with a plea not that the punishment of Christians be terminated, but that the charges against them be examined; and it ends by quoting Hadrian's rescript or directive (*c*. 125) prohibiting the punishment of Christians except on charges proven in open court. The tone of the whole document is mild, conciliatory, persuasive. Their very name, Justin playfully hints, suggests the falsity of the charges of immorality brought against them: they are indicted as Christians—but the word *chrestos* means kind and good (4). As for the charge of atheism, Justin admits it (5f.). But only in the sense that, in making a distinction between evil demonic spirits and good godlike spirits, as both Socrates and the incarnate Logos enable us to do, Christians withhold worship from devils imagined to be gods, and offer it only to the most true God, Father, Son and Spirit. Justin resumes the defence of Christians at this point in his *Second Apology*. Here he embarks upon a comparison of Christian moral teaching with that of the pagans including the Stoics, and shows its superiority: what Socrates declared only as an ideal, he says (10), Christian morality has realized on earth.

We hear more about the charges made against Christians in the *Supplication for Christians* by **Athenagoras** (which must have been written between 176 and 180). If atheism is anywhere to be found, it is not among the Christians but rather among the Greeks who have largely abandoned the traditional polytheism. Athenagoras gives an account at some length of the very different beliefs which Christians hold; for they proclaim a God who has spoken by the Holy Spirit through messengers in the Old Testament, and who is one but not undiversified unity. For the Son of God is the Father's Logos, and the Holy Spirit flows divinely from him. Besides, the ethical teaching of Christ lays the foundation for the conduct of Christians. The charge of licence and debauchery is groundless. On the contrary, Christians are dedicated to chastity. So far from being murderers, they condemn and renounce abortion, exposure of children, and even the gladiatorial shows.

**Tatian** (*c*.160) is famous for his *Diatessaron*, the first attempt to weave the records of the four Gospels into a single continuous narrative. In his *Discourse to the Greeks* he carries further the comparison of Christianity with surrounding paganism. He delivers an attack of unusual force upon the contemporary world: he can find nothing but evil in its religion, its ethics, its philosophy and its culture. Because of the violence of its tone, the work is valuable more for the evidence it supplies of the Graeco-Roman world of the day than as Christian apologetic.

The answer offered by the Apologists to Jewish objections has more lasting apologetic value. The central thesis is simply that the expectations and anticipations written into the Old Testament have been apprehended, understood and applied by Christians, and in the Christian faith have been fulfilled and realized. Here we have in a pure form the classic apologetic argument from prophecy. As has been seen, this pattern of defence has precedent in the New Testament itself; and in the course of apologetic activity it is in different forms repeated again and again. Justin Martyr in his *First Apology* devotes a good deal of space and attention to it. He bases his proofs of Christ's divinity not so much on the reports of men as on "the prediction of prophets" (27). The Jews, he says (44), will themselves grant that the prophets were inspired by the "divine Wisdom or Logos." But the Old Testament itself supplies indications not only that the Logos would be incarnate (Isa. 9.6), but also where this would take place (Mic. 5.2). Even the historical crisis bound up with this appearance (e.g. Zech. 9.9), the reception it would receive (Isa. 1.3f.), and especially the end to which it would lead (Ps. 22.16, 18; Isa. 65.2, 50.6-8) are anticipated. It will be noted that Justin is untroubled by the complications with which biblical criticism has invested the whole subject of prophetic prediction and the proof based upon it. Today we feel obliged to distinguish the general principle involved and the detailed application of the principle. Recently there has been a significant return to the general principle that there is a predictive or expectant element in the Old Testament which provides a framework into which what is recorded in the New Testament fits as fulfilment, even if we think it necessary to be more sceptical about the detailed point to point correspondence of which Justin makes such uninhibited use.

In his *Dialogue with Trypho* (c.160), Justin Martyr develops his general argument in greater detail, paying special attention to the Jewish criticism that Jesus set aside the law contained in the Old Testament. The relation of Jesus to the law, Justin writes, is not an act of infidelity: his unique position entitles him to transcend the law in fulfilling it. In this sense, he insists, Gentiles are properly admitted into the Christian Church without being obliged to obey the law in all its detailed requirements. This point of view is further developed by **Aristides** in his *Apology* (possibly 164), who addresses himself particularly to the Jewish opposition to Christianity. He divides mankind into the barbarians, the Greeks, the Jews, and the Christians, the differentia being the object to which worship is addressed. While the barbarians worship material bodies, and the Greeks, gods who too obviously manifest human faults and passions, the Jews at least worship one God, though their attention has been falsely directed to invalid reverence for angels, sabbaths and seasons. Christians on the other hand, the "third race", apprehend the truth about God, recognize his moral character, and admit the moral obligation which this enjoins upon them.

The attitude of the Apologists to the current pagan philosophy is of crucial importance in the development of Apologetics. Here we have the first attempt to work out a relationship between Christianity and a prevailing climate of thought which we should today designate as secular. Pagan religion and cult are denounced and ridiculed, but pagan philosophy is accorded great respect. We repeat: the general policy (not, however, adopted by Tatian) is to seek common ground rather than to provoke conflict. Christianity accordingly is represented not as the inexorable opponent of the philosophical heritage of the Hellenistic world but as its most reliable vindicator and exponent. Justin Martyr does not hesitate to appeal to the authority of the classical philosophers. The name of Socrates has already been cited. But he appeals also to Plato and the Stoics, Menander and the poets. The place they hold in his scheme of things is exemplified in what is said about Plato. According to Justin, Plato both read and borrowed from the Hebrew Scriptures, for example in the account given by him in the *Timaeus* of creation (*First Apology*, 76f.). This "bizarre notion"[3] is now quite discredited. More generally Justin is content to show that Christianity is congruous with and adds nothing beyond the teachings of Plato (*op. cit*, 28). In an important passage in the *Second Apology* (10) he gives the ground for this. According to him, if the philosophers have been able to anticipate truths embedded in the Christian faith, it is because they partake of the *logos spermatikos* or seminal Logos. Christ "was partially known even by Socrates; for he was and is the word who is in every man, and who foretold the things that were to come to pass, both through the prophets and in his own person." Pagans and Christians alike are indebted to Christ who is the source of all truth. The knowledge possessed by the former is only fragmentary and is confined to philosophers and scholars, while the fuller Christian knowledge is enjoyed by artisans and uneducated people.

So Justin Martyr appropriates in the name of Christ all that is of value in the secular thinking of his day. No very great care is taken to prove identity between the truth expressed by the pagans and that incorporated in Christianity. Since the supposition of correspondence based on Plato's acquaintance with the writings of Moses cannot be sustained, all that remains amounts to saying that, because Christ is truth, anything that is truly said anywhere must ultimately be traceable to him. The argument does appear to prove something, and it certainly does honour to the supremacy of Christ. But it is doubtful whether a convinced Platonist would be profoundly moved in the direction of Christianity by having his learning thus taken over, given the appellation of Christian and arrogated to Christ.

The work of the Apologists is often decried as a betrayal of Christianity to the enemy, declared and undeclared: the spirit of the age debauched the faith. Harnack gives expression to this view in his monumental *History of Dogma* (1886-89, Eng. 1894-99): Christian theology suffered distortion through Hellenisation and the early intrusion of elements of Greek metaphysics. However, we should perhaps reflect that such judgments are necessarily more or less partisan, in the sense that they represent a knowledge of one side of the case without face to face acquaintance with the other. The Apologists at least knew both sides equally well. The world in which they lived was saturated in Hellenism, but they had devoted themselves to the Christian faith. No one following them could ever be in quite the same position again. Distance lends perspective as well as enchantment; and today we certainly see some things more clearly than did the Apologists. Their understanding of the connection between Hellenism and Christianity was certainly far too *simpliciste*. If there is a relation it does not consist in an interchange of ideas through the medium of the writings involved; nor in a repetition, the one on an elementary and the other on a more advanced level, of ideas that are identical. There is a similarity between Prometheus chained to his rock and Christ nailed to the cross and both refusing to denounce their executioners. But the two figures belong to quite different areas of reality and the similarity is only superficial. The point of contact between Christianity and Hellenism, if there is one, is located at a more profound level, where indeed all that is certainly true is certainly of God.

Chronologically the four great names that follow next in the story of Christian theology are those of Irenaeus, Clement of Alexandria, Tertullian and Origen. By the time that these theologians have said their say and made their contribution, the corpus of Christian theology has been greatly extended and immeasurably strengthened. The days of rather awkward schoolboyish fidelity to the teachings of Jesus and the works of St. Paul, often revealing a genuine love and a deficient understanding of Scripture, are over. Christian theology now clearly stands on its own feet. Of course it remains faithful to the Apostolic writings as these were slowly consolidating themselves as a norm for Christian thought. But it expounds, interprets, applies and employs them with a freedom based on appreciative understanding. Yet there is no clear break with those who had gone before. The hundred years enriched by these four theologians overlap at their beginning with the time of the Apologists. The situation to be apologetically addressed does not change overnight. Irenaeus confronts Valentinus who contributed to the situation Justin Martyr faced. Tertullian singled out Marcion the quasi-Gnostic, as his opponent. The formidable attack of Celsus upon Christianity in the third quarter of the second century has to wait some 70 years until it meets in Origen a Christian of the calibre required to refute it. In these three theologians Christianity found defenders who are sure of themselves and of the Christianity they defended, and who are moreover equipped with the intellectual ability enabling them to avoid both a too querulous denunciation of their opponents and a too eager compounding with them. Yet among the four names is that of **Clement of Alexandria** (*c.*150—*c.*215) and he exhibits more of the spirit of the Apologists and earns from Henry Chadwick[4] the title of "the liberal Puritan". This chapter will appropriately end with him.

In Clement, Christianity for the first time achieves scholarly exposition. True, the works he leaves behind are, at best, loosely constructed and at worst, downright rambling. But they show an immense knowledge of past and present thought and of philosophical and poetic literature, even if the acquaintance seems to depend a good deal on anthologies from which he cannot resist quoting freely and extensively (see *Stromateis*, 1.2 for his own defence). The situation in Alexandria placed Clement between two fires. On the one hand were the ordinary orthodox Christians, anti-intellectual, moralistic, obscurantist; on the other the intellectuals strongly attracted by Valentinian Gnosticism and the Platonized version of Christianity it offered. Between these two contrasting elements Clement plays the part of skilful mediator and urbane reconciler. He seems deliberately to design and assume this role himself. The Word, he says (*Paedagogos*, 1), conducts us to salvation by first exhorting, then training, and finally teaching; and it looks as if Clement was led to follow a similar plan in his writings. For he follows up the *Protrepticos* (or Exhortation) with the *Paidagogos* (or Instructor); while the third work, *Stromateis* (or Miscellanies, literally "carpetbags"!), in some degree discharges the third part of the plan, even if Clement's incorrigible discursiveness plays havoc with any intended systematic exposition. But the apologetic purpose of the works is already clear: the heathen Clement will exhort "to abandon the impious mysteries of idolatry for the adoration of the divine Word and God the Father" (*Protr*, 1); the faithful are ready for instruction in how to conduct themselves as Christians (a strange medley of morals and mere etiquette); and the teaching follows in the inconsequential form of the Miscellanies.

Clement manifests a considerable measure of agreement with the Gnostics. For him truth is one. Philosophy is illuminated by the light which is Christ. The trouble with the philosophical sects is that each claims the portion it possesses is the whole truth. The remedy for sectarian divisiveness is to pool the word of truth from each (*Str*, 1.13). But Clement refuses to be submerged in the sea of Gnostic syncretism. Certainly God is the cause of all good things, and of course of all truth. But in the Logos, the second person in the Trinity, the supreme revelation of God has been given, and Christianity, accordingly, is the perfection of what the systems of philosophy grope after. But they make their own contribution: philosophy was given to the Greeks as a schoolmaster to bring the Hellenistic world to Christ, just as according to St. Paul the law was given to the Hebrews (*Str*, 1.58; 2.23, 25): "philosophy is the handmaid of theology" (*op. cit.* 1.5).

His opponents thus placated are invited to allow the Logos to make its own impression on them. He strongly criticizes paganism: the religious myths are absurd, the practices impious, the images shameful, and the opinions about the gods of many of their philosophers are ignorant and erroneous. His appeal consists in an exhortation to abandon such teachings for the sublime truths of the Gospel. These are commended to all reasonable men by the Logos itself: "the heavenly and truly divine love comes to men, when in the soul itself the spark of true goodness, kindled in the soul by the divine Word, is able to burst forth into flame" (*Protr*, 11).

Like the Gnostics, then, Clement's theology supposes a spark of the divine in man, and this the Logos of Scripture (*Str*, 1.1) can fan into flame. But he goes further in characterizing this element in man in the account he gives, or rather the scattered remarks he makes, about faith. Faith indeed rests upon presuppositions. But then so do also philosophical systems. Faith has to be distinguished from mere acquiescence. Basilides is wrong in supposing that faith is simply a natural gift. But so too are anti-intellectualist Christians wrong in thinking of it as capitulation to sheer authority. Rather faith is a matter of assent to God who is worthy of trust. This involves an exercise of will, and implies not only knowledge but also ethical activity.

Clement is less critical of Platonism than for example Justin Martyr. Yet at a decisive point he sees that a distinction must be drawn. He makes clear the line separating the Creator and the creation. This conviction nerves him to contradict Plato when he asserts that the heavenly bodies have souls. Yet if he construes Plato's doctrine of the creation by means of Genesis to mean that the cosmos is created and not eternal, he is himself not entirely unequivocal. For while he more than once declares that the world is made "out of nothing", the Greek form of words he uses suggests he is thinking of its being made not from what absolutely does not exist, but rather from relative non-being.[5] On the other hand, he is quite sure that the Gnostics are wrong in supposing the world to be the work of a less than beneficent demiurge, that neither is the soul by nature good nor the body evil, and that immortality is not an inherent attribute of the soul but the gift of Christ.

Thus Clement roams round the rich intellectual world of his day with a far greater sense of mastery than Christian theologians had hitherto shown, fearlessly rebutting such elements as are incongruous with the Christian faith, and just as eagerly putting others to apologetic use. The broadest area of agreement which he shares with Gnosticism is found in his conception of salvation. For him, as for any of the Gnostics, salvation is by *gnosis*, and the knowledge or illumination implied is supremely offered in Jesus Christ who became man to impart it.

# CHAPTER THREE

# TOWARDS NICAEA

FOR intellectual power and theological ability, Irenaeus and Origen rise head and shoulders above all other Christian writers before 325. But the contribution each makes is different from the other and highly individual, and this is true not least of the apologetic aspect of their work. With **Irenaeus** (c.130—c.200) the apologetic task comes to be identified and defined with greater clarity. Even more important, for the first time an attempt is made to go beyond unsystematic apologetic practice and to define the principles of Apologetics. Irenaeus is not content simply to select from the riches of the classical world what suits or is congruous with Christianity and to reject what contradicts or conflicts with it. He passes beyond such eclecticism to study not only what is heretically said, but also what heresy in itself is; and he proceeds not only to approve particular elements in the non-Christian world, but to construct a strategy of Christian defence. Scientific Apologetics begins to take shape and to replace amateurish apologetic activity.

This greater maturity of apologetic outlook appears in Irenaeus's deliberate selection of the enemy he will challenge and the carefully directed and sustained counterattack he makes. Of his two surviving treatises the longer and better-known is from the title onwards a deliberately apologetic work. It is now referred to as *Against Heresies* (*adversus Haereses*); but Irenaeus himself supplied a longer title: *Five Books to unmask and overthrow falsely named Gnosis*, citing 1 Tim. 6.20. Book 1 is an account of the doctrines he proposes to expose and refute. It is a mine of information about what the Gnostics believed. Irenaeus refers at the beginning to "certain men," "disciples of Valentinus", who have set truth aside, and he quotes 1 Tim. 1.4 against them. His original intention seems to have been to deal with Ptolemy, a Valentinian Gnostic. But the front on which he engages widens to include Valentinus himself. He then moves forward in time to deal with other followers of Valentinus, and also backwards to tackle the earlier Gnostics from Simon Magus (of Acts 8.9-24) onwards. It is indeed a strange world of thought into which the reader is plunged as Irenaeus describes it in preparation for his attack. Thirty aeons produced for the glory of the Father being wrapped up in silence, for which reason the Saviour did no public work for thirty years (1.1.3); the soul in distress calling out: Oh, and thus unconsciously honouring and claiming assistance from the seventh heaven which has uttered the element Omega (1.14.7f.); and so on. One has sympathy with Irenaeus when he denounces such unedifying speculations as ravings, and is tempted to agree when at the end of Book 1 he passes judgment (1.31.3): *adversos eos victoria est sententiae eorum manifestatio* (to describe such sentiments is to refute them).

Yet he does not merely allow the Gnostic challenge to collapse under the weight of its own fantastic elaboration. He is better than his word, and proceeds in Book 2 to "overthrow their whole system by means of a longer treatment" (2.Pref.2). Here the outlines of positive orthodox theology appear. God is one; the world is formed by the Father through the Logos; the system of aeons is totally unnecessary and hopelessly inconsistent; argument by means of numbers, letters and syllables is a delusion. Irenaeus advocates as antidote to the Gnostic absurdities "a sound mind devoted to piety, and the love of truth" (2.27.1); "by means of love we attain to nearness to God" (2.26.1).

But Irenaeus is impelled by his own interest and concern to undertake an even more searching and fundamental critique. He adds three further books in which, with acute observations on many other points, he apprehends and sets out the principles of a proper Apologetics. Instead of opposing Gnosticism with a better Christian *gnosis* as Clement did, he formulates three principal criteria for distinguishing true Christian doctrine from heretical propositions. The Church's proper retort to Gnostic speculation is in terms of continuity. First, the plan of salvation comes down to Christians in the Gospel attested in the Scriptures which are the ground and pillar of the faith (*cf.* 1 Tim. 3.15, though in fact it is the Church that is described there) (3.1.1.). We note that Irenaeus is not above relapsing when it suits him into the type of numerical argument for which he ridicules the Gnostics. For he shows the necessity of there being four Gospels, neither more nor less, to correspond to the four quarters or zones of heaven, the four-faced cherubim, and the four covenants with Adam, Noah, Moses and Christ (3.11.8). Secondly, there is tradition, originating with the Apostles, and preserved by means of the "successions of presbyters in the Churches" (3.2.2). Thirdly, there is the perpetual succession of bishops, instituted by the Apostles, and continuing down to contemporary days—they have been guardians of the Apostolic tradition. Here Rome, the Church founded by the "two most glorious Apostles, Peter and Paul", has a "pre-eminent authority" (*potiorem principalitatem* (3.3.2), but both text and meaning are disputable).

This notable exposition puts Irenaeus in the first rank of apologists for the Christian faith, just as the contribution he makes in other areas of theology assures him a place of honour amongst the theologians. He stands above the course of events and the stream of contemporary thought, and he grasps the essential historicity of the Christian faith. It is a theological principle of supreme importance. Theology can never make an entirely new start, for this could only happen on the basis of another incarnation. Apologetically used, the principle exposes the essential weakness of the Gnostic versions of Christianity. They are faulted on each of the three principles. Their supposition that there are hidden mysteries which were only verbally imparted to "the perfect" among men is simply false (3.3.1). With the application of the three principles their system collapses in ruins.

**Origen** (c.185—c.254) must be classed among these sometimes called "blue water (or speculative) theologians." Both he and Irenaeus are aware of the limitations of reason in investigating the transcendent, but they differ widely about where the boundary line is to be drawn beyond which reason is at a loss. With his emphasis on Scripture and tradition as defences of true faith, Irenaeus is the prototype of the orthodox traditionalists. Origen on the other hand pushes back the boundary with a much more intrepid hand: where Scripture is silent, reason guided by grace can speculate. This dissimilarity lies for the most part outside the concern of Apologetics. Like Irenaeus, Origen has one main work which in both title and contents is explicitly apologetic in character. This is the work known as *contra Celsum* (mid third century) in eight books. But this writing offers not only an apologetic reply to Celsus. It is given in such careful detail that, though Celsus' original attack no longer survives, nine-tenths of it is preserved in the quotations Origen supplies. This is the earliest case in which we have so full a record of all the evidence led for the prosecution and defence of Christianity. While Irenaeus is daring enough to take on "all heresies", Origen launches his attack on a narrower sector of the front where Christianity was in contact with the ancient world. The point is not unimportant. Origen shows himself quite competent to identify and appreciate what is inimical and injurious to Christianity on a limited scale and to deal with it effectively. But the cast of his mind is inclined to be sympathetic towards views and opinions of a more marginal and less clearly orthodox kind. He offers them hospitality rather than hostility. Consequently violent controversy arose concerning his orthodoxy, and continued for centuries. Not many Christian writers have such a stature that they are studied for 300 years before being condemned by the Church! (Council of Constantinople 543). Yet Origen clearly desires to be truly Christian, and declares that error in doctrine is more reprehensible than moral fault. He is neither latitudinarian nor free thinker, but he evidently stands for a more liberal employment of the mind in the interests of theology; and this is one way in which Apologetics may be done.

**Celsus** launched his attack on Christianity *c*.177—180 in his *True Discourse* (*Alethes Logos*), a work in four books. In the first the objections offered are expounded by a Jew who, faithful to the Old Testament, maintains that the Messiah of Christianity is not the fulfilment of Jewish hopes. In the second it is a pagan who presses home the attack by demonstrating that the Jewish hopes of a Messiah are themselves absurd. Celsus' own criticism of Christianity, of both its beliefs and its ethic, is formulated in Book 3; and in the fourth book he passes over to a restatement of paganism as a defensible alternative preferable to Christianity.

The work constitutes a landmark. Until its appearance explicit opposition to Christianity had not reached systematic literary expression. The Christian theologians already mentioned certainly went in to the attack on ideas which would pervert or destroy Christianity. But they had to seek out the enemy, either in a paganism in which opposition was only latent, or in Gnostic systems which sometimes ostensibly claimed to be Christian and which in any case would cheerfully have compounded with anything less intransigent than Christianity was proving to be. Celsus comes out into the open with a direct challenge. War is expressly declared, and by a formidable foe.

The cardinal error Celsus makes is to underestimate the Christianity he challenged. He apparently cannot bring himself to believe that there are or can be any educated believers. Had he lived to read it, the reply which Origen constructs must surely have shaken the obstinacy with which he depicts Christian intellectual ineptitude. For at the instigation of Ambrose,[1a] as he tells us, and rather against his will, Origen devises a riposte which, for all its rather tedious prolixity and formlessness, is mild in tone, reasonable in character, and in effect devastating. One by one, in almost interminable array, the points Celsus makes against Christianity are assembled, and to them Origen quietly and confidently makes his reply. Celsus mocks at the Christians who can or will give no reason for their belief, "repeating: 'Don't examine, only believe', 'your faith will save you', and 'the wisdom of this life is bad, but foolishness is a good thing'." "In the Christian system", answers Origen, "there is at least as much investigation into acts of belief and explanations of dark sayings" as in other systems (1.9). But then the whole eight books of Origen's reply is a more monumental witness to both the willingness and the ability of Christianity to give a reason for its beliefs.

From the philosophical point of view, Celsus proposes an interpretation of the affinities between Christianity and the philosophical thought of antiquity different from that usually suggested, for example by Justin Martyr, whose works Celsus may have read. Plato is not dependent on Moses, nor is pagan philosophy an elementary stage on a road that terminates in Christianity. In fact the opposite is true: Jesus borrowed from Plato and Paul from Heraclitus. Not only is Christianity dependent on classical philosophy: it misunderstands and corrupts what it uses (6.16, 12). Perhaps some contemporary pagans had laughed up their sleeves when Justin suggested that Plato had read Moses. But Origen can here turn the tables on this new advocate of paganism. What educated person would not laugh at Celsus for suggesting that Jesus, who had "never learned" (John 7.15), had studied Plato, quoted from him, and perverted what he quoted (*ib.*)? Origen suggests that Celsus could only have come to such an estimate by reading the Gospels in a spirit of hatred and dislike, and one feels the comment is accurate and just.

The chief theological point at which Celsus must be answered concerns the view of God which he holds and presses home sometimes with great acuteness. Indeed many of the objections he makes are indistinguishable from what are still today sometimes advanced as difficulties. For example he complains that Christians talk of God as if he had hands and limbs, as though he spoke with a mouth and voice, as though he grew fatigued (6.61ff.). In reply Origen makes the simple distinction between a literal anthropomorphism and a figurative necessity: if we talk at all we must do so by means of analogies. Again Celsus' criticism that, if God lacks nothing, then all feasts in his honour are useless, reveals him as a mocker of all religion—as though, says Origen (8.21), everyone did not know that, while God is not enriched by such rites, men offer enlightened worship by means of them, and the Christian keeps certain days *because* he knows that all days are God's.

Above all, the incarnation presents Celsus with an opportunity for ridiculing Christianity. The Jew is his mouthpiece in declaring that the Christian Messiah does not fulfil the Old Testament expectations, and the pagan in showing these same expectations to be in any case ridiculous. Besides, the incarnation itself is full of contradiction. Does God come to improve his knowledge of the world? (4.3). God must be subject to change if the incarnation is real, and deceitful if it is only an imagination of the believer (4.18). And what about heaven left empty when God departs in order to become a man (4.5)? Even the problem of contingency is raised: the Christian talks of the cross as "a tree of life"; but if Jesus had died by falling over a precipice, would he talk of a precipice of life beyond the heavens (6.34)? Origen in his reply brings to bear in simple and dignified language the growing resources of Christian theology and the assurance of personal faith. He is quite sure that God loves the human race, that the incarnation is a real condescension on his part, that it was designed for our good, and that specious problems of how God could do so while remaining God are answerable in terms of what he calls "the economy of his providence" (4.14). Celsus has not worked hard enough to learn what Christian theology has to say. He simply skims off verbal phrases and invests them with interpretations both superficial and erroneous.

At no point does Celsus more clearly reveal not so much the inadequacy of Christianity as his own stuffy and supercilious character than where he ridicules Christianity for its vulgarity, its depreciation of human values, its anti-cultural tendency and practice, and the ineffable commonness of the people who adhere to it. In a well-known passage he declares: "Let us hear what kind of persons those Christians invite. Everyone, they say, who is a sinner, who is devoid of understanding, who is a child, and, to speak generally, whoever is unfortunate—him will the kingdom of God receive" (3.59). And again: "it is only foolish and low individuals, and persons devoid of perception, and slaves, and women and children, of whom the teachers of the divine word wish to make converts" (3.49). Origen's retort has a true and humble magnificence: "Christ is the Saviour of all men whether they be intellectual or simple; those that are instructed and wise can come here and be satisfied; those that are foolish or sick or sinful can approach in order to be cured." (*ib.*)

With **Tertullian** (*c*.160–*c*.220) the science of Apologetics attains a new level of comprehensiveness and pertinacity. Perhaps one should rather say the art of Apologetics, for Tertullian excels especially in the practice and application of the activity. Well educated in both rhetoric and law, a master of Greek, for some time a noted lawyer and then a convert to Christianity, he plunged into a literary career dedicated to the vindication of the Christian faith on almost all imaginable fronts. To this chosen task he devoted the ability of the jurist, the ardour of the convert, and all the intelligence, elegance and wit with which his passionate nature was equipped. The Latin in which he writes is dry and terse, but he fashions it into a splendid instrument for the dialectic in which he engages and the paradox which he so much enjoyed. The argument he sustains is formidable, rather overpowering, and a little hectic, resembling "a display of fireworks", as F. L. Cross remarks,[1] "dazzling rather than convincing", says B. Altaner.[2]

It is usual to divide his writings into three groups: apologetic, doctrinal and polemical, and moral and practical. In fact, "all his writings are controversial."[3] Certainly, if apologetic writing means in general the commendation of the Christian faith, having a very wary eye upon the unbelieving world, and including both statement of the Christian faith and refutation of opposing doctrines, then the first two groups fuse into a sustained apologetic.

To the already recurring question concerning the possibility of a *modus vivendi* between Christianity and contemporary culture, it is the office of Tertullian to supply a new answer. His contemporary Clement proves himself the faithful but thoroughly hellenized Christian, while a little later Origen shows his hand in his massive repudiation of Celsus' basic thesis that Christian and Hellenistic strands will not blend. The proposal Tertullian makes constitutes a redisposition of traditional attitudes. He takes his stand with Celsus in declaring the incompatibility of Christianity and Hellenism, but he remains fervently Christian while doing so. "What has Athens to do with Jerusalem?", Tertullian demands shrilly (*de Praescriptione Haereticorum*, p. 7); "what concord is there between the Academy and the Church? Away with every attempt to contrive a piebald Christianity, with Stoic, Platonic and dialectical ingredients. Knowing Jesus Christ we need no speculative enquiry; and possessing the Gospel no further research". His adherence to this thesis of radical incompatibility is unwavering. Sometimes it infects his manner with truculence. But at least he is always prepared to argue his way step by step; and the invective he employs seldom or never degenerates into disdain or contempt of those opposed to him.

His most famous utterance concerns the crucifixion of the Son of God: "it is by all means to be believed because it is absurd; the fact is certain because it is impossible" (*de Carne Christi*, 5). Thus, in his strident way Tertullian throws his challenge in the teeth of philosophy. Yet Tertullian's thought wears a different aspect too. He is no radical anti-rationalist. Christianity can expect nothing from philosophy; it seems rather to make alliance with the absurd and the impossible. Nevertheless Tertullian makes an unhesitating appeal by means of reasoned argument to a certain inchoate, untutored, but basic intuition of God possessed by men, an unreflective "testimony of the soul". In his *Apology* (17) he speaks of the "*anima naturaliter Christiana,*" and his little discourse *de Testimonio Animae* constitutes an excursus upon the phrase. True, "a man becomes a Christian, he is not born one" (*de Testimonio Animae* 1).

Yet the uninstructed soul "testifies to the truth" (*op. cit.* 6). To prove the point Tertullian summons in evidence the spontaneous exclamations of pagans, their belief in the survival of the soul, their hope for the departed, their belief in evil spirits, their fear of ultimate retribution; and he finds even in their denial of God an oblique testimony to his reality.[4]

The variety of fronts on which Christianity was to be defended and the versatility of the defence Tertullian offered can be shown by reference to a few of Tertullian's chief works. The *Apology* confronts the authorities of the day and shows the ignorance and injustice with which they dealt with Christians. They are constantly charged with "secret crimes" (*op. cit.* 6), infanticide and cannibalism, incest and obscene feasting. But no enquiry is made and the charges rest on rumour alone (8). More serious but equally without foundation are the charges of contempt for established religion, lack of patriotism (28), and even treason (29). In this juridical sphere Tertullian is thoroughly at home. The sole crime that is really charged is the *nomen Christianum*. But, Tertullian points out, this implies that there is apparently one law for common criminals who are allowed defence, and another for Christians; one law for philosophers who may embrace atheism with impunity, another for Christians who are for the same reason brought to trial. Yet these outrages do not mortally injure Christianity: *plures efficamur, quoties metimur a vobis, semen est sanguis Christianorum* (the more we are cut down the more we abound; the blood of Christians is seed) (*op. cit.* 50).

Against heresies Tertullian takes up the cudgels in his *de Praescriptione Haereticorum*. For title Tertullian chooses a legal term deliberately. In Roman law a *praescriptio* awarded to a defendant rejected the claim of the prosecution *a limine* and thus obviated the need for trial. Tertullian's *praescriptio* sets forth the grounds on which the claims of heretics should be rejected. The heretics whom he specifically has in mind are exemplified by the names mentioned in the treatise, Valentinus (said to be of Plato's school), Marcion (of the school of the Stoics), and Apellas a rather less well known Gnostic. His reply to them follows lines similar to the argument of Irenaeus; and he deals at greater length with them in other smaller treatises devoted specially to them. The real importance of the *Praescription* lies in its definition of the principles by which heresies are proved to be in error. Truth has been committed to the Catholic

Church alone. Possession of the Scriptures, the ancient tradition handing on the Apostolic teaching, and in a less emphasized degree the succession of bishops have preserved within the Catholic Church the purity of Apostolic doctrine. The acid test to be applied to heresy is whether it can prove itself Apostolic, and by this test heretics fail (see *op. cit.* 15f, 19, 21f, 32, 36). There is no secret tradition, as the heretics pretend (26); it is not even permissible for heretics to interpret the Scriptures (15). The contents of the faith are defined by the rule of faith, which is constituted by Scripture and the Church's right interpretation of Scripture. "To know nothing against the rule of faith is to know all" (*adversus regulam nihil scire omnia scire est*) (*op. cit.* 14).

Against Marcion (*adversus Marcionem*) Tertullian wrote his longest and apparently most painstaking work. From it is derived most of what we know about this quasi-Gnostic. He takes up in turn the salient divergences from orthodox belief that Marcion proposes and deals with them thoroughly. Marcion had this at least in common with the Gnostics, that the world is thought of as the handiwork of a demiurge. This Creator God is revealed in the Old Testament and appears as a God of law. With the God of love revealed by Jesus and the New Testament the Old Testament God has nothing in common. This thesis Tertullian attacks in Books 1 and 2, showing that the distinction Marcion makes is unfounded: the Creator of the world is identical with the good God of the New Testament. Marcion indulges in a docetic Christology. For Christ is an emanation from God, an aeon as the Gnostics also declared. His body is thought of as mortal, and he suddenly appears for the first time preaching at Capernaum. Tertullian devotes Book 3 to showing that Christ is really the Messiah foretold in the Old Testament, that he is no aeon but the unbegotten Son of God, and that his incarnation is real and corporal. Marcion was led in justification of his main thesis to draw up a novel canon of Scripture: the Old Testament is wholly rejected; and of the New Testament he allows the ten Pauline Epistles because Paul appreciated the distinction between law and Gospel; and to this he added a truncated version of Luke. The line followed by Tertullian in Books 4 and 5 is to demonstrate that the contradictions Marcion finds between Old Testament and New Testament are illusory.

Marcion had already been the object of attention on the part of

Irenaeus (*adv. Haer.*, 1.27) and others. His divergent version of Christianity constituted a grave threat to orthodox Christianity, as the attention paid to him in all parts of the Christian world testifies. Marcionism survived the exposure of his doctrines well into the 3rd century, but by its end the threat it offered subsided and disappeared.

Two other works of Tertullian call for brief mention because of their apologetic intention. In *adversus Judaeos* he replies to Jewish objections to Christianity, defining afresh the relation between the law of justice and the law of love which Marcion had so misrepresented. He shows that the promises given to the Jews have indeed found their fulfilment in the New Testament and are thereby made available to Gentiles. In this fulfilment the law of the Old Testament has been superseded by the law of love.

Finally the *de Carne Christi* presents Tertullian more clearly as a dogmatic theologian. He is here concerned to expound the full humanity of Christ and the reality of the flesh he assumed. The argument is developed in the form of a spirited apologetic reply to the Gnostics, Marcion, and other docetic Christologists who represented Christ's body as merely phenomenal.

# CHAPTER FOUR

# NICAEA AND ATHANASIUS

THE "Patristic Age" is usually thought of as lasting from the end of the first century, when the Apostolic age was closing and the New Testament books had been written, up to the end of the eighth century. This period is divided into two parts by the Council of Nicaea in 325. The Apostolic (or Subapostolic) Fathers form the critically important link connecting all later Christianity with the time and events of the incarnation. The Ante-Nicene Fathers who follow them discharge the same function in the succeeding age. Here too it is of importance that Christian thinkers were able to defend the Christian faith, with indeed varying success and decisiveness, to transmit it faithfully, and to beat off the enemies, deliberate and indeliberate, external and internal, that threatened it. The Council of Nicaea is particularly concerned with the chief issue, though it has other interests too. In the turbulent flow of Christian thought it stands out as a rock of temporary refuge where it was possible for Christian theology to consolidate, reorganize, and prepare for what was to come. To change the metaphor, the Council is the precipitation of the dogmatic and apologetic activity hitherto conducted by the Church; and the Church in the future was to draw upon this deposit for later apologetic enterprises.

We have already looked at the great champions of the Christian faith in the years before the Council. They are followed in the theological succession of the Post-Nicene era by others, in increasing numbers and with extending diversity of concerns and gifts. In this second part of the Patristic Age two of them call for notice here because of their outstanding importance as theologians and their contribution to the defence of the faith. Here too strict division into periods is arbitrary. For one thing, the Gnosticism prevalent in the second and third centuries propelled itself into the fourth and evoked new replies from Christian theology. Besides this, the concern which precipitated the Council was one that agitated the Church for some years before it was summoned; the chief protagonist of Christian orthodoxy wrote his two major works of apologetic interests before the Council was convened; the orthodoxy which he led to success at the Council continued to be vexed by the same issue for long after the Council; and orthodoxy, convulsed and deeply divided during this later period, was championed through thick and thin, in prosperity and adversity, in office and out of office, by the same protagonist as had earlier done duty in its name.

This individual is **Athanasius** (*c.296–c.373*). *Athanasius contra mundum*[1]—the words conjure up the picture of the courageous defender of Christianity standing alone for orthodoxy, in a world rapidly defecting to the other and Arian side. The picture is true enough, but it is on too small a scale to show the detail without which the situation is apt to be misunderstood. For one thing, it was often attacks against himself that Athanasius was engaged in beating off. For another, it is altogether too romantic to suppose that the warfare, the weapons, the motives and the objectives were all theological in character. Of course theology entered pervasively into the matter, and Athanasius did pit himself against those who labelled themselves by a name connoting a divergent theological point of view. But it is not all high-souled theological debate that goes on. All too often it is party strife, squalid and ruthless; jockeying for position and power, bidding for imperial favour, and "fixing" majorities. Athanasius has as often to rebuke his opponents for dirty tactics as for erroneous theology. But at least he contributes to this warfare on a theological level. Another odd circumstance has to be observed. One may say that his preparation for the apologetic struggle was more notable than his actual participation in the work of the Council. In two works, *contra Gentes* and *de Incarnatione*, sometimes regarded (as by Jerome) as constituting a single work in two parts, he laid the foundations of a theological position which, though later expanded, he never found reason to abandon; and from it he carried out the other apologetic activities which occupied most of his life. But while in them he must be seen as preparing for the grievous struggle that lay ahead, the works themselves constitute an apologetic of capital importance; and the opponents he picks on are philosophical and popular paganism, and in a lesser measure the Jews.

The *contra Gentes* is a thoroughgoing assessment and refutation of paganism. The key to the whole situation is man's abuse of free-will, for this is the origin of evil. Man is made in the image of God, reflecting the Logos of God and possessing a knowledge of God, and so is a rational being. The essence of evil consists in man turning his back upon the Logos or image of God. His whole being thereby suffers a radical distortion. It is not so much that he forthwith becomes simply non-rational; it is rather that he no longer thinks straight. Then, losing the knowledge of God, he replaces it by the illusions of idolatry; and these illusions he even supports and justifies by argument and proofs. Athanasius reviews these philosophical and popular accounts and refutes them. God is simply not identifiable with nature, whether in part or in whole. He remains transcendent of it but not inapprehensible by at least one element in it. This element is man, and Athanasius proceeds to show that man, though plunged into degeneracy and decay, through his own fault, is none the less essentially rational and immortal, and so is capable of knowing God. Moreover the traces of order and harmony apparent in the world are due to the Logos which is their initial and sustaining ground. Accordingly the need is for the restoration of man to that affinity to the Logos in which he was first conceived by God. In this way alone the world and man will be brought back to that original relationship of congruity with their Creator from which sin has so violently dislodged them.

The frame is thus constructed into which the *de Incarnatione* fits the substance: "The renewal of creation is the work of the self-same Logos that in the beginning made it" (*de Inc*, 1.4); and "the Logos was made man in order that we might be made divine" (*op. cit.* 54.3). The *de Incarnatione* is no doubt primarily a treatise in Dogmatics. But it is composed with a vivid awareness of competing contemporary systems and deliberately at certain points sets out to confute these contemporaries. If that were not enough, it constructs a theological and especially a christological position from which Arianism could only be opposed root and branch. Therefore we are bound to take account of it here. It deals apologetically with the contemporary and past, and it prepares apologetically for the future.

If the Father works the salvation of the world by the same means he used to create it (*op. cit.* 1.4), it is appropriate to begin with the doctrine of creation. Here Athanasius rests confidently upon the testimony of Genesis, that "in the beginning God created the heavens and the earth" (Gen. 1.1); and this he interprets as meaning absolute creation: he made it out of nothing. On the way to this affirmation, Athanasius briefly refutes three variant views. The Epicurean view is materialistic and depends on the notion of fortuitous generation—but it fails to account for the differentiation of created things. The Platonic view, as Athanasius understands it, supposes a pre-existent matter out of which God makes the world—but this diminishes God by making him share eternity with another, and by giving him the role of a mere artificer. The Gnostic view is characterized by dualism, and the Creator God is separated in Gnostic thought from the Saviour God. This is in defiance of the New Testament witness which clearly identifies the God who in the Old Testament made male and female with the God who in the New Testament joins them together in matrimony.

In the Christian view, then, God assumes total responsibility for the making of the world. In this world there is an unstable element (*op. cit.*, 3.3). God not only created man, but made man after his image, granting him the promise of enduring blessedness conditionally upon man remaining within his grace. This condition being violated, restoration of the disrupted order can only be accomplished by God. Hence the Logos comes to us, assuming a body no different from our own (8.2). Thus it is possible for him to reverse the two chief consequences of man's defection from God's original plan for him. The corruption in which man by his action involved himself is brought to a halt; for the mortal body the Logos assumes partakes in the immortality of the Logos that assumes it, and this immortality is imparted to men with whom his assumption of a body makes him one. Then too man by his action had consigned himself not merely to loss of the knowledge of God, but to loss of the principle of reason by which God was to be known. Once again it is only a Logos becoming flesh that can break the entail of man's infidelity and throw the process of corruption into reverse. The Logos by becoming man attracts men's attention away from the things of sense and supplies them with a fresh revelation of God which confronts and supersedes all the superstitious surrogates with which their ignorance had supplied them. Moreover the Logos becomes man in order to create afresh in man the image of the Father, and to restore in him not only the fruits of knowledge but the principle of knowledge itself or reason.

Athanasius conceives of a "necessity" governing the death of Christ and his resurrection—a thoroughly rational necessity of course, in the light of which he expounds how appropriately what happens accomplishes the purpose for which it was designed (20ff). We note in passing that here Athanasius supplements his hitherto largely ontological argument with one that is essentially ethical. Not only is our salvation accomplished by the Logos becoming incarnate and so identifying himself with us. Another strand is now added to the argument: the debt man morally incurs by his defection from his Creator's purpose is discharged by the Logos that becomes incarnate. Athanasius rises above the categorization that is so often used to distinguish between an Eastern and Greek theology that talks only in terms of incarnation and God's consequent oneness with man, and Western and Latin theology obsessed with crucifixion and its propitiatory or expiating effects.

In the last chapters of the *de Incarnatione* Athanasius sharpens the apologetic point of his treatise. The Jews are invited to consider afresh the witness of their own Scriptures. The Saviour has come: what is said about the life, the career, and the death of a coming Messiah throughout the course of the Old Testament has manifestly its correlate in reality in the Christ. Further, the consequences following upon the coming of the Messiah that are predicted in the Old Testament are now accomplished facts. For the fount of prophecy has dried up, the destruction of Jerusalem has taken place, and the conversion of the Gentiles is under way (33–40). A different apologetic is directed to the Gentiles, and this too is argued in two parts. Contemporary philosophy knows very well of the existence of the Logos, and it has frequently been said, as by Plato, that the universe is a great body in which the Logos is to be apprehended. Why should the Logos not unite himself with part of that universe— with man that is so significant a part of it? Athanasius then argues that in principle philosophy should have no difficulty in accepting an incarnation. We may believe that he is aware that there is wide discrepancy between philosophy's admission of a generalized presence of the Logos in the world (which in fact Athanasius had already criticized in the *contra Gen.*, see above) and a hypostatic or personalized union of the divine with the human such as the incarnation implies. The argument is no doubt deliberately *ad hominem*. The Gentiles should also take account of the facts. For the worship of idols, belief in oracles, the authority of the pantheon have all declined into discredit since the advent of Christianity. The pretentious works of Greek philosophy convinced a few; the Gospel of Christ wins men of all kinds all over the world. In morals Christianity has unloosed a new private continence and an unprecedented public peaceableness by means of the teachings of Christ. All this is proof that Christ is God, the Word and the power of God (55); and if more detail is desired, it is to be found in the Scriptures.

Athanasius is thus able to bring his early pre-Nicene theological work to a sanguine conclusion. He sees paganism in decline and the Christian apologetic in advance. He is confident about the future and the further and extending triumphs that await Christianity in it. Judaism indeed remains, intransigent in its disbelief and incredulity. Athanasius' buoyancy is muted here. As he comes to a finish he enquires what Christ can more do to complete his fulfilment of their expectations, but he brings no evidence to show that Judaism is either retreating or relenting. Yet the note on which he ends is optimistic.

For us who look back from the point of view to which sixteen hundred years have led us, two things stand out with some clarity. The first is that Athanasius has good reason for his optimism. There had been three hundred years of Christianity. It had begun with eleven men committed to it as totally as it has ever been given any men to be; plus a few women on the edge of the circle; plus an indefinite number of people ranged at a greater distance from the centre and attracted in different degrees. From this beginning onwards, Christianity has had a warfare on its hands, a campaign in which it was made acutely aware by the growing circle of its own adherents of other classes and systems that for various reasons resisted its message. Now by the time of Nicaea, Christianity was written indelibly upon the map of the known world. Moreover it showed signs of undiminished vitality in its practice, its conduct and its thought. It had won through. The day was dawning when it would enjoy imperial favour. It is customary nowadays to view sardonically the entry of Christianity upon the Constantinian age. No doubt there is good reason for this. Yet it represents a remarkable achievement. A religion that had passed through the vicissitudes of neglect, persecution, proscription and legalization, had so forced itself upon the attention as now to win imperial preference and a kind of establishment. Those who had proclaimed and those who had defended had at last won this outward mark of greatness.

The second thing that from our point of vantage we cannot fail to note is that Christianity had now reached a watershed. When all necessary qualifications have been made, it is clear that up to this point Christianity had been on the apologetic front crucially engaged with external enemies. In the period that succeeds, it was to be as crucially engaged with internal foes. Of course internal foes had already been confronted and against them it had had to conduct its defence; and external enemies, some of them old enemies and some of them new, would still have to be engaged—this is what is meant by the necessary qualifications. But at this point of the apologetic enterprise the relative importance of these two types of opponent changes. The career of Athanasius affords illustration of this. For it fell to him to do apologetic duty on both sides of the watershed. With the events that gave rise to the Council of Nicaea and the repercussions they produced after the Council, Athanasius turns his attention from the threats that menaced Christianity from outside to a no less formidable danger that arose from inside, with which is associated the name of Arius.

During the third century Christian thought had become by no means simply content to repeat without modification or supplement what belonged to the orthodox statements of the Christian faith. The witness of Scripture remained intact and inviolate (except when Marcion dismembered it and reassembled only some of the fragments). But how was this witness to be interpreted? How was it to be apprehended and then proclaimed that God was in Jesus reconciling the world to himself? Attention focused on the person of Jesus: how was it to be understood? One trend of thought we have already come across. There were those so emphatic that Christ was indeed from the side of God that, influenced by the Gnostic thought that the world is essentially evil, they could only suppose that the body Christ assumed was phantasmal, a mere appearance—Docetism. But on the other side there was a quite different trend of thought, facing the same issue but resolving it in different terms. Jesus was, they felt assured, really and truly human, the Son of Joseph and Mary. According to the Scriptures, the man Jesus was raised to the status of Son of God by, many supposed, the descent of the Holy Spirit in the form of a dove upon him at his baptism—Ebionitism. In the third century further developments took place. Monarchianism was put forward to safeguard the unique and inviolate unity of the Godhead, by excluding such representation of the Son as would imply either that the Godhead was divided or that there was more than one God. The Dynamic Monarchians held that Jesus was God in the sense only that a power or influence from the Father was vested in his human person. The Modalist Monarchians sought to preserve the unity of the Godhead by conceiving of Jesus as no more than a mode or aspect under which it pleased God to appear and which corresponded to no real correlate differentiation or distinction within the Godhead itself. These variant views had not so far threatened to divide the Church or to confuse and undermine its essential message, though Tertullian in his *adversus Praxeam* reacted sharply against the last. But the time had now come when the latent diversity of theological opinion was to rock the Church to its foundations.

It all began with a lecture by Alexander, the Bishop of Alexandria, on the mystery of the Trinity in unity. To this **Arius** (*c*.250–*c*.336) took instant exception, declaring that the distinction of the three persons in the Godhead had been obliterated, and that in effect the statement implied, like Sabellius, that the only distinction was between mere modes. In opposition to this view Arius undertook to restore the reality of distinction in the Godhead, exaggerated the elements that differentiated the second person in the Trinity, and eventually, to secure this end, replaced the concept of Sonship by that of creaturehood. Christ belonged to the created side of things; and the coeternal and coessential deity of the Word was surrendered. This novel view of the relation of the second person in the Trinity to the Father apparently struck a sympathetic chord in the hearts of many of the newer converts to Christianity who had come over from paganism to the now imperially favoured religion without any very thorough grounding in the faith, and in whom the elements of paganism had by no means been thoroughly eradicated. When Arius adopted the imaginative tactics of propagating his variant version of the faith by means of popular ballads (*thalia*, as they were called), they fell an easy prey to its seduction. The rift between Arians and non-Arians became so serious and so disturbing to both unity and order that even Constantine became alarmed. Accordingly the First Ecumenical Council of Nicaea was summoned in 325.

Here Athanasius, at the time no more than deacon-secretary to the Alexandrian Bishop Alexander (and functioning like one of the *periti* of whom so much use was made at the recent Vatican Council II), played a critically important role. Largely through his resolution and competence, the Council defined the faith in terms of the co-equality of the Father and the Son, and asserted that the Son was consubstantial (*homoousios*) with the Father. Arius and other bishops who shared his views were banished. For the first time in history a Council of the Church had been convoked to defend the faith against a variant form which constituted a mortal threat.

As for Athanasius, he had now behind him the work by which above all he is remembered with gratitude by Christians in succeeding ages, and also a personal triumph in stabilizing the Church in fidelity to the essential Gospel at a moment of crisis. Yet only a small part of his life's work had been accomplished. His most important theological work, the orations *contra Arianos*, had still to be written. But it remains true to say that the *de Incarnatione*, his best known work, is determinative of the part he played both at and after Nicaea. It showed him to have grasped the reality of God's becoming man for man's sake which he neither relinquished nor compromised. This being firmly held and capably argued, it could only appear to him that Arianism, in conceiving the Saviour as some kind of *tertium quid*, neither God nor man, and as a creation of God, albeit a perfect creature and so not merely one of the larger class of creatures, was undermining the basis of man's salvation and making it dependent on something incapable of sustaining the role of Saviour. Arianism, like most serious heresies, had simplicity on its side. How much easier to think of God working for man through an intermediary that is properly speaking neither God nor man! Athanasius resisted this false simplification, in his own way championed the essential Gospel, and unhesitatingly plunged into the theological fray in which this attractively simple variant was finally overthrown.

From the same impregnable position he exerted a determinative influence in the decades that followed Nicaea. For the struggle with Arianism was to drag on for another half century. The story of his five banishments belongs to history, that of the manoeuvres of the Arian party, to the seamier side of ecclesiastical politics. In the end the Semi-Arians, addicted to the term *homoiousios*, of like but not the same substance with the Father, which Origen had used, were won over partly by the alarmingly great success of the Arians. "The whole world groaned and marvelled to find itself Arian," says Jerome; and such success frightened many on to the side of orthodoxy. But the persuasive and resolute arguments of Athanasius played a notable part in achieving victory for the orthodoxy he championed. The story belongs to Dogmatics rather than Apologetics. In the Constantinopolitan version in which the so-called Nicene Creed is known today, the Church settled for *homoousios* as the fittest term to designate the distinctiveness of the Son and his essential unity of essence with the Father. In the terms that were then available, anything else would have impaired the Gospel. The battle was well worth fighting. The solution was not unsatisfactory, even if today we must have reservations about the adequacy of terms like substance to convey what after all is the personal favour, grace and forgiveness which God offers us in Jesus Christ.

# CHAPTER FIVE

# AUGUSTINE

DURING celebrations held to honour his 80th birthday, Karl Barth is reported, in characteristic vein, to have said: "There are no great theologians—only theologians obedient to the Word of God". If we were to relax this rule and allow the question as to who is the greatest theologian that Christianity has known, **St. Augustine** (c.354–c.430) ranks as the only possible candidate. "The most illustrious doctor of the Church," writes E. Portalié;[1] "one of the writers whose thought has exercised the most powerful influence upon Western religious thinking." This is not the place to argue the case, or to enumerate the personal qualities which thrust Augustine forward into the first rank. But if we look behind him at the course of thought already outlined, it is evident that he towers above the thinkers so far considered. Of course they equally belong to the stream of the Church's transmission of the faith. But their names remain in comparative obscurity for most ordinary Christians, while that of Augustine is a household word. As for the scholars and academic theology, the earlier writers will be referred to for evidence or authority on this or that point, but Augustine for whole doctrines. He moulded the theology subsequent to him for 800 years. He survived the reaction against Augustinianism occasioned by the rediscovery of Aristotle and the employment of the new knowledge by St. Thomas Aquinas. He was appealed to by the Reformers, and also on the Roman Catholic side by the Jansenists, while, with the exception of Luther and Calvin, no other writer is so frequently mentioned by Karl Barth in our own day. To quote Portalié again, his teaching "marked a decisive epoch in the history of Christian thought, and ushered the Church into a new phase."

From the point of view of Apologetics, Augustine's life is of singular importance and interest, simply because he was the target of apologetic Christianity before ever he became an exponent of it. Of his spiritual pilgrimage the *Confessions* offers a record—a work with which most people are acquainted. Whether it relates trustworthy history is doubted by such critics as A. Harnack; and F. W. Farrar can poke fun at the too scrupulous remorse with which the youthful Augustine reflected upon the incident when he stole pears from the orchard.[2] But the more discerning reader will easily perceive that it is the apparent lack of motive for the deed that shocked the theologian. No doubt the *Confessions* represents a stylized account of Augustine's spiritual odyssey, but more recent sober critics tend to recognize its positive historical value.

In any case we are not dependent on this personal testimony alone. It embodies apparent facts, and these establish sufficiently the way he travelled, through indifference, contempt, doubt, conviction, to eventual conversion and confession of faith. Born in a Christian household (his mother Monica was a devout Christian, his father was baptized only shortly before his death), he was little impressed by his mother's religion which he described as "an old wives' tale," Trained in rhetoric, he fell in love with philosophy. His first commitment was to Manichaeism and he enrolled as an auditor. But doubts about the adequacy of Manichaeism, about its cosmology, its dualism, and its notion of God, increased and plunged him into philosophical scepticism. Now the sermons of Ambrose Bishop of Milan, with their allegorical interpretation of the Old Testament, supplied him with an answer to Manichaean objections to the Old Testament. In this period of doubt he became attracted to the treatises of Plotinus and learned that God was pure spiritual substance, and evil only the negation of good. From Simplicianus, a neo-Platonist priest, he was taught how the best in Plotinus was completed by the Johannine account of the Logos. Philosophy was preparing Augustine for faith in the Logos-God. When Simplicianus drew his attention to the writings of St Paul, he learned that union with God was not the achievement of philosophical mediation but the gift of God's grace. The hour for decision had come. In a mental and spiritual turmoil, he tells us, he ran out into the garden, where the voice of a child repeating the words: *Tolle, lege*, impelled him to open the Scripture, where he read Rom. 13.13f. Conviction swept uncertainty away, and in 386 he enrolled for baptism.

It is a remarkable story—philosophy exposing the inadequacy of a deviant form of Christianity, scriptural exposition the inadequacy of the pretensions of philosophy, and in the end simple Christian witness, as exemplified in Marius Victorinus and the hermit Anthony, brushing away the final hesitancy. Sometimes directly, sometimes indirectly, Christianity had commended itself triumphantly, and the victim of unbelief becomes the defender of the faith.

Augustine's chief apologetic work is the *de Civitate Dei* and of this something must be said later. But only the first ten books are devoted to the defence of Christianity against objection and reproach. Books 11–22 develop a theme important in its own right and not addressed specifically to objectors to the Christian faith. This is characteristic of Augustine's writings. The subject he undertakes is carried forward by the powerful drive of his thought beyond the point to which it had hitherto been taken. It is not enough for him merely to answer objections: he must cross the indefinite line that separates Apologetics from Dogmatics and add his own independent contribution. This is evident not only in the *de Civitate Dei* but in the works that may be listed as controversial. These fall into three main groups, according to the situation to which he addressed them. He felt himself obliged to take on the Manichees—and demolishing their doctrines, he moves on to offer positive doctrine, chiefly concerning the nature of evil. He finds it necessary to confront Donatism, a Christian deviation of a mostly practical order—but he does not lay down his pen without making a permanent positive contribution to the Church's understanding of its own nature and practice. Later he undertakes to defend the faith against the heresy of Pelagianism—and he advances his positive doctrine of grace and predestination.

Three qualities may be said to form the basis of Augustine's permanent importance for Christian Apologetics. There is the accuracy of his acquaintance with the doctrines he opposes—in the case of Manichaeism, for example, which he knew with the intimacy of a former committed believer. Further, as already said, he is not content merely to destroy the false doctrines he considers, but develops an independent contribution in the field thus cleared. The original subject then bursts the limits within which it has hitherto been treated, rises to its full stature of implication and consequences, and can from this time on be sensibly discussed only in the new perspective in which it has been surveyed. Besides these qualities, Augustine as a writer possesses a remarkable ability, as we should say today, to communicate, and the intensity with which he writes kindles both understanding and interest in those who read.

No religious movement can have attracted a greater range of varied descriptive adjectives than **Manichaeism.** It had been called barren, inhuman, absurd, puerile. Yet it also possesses grandeur, fervour, and moving lyricism; and as G. Bonner says[3], it "remains impressive even in its ruin." A "hotch-potch of many long dead heresies",[4] and "more fantastic than the Arabian Nights",[5] its spread and longevity are both astonishing. Its founder was martyred by the fire-worshippers of Persia; but the faith he professed spread over the great land mass from the Atlantic Ocean to the China Sea. It endured through twelve centuries, and twice in this long period, once under the Roman Empire and then again during the Middle Ages, it "constituted a serious menace to the Christian Church."[6]

It was eclectic rather than syncretistic. Its founder Mani was a Persian, and from the Zoroastrianism prevalent there his system adopted the dualism it propagated. From Buddhism it borrowed its belief in the reincarnation of souls. From Christianity came the reverence it accorded to the name of Jesus, whose principal and final apostle Mani claimed to be, while his followers identified him with the Paraclete Christ had promised. It is this borrowing from Christianity, distorted as it of course was, that caused the Fathers of the Church to regard Manichaeism as a Christian heresy. It had much in common with Gnosticism, and like Gnosticism it offered illuminative knowledge as the key to salvation. *Gnosis* is *epignosis*, says H. C. Puech[7]—a knowledge complete and entire, embracing both God and self.

How did it happen that Augustine came to throw in his lot with a philosophy so bizarre? To us it seems almost incredible that he should do so. Yet Manichaeism had an impressiveness of its own, as its pervasiveness and longevity sufficiently testify. It was woven into the religious texture of the time, and for such a restless questing mind as Augustine's it had some attraction. It was imposing and comprehensive, and into it the details of the world could be fitted and explained. In a word it seemed to explain the appearances.

Dualism was a salient feature of the system, the representation of the cosmos as the cockpit where two powers are locked in mortal combat, the power of light against the power of darkness, of good against evil. It must be remembered that dualism, whether finally satisfying or not, does offer an attractively plausible and simple explanation of the perennial problem concerning the existence and nature of evil and of man's involvement in it. Further it was the claim of Manichaeism to commend itself by hard reasoning. Of course it did not practise science as we understand it today, but then myth had at the time to do duty for observation. Augustine's own scientific knowledge was negligible, and he could hardly do other than accept the conventions of his age. Within these limits, Manichaeism promoted itself by argument and demonstration. This to one of Augustine's critical bent of mind provided an agreeable alternative to the acceptance of doctrine upon the bare authority of the Church. Besides, Manichaeism mounted a shrewd attack upon the Scriptures of the Church and so, at least for a time, until Augustine realized the bankruptcy of their handling of their own scriptures, it anticipated and destroyed the possibility of his resort to them.

Did Manichaeism provide Augustine with ethical satisfaction? It must be remembered that Augustine never passed beyond the status of auditor, and disclaims knowledge of what happened at the Manichaean eucharist of the so-called "perfects". Later, when submission turned into rebellion and then attack, Augustine has bitter things to say about the conduct Manichaeism promoted or allowed. At points the apostate from Manichaeism possibly overdoes the violence of his criticism, and invective takes the place of argument. But it is tolerably clear that, as is common in sects that combine an austere rule of life with a radical dualism between spirit and flesh, Manichaeism in at least some of its forms permitted wild licence. It looked on sexual intercourse with abhorrence, but it permitted auditors to practise it so long as it remained infertile. It is significant that the birth of Augustine's son Adeodatus occurred before his acceptance of the system and accordingly cannot be cited as proof of his approval of its ethical teaching or practice. It may further be surmised that the dualism of Manichaeism provided relief for Augustine—a kind of alibi. The real conflict taking place is of cosmic dimensions and the parties engaged are the two opposing powers of light and darkness. In this perspective the culpability that can be attached to the individual is sensibly diminished. What after all is he more than one little corner of the field where the cosmic battle rages? If then evil overcomes good, it is not the individual in final analysis that is to blame. It is the battling cosmic powers that win and lose the day. To a nature torn with tumultuous and uncontrollable passions, the chance of disowning responsibility in this way must have had overwhelming attraction.

Augustine later refers more than once with distaste to the Manichaean practice of sexual intercourse as the means for release and purgation of the divine element embedded in man. He denounces this as a "foul heresy", though admitting that the Manichaeans say in their defence that this was the view of only a splinter group.

It appears, however, to have been not the ethical weakness of the system, but rather a growing sense of the ineffectiveness to explain all that its impressively grandiose scheme had taken on that constrained Augustine to withdraw the adherence he had rashly given. The feebleness of one of its exponents had possibly a part to play here; for it appears that the famous Manichaean Faustus, bishop of Milevis, disappointed him and Augustine thought him a rather uneducated babbler.

Of all the enemies to whom Augustine pays attention the Manichaeans were the most easily assailable, vulnerable and vincible. The lordly air of comprehensiveness and omnicompetence was impressive. But once criticism had pierced the outer walls, the interior was discovered to be not empty but full of a ragbag miscellany of notions which could not stand up to serious scrutiny. One wonders whether the violence with which Augustine later proceeds to demolish the Manichaean system may not have been due to inner mystification and resentment that he had been so taken in by it. At all events Augustine's polemic did not only chalk up a victory on the scoreboards of the faithful; it induced, for example, the Manichaean Felix to denounce publicly Manichaean doctrine and to embrace the Catholic faith.

Augustine's attack on Manichaeism is developed chiefly in his *de Haeresibus* (c.428) in which 88 heresies are enumerated; but he returns to the attack before and after this date in something like 20 of his published works. The issue chiefly at stake concerns evil. Augustine's own conviction of the formidable reality of evil was strengthened by his own experience of the uncontrollable excesses to which concupiscence impelled him; and this conviction was ratified and given a temporally satisfactory rational basis by Manichaean doctrine. This early conviction Augustine never relinquished: with evil one cannot come to terms. At the same time he came increasingly to realize that, though Manichaean dualism represented the reality of evil with dramatic vividness, in the last resort it was inadequate as a philosophical account. "I kept seeking an answer to the question: Whence is evil?" says Augustine (*Confessions*, 7.5.7); and more radically: What is evil? (*op. cit.* 7.2.3). The answer in terms of dualism was initially attractive. It might be that the Manichaeans if they had pursued a more strictly logical road might have had greater philosophical success. But this was prevented by their adherence to Christianity. They shied away from positing two absolutely distinct and equal powers, in the interests of maintaining that the Father of goodness had such priority that the powers of darkness could only be regarded as rebels. The Monarchian inclination of the Manichaeans could not be suppressed, and in its interests they were willing to sacrifice the credibility which tight logic might have imparted to their system. On the other side too it was found difficult to make credible the literally absolute and unmitigated evil character of evil. The imposing character of the rule and power of darkness implied qualities of health and stability which are not in themselves evil. This discernment suggests that another solution must be found and, if we may read between the lines, Augustine seems to have found here the clue to a different interpretation and the Achilles' heel for his assault.

Whether a more imposing logic would have had the power to retain Augustine is one of the ifs of history that no one in his senses would care to pontificate about. The fact is that Augustine found another and preferable solution whose origins are traceable to the Neo-Platonism that captivated him at one stage in his career. The very notion of corruptibility implies deterioration; and deterioration implies the process from what is good to what is less good. If substance is incorruptible, then no question of its corruptibility arises. If it is corruptible and corruption does set in, the process is a movement away from a state of goodness. Accordingly evil in itself is not a substance, not as we should now say something positive. It consists rather in the absence of something, in the lack or privation of goodness. So Augustine holds it to be most certain that things are evil for want of goodness, and that the entire absence of goodness would entail their ceasing to exist. Thus he provides himself with a fairly satisfying answer at the point where the Manichaeans were defective: God the Creator is good; and his creation is not evil but only defectively good.

There still remains the question why evil understood even in this sense is there at all; how the privation involved gets a first foothold. If Christianity cannot give some kind of answer to this, then the force and inherent simplicity of the frankly dualistic view is bound to reassert itself and extend its influence over the unconvinced. Augustine is clever enough to supply an answer, and at the same time wise enough to realize that it is an incomplete one. He makes use of what is really an extension of the idea that evil is privation, to point out that goodness can reside in a whole even when the parts of which it is composed are not or do not seem to be good in themselves. This is the "in the long run" view.[8] In the long run the goodness, with which in the beginning God equipped the world, will be evidently restored, not so much by the alteration of what now seems to be evil, but by incorporation of it or its consequences in a larger whole. As Augustine suggests,[9] light is not evil because it hurts those who have weak eyes. The bother about this kind of argument is of course that, while it may contain some truth, it supplies little immediate comfort to the sufferers, and it promotes a conception of a God who is so preoccupied with big-scale operations that he seems indifferent to the small and individual component parts of the whole enterprise.

But Augustine does not think that this explanation covers all the facts, and he presses on to affirm that essentially evil is the consequence of sin and the result of the abuse of man's freewill. The special strength of his exposition is his acute awareness (not always apparent in others making use of a similar argument) that much that is evil cannot possibly be attributed to what men do at all and hence cannot be represented as having its source there. Augustine supplements the more ordinary account of man's sin and its consequences with a resolute discernment that evil perpetuates evil, and once the entail is set up evil consequences accumulate. The source of sin is located in the will; and the train of consequences that the evil act of will initiates stretches on and on, to right and left, over guilty and innocent.

In the last resort even this consideration, Augustine realizes, does not dispose of the matter of evil. For the question springs up after evil has been located in the will: Why does the will manifest this defect? Here Augustine very sensibly declines to press too far: he has no real explanation to give for that turning away of the will from the good towards evil. All he allows himself to say is: "All good is from God. Hence there is no natural existence which is not from God. Now that movement of 'aversion' which we admit is sin is a defective movement; and all defect comes from nothing" (*de libero Arbitrio*, 2.20.54).

In Augustine Christianity found a worthy protagonist in face of the surprisingly serious threat that Manichaeism offered. If we come to the conclusion that he outfights and outwits his opponents at all significant points, this should be attributed not merely to the superlative qualities which Augustine undoubtedly displays and exercises, but also to the resources of the Christian faith upon which he could draw. In doing battle Augustine utilizes material from other sources, but, one may venture the judgment, never without a significant modification in a Christian sense. Plotinus held that evil is non-being. Over against the Manichaean dualism this was a more supportable rendering of the facts. But Augustine realized that it was not far enough removed from dualism to provide a safe battle-ground; and he protects himself against slipping in that direction by his insistence upon the privative character of evil. On the other hand there are close resemblances to Plato in the view he adopts. But characteristically Plato stated his view repeatedly in the form that "all wrongdoing is involuntary". But the weight and agony of Augustine's experience of evil forced him to remould this inter-pretation. The experience recorded in the *Confessions* showed up the triviality of any explanation of evil that defined it in terms of ignorance and left out the element of responsibility and guilt. In his insistence that sin be located in the wrong direction of the will Augustine penetrates to the heart of a human predicament that is of central importance; and he is characteristically willing, when this argument has carried him as far as it properly can, to admit that beyond this point is something mysterious. The story of Augustine's defence against Manichaeism would be incomplete without at least a brief reference to the position which, under attack, Augustine was constrained to take up with respect to Scripture. It may be supposed that the real reason why Manichaeism was disposed to reject the Old Testament was simply that it conflicted with the revelation that had come to them through the agency of Mani. But numberless believers and unbelievers have found that the Old Testament on the face of it offers very serious difficulties of belief. Manichaeism in the person of Faustus (who was to be answered later by Augustine in a work of 33 books!) complained that to accept the Old Testament was to be bound by its ceremonial and he added to this an objection to the frequently scandalous behaviour of the patriarchs. In reply Augustine employs an argument which he did not himself invent and which he was not the last to use. Scripture, he says, in *de Utilitate Credendi*,[10] has a four-fold sense: historical, aetiological, analogical, and allegorical. This four-fold sense supplies us with rules by which to understand what Scripture is saying. Thus sometimes, as Augustine goes on to say, Scripture tells us what happened or was done. Sometimes there is a specific reason or cause for what it says, as when Jesus explains the Mosaic permission of divorce "because of the hardness of your hearts" (Matt. 19.3 ff). The similarity and parallelism between the Old and New Testaments is explained by analogy. Other things have to be understood as not literally but figuratively intended, as when St. Paul uses Abraham's two children to symbolize the two covenants. This method of interpretation enables Augustine to uphold the validity of the Old Testament in face of the objections made against it. But it also supplies him with a ground for maintaining the authority of Scripture in general. Once again we have an example of Augustine being better than his word. His apologetic statement of the faith thrusts forward to disclose new insights. His answer is designed to reply to objections, but it moves swiftly on to erect upon the bare answer a positive contribution to understanding the larger issues involved. Scripture thus justified and validated immediately takes its place as an instrument for commending the Christian faith.

If Manichaeism had earlier appeared to Augustine attractive because it appealed to proof and reason, how much more the Christian faith when firmly based on Scripture! His apologetic invitation to the hostile and the indifferent is contained in the lapidary phrase: *Intellige ut credas; crede ut intelligas* (understand in order to believe; believe in order to understand) (*Sermo*, 43.7, cf. *Ep*, 120.3, *de Trin*, 1.1.1). Here faith and understanding are held in fruitful tension; and here too Scripture has a crucially important role. "The Holy Scriptures," says Augustine (*Ep*, 120.3.13), "which persuade us to have faith in great matters before we understand them, cannot themselves be useful to you unless you rightly understand them." Augustine never trivializes, and he never over-simplifies. He will neither endorse the peremptory demand for a *sacrificium intellectus* (that intellect be sacrificed), nor concede the claim that understanding must precede belief: he will side neither with the later existentialist who proposes a trivial Pascal's wager,[11] nor with the rationalist who insists on knowing all from outside at the very start. His view rather is: "Authority has precedence in time, reason in inner reality" (*de Ordine*, 2.9.26). It is in the light of this clear understanding of the issues involved that we have to interpret his famous phrase on which Roman Catholics and Protestants are apt to come to loggerheads if not to blows, that *ego vero evangelio non crederem, nisi me catholicae ecclesiae commoveret auctoritas* (I should not believe the Gospel unless the authority of the catholic Church moved me thereto). Augustine touches here what is perhaps the crucial issue in Apologetics, and as we might expect does not fail to illumine it. The former adherent of Manichaeism who preferred argument to the authoritarianism he found in the Church is not likely to surrender the value embedded in this position upon his conversion to the Church's teaching. On the other hand he has too great insight to think that God constrains men to belief by mindless pressures.

In the general development of Augustine's thought the dispute with **Donatism** must be ranked in importance with the debates he carried on with the Manichaeans and the Pelagians. However, for Apologetics the controversy is of lesser significance. The reasons are plain enough. If Manichaeism or Pelagianism had not been contained and overcome, the Christian faith would have shifted from its moorings in the Apostolic tradition and would have been irreparably damaged. But if Donatism had triumphed, Christianity would not have been lost, though the Church would have come to do things in a different way. The distinction here is not absolute but it is real enough. In none of the three major disputes did Augustine contend with those who stood deliberately outside the Christian faith. But Donatism is more clearly a deviation within the Christian Church. It was a domestic difference of opinion. In the end the distinction Augustine himself was to make is justified: he had here to deal with a schism rather than a heresy. For this reason a brief reference will here suffice.

During the persecution instigated by the Emperor Diocletian (284–305), some African Christians had surrendered their Scriptures when possession of them had been proscribed. Felix the Bishop of Aptunga was believed by some to have been one of those *traditores* (betrayers). Accordingly they withheld acceptance of Caecillian the Bishop of Carthage whom Felix had consecrated (311), and had Majorinus and Donatus consecrated instead. Those who rallied round Donatus were rigorist in outlook, held that the Church was for saints, and considered that sacraments performed by *traditores* were invalid. The Catholic Church with the Bishop of Rome at its head ranged itself against the Donatists, but the adverse judgments that various Councils passed against them failed to resolve the dispute or convince the Africans. Non-theological factors were powerfully at work: the Donatists were stiffened in their opposition not only by theological conviction but by African nationalist feeling. Coercion failed to bring the schismatics to heel; they retorted by means of gangs of *circumcelliones* (ruffians) who terrorized the Catholics; and renewed coercion was equally unavailing.

With Augustine's intervention the theological issues came to the forefront. There was first of all a question of fact: was Felix or was he not a *traditor*? The Catholic Church and the Donatists answered the question differently, and the affair could evidently not be resolved at this point. Augustine brought the matter on to other ground. Even if Felix had been a *traditor*, he maintained, what he did had none the less validity in virtue of the office or order into which he had been installed. Augustine was propounding a theological principle of importance: the validity and efficacy of sacraments did not depend upon the worthiness of the minister celebrating them; and the ultimate ground for this is that Christ himself is their true minister.

Again Augustine, applying himself to a limited problem, succeeds in eliciting its concealed implications and deploys them in their full range. The Church is not a closed circle of already perfected saints; it is a visible community comprising saints and sinners. To this mixed community Christ its head has himself committed the sacraments of grace. Hence grace is not tied to the worthiness of those who minister. The central theological principle for which Augustine contends is the freedom of God in conferring grace. To this end he severs the dependence of grace upon human qualities and abilities: God gives it freely, not *Ex opore operantis* (not because of the person acting). In its place he posits a connection between grace and the sacramental means of its conveyance. But he does so without disparagement of God's freedom. That God wills that grace be conveyed by those means does not imply that he has tied his hands. Grace belongs to God, and God it is that bestows it.

The controversy prompts Augustine to take a stand of historic importance at two further points. He declares that the Donatists are chiefly to be faulted not for their inadequate doctrine but for their lack of love. Bad doctrine makes the heretic, but lack of love the schismatic. Augustine felt deeply the want of charity that disposed the Donatists to drive the wedge of division into the body of Christ. One may conjecture that this above all he found hard to forgive. No doubt this lies behind an action less commendable—his appeal against the Donatists to the civil arm. There are mitigating circumstances certainly. Augustine was understandably stung by the intransigence with which even his eirenic overtures were met. He was vexed by the continued activities of the *circumcelliones*. Moreover the Donatists themselves did not scruple when it suited their ends to accept the intervention of the civil authority. At all events, Augustine invokes the *compelle intrare* of Luke 14.23 as justification for exerting coercion. Even so we must not exaggerate, and the representation of Augustine as an early Torquemada is simply fantastic. Yet compulsion is clearly not an apologetic device; it is rather the abandonment of Apologetics.

The debate with **Pelagianism** in which Augustine was implicated in the later stages of his career is of great interest to the Christian apologist. For one thing the issues involved are profoundly important; for another it is not trivial in-fighting that the Church conducts here, but war against an opponent that had in the end to be extruded under judgment of heresy from the Christian community. The student of Augustine will appreciate that in such a controversy the powers of the *doctor gratiae* (*the* teacher of grace, as he has been called since the Middle Ages) were given immense scope to extend and display themselves, and of this he took full advantage.

The controversy has a singular significance for Apologetics. Considering the importance of the issues raised, the campaign was brought to a close with surprising rapidity and conclusiveness. Pelagius, a lay monk from Britain, who came to Rome about the year 400, began to formulate disturbing theological opinions shortly after. He was challenged by Augustine from 410 onwards, and after some papal indecisiveness was excommunicated in 418. Only a tiny minority continued to propagate Pelagianism, though it prolonged itself in the form of Semi-Pelagianism. A hundred years later it was again unconditionally rejected and as a formulated body of doctrine disappeared. The victory won by orthodoxy was unusually swift and complete and organized Pelagianism dropped out of account. Yet no deviant form of the Christian faith has propagated itself with such persistence. Defeated officially, it still contributes unofficially, indeliberately, and even unconsciously to the formation of opinion and affects Christian thought. Apologetic activity has been undertaken more frequently and continuously against latent Pelagianism than against any other heresy. The baton of a marshal of France may or may not be in the pouches of every French soldier; it is quite certain that a Pelagius lives actively in the heart of every Christian.

It appears that it was a quotation from Augustine himself that sparked off the whole affair. A bishop in Pelagius' hearing read a passage from the recently published *Confessions* (10.29.40) in which Augustine praises the mercy of God by which he had been delivered from the bondage of incontinence. "Thou commandest continence; give what thou commandest, and command what thou wilt" (the famous: *da quod iubes, et iube quod vis*). According to Augustine (*de Dono Perseverantiae*, 20.53), this evoked a furious protest from Pelagius, who could hardly be restrained from violent altercation with the bishop. The incident has no doubt become stylized in the narration. Certainly it was misgivings already entertained by Pelagius which erupted. His mode of training and conduct could only make him hostile to views that seemed to disregard the need for rules to guide men and discourage the effort to comply with them. Nor was it a merely narrow legalism that lay behind his antipathy. Pelagius, as scholarship has recently established, was moved by a moral earnestness that is at least commendable, and this concern he underpinned with biblical foundation.

It seemed to him unworthy that the more difficult injunctions in Scripture, e.g. the dominical "Be ye perfect" of Matt. 5.48, should be evaded by clever allegorical interpretation. Two implications seem to follow immediately upon the despondent report which Augustine compiles against human ability. The first affects God: he is inconsistent if he enjoins commands upon men that they are unable to perform. The second concerns men: to admit inability represents a severe discouragement to all moral endeavour and an invitation to indolence and indulgence. The view that Pelagius positively substitutes is easy to anticipate. When charged with teaching that "man can live without sin, in obedience to the divine commands, if he pleases", he claimed that this accurately represents his teaching. He credited man with powers of self-determination, and this meant the denial of the radical corruption of human nature. It follows that neither sin nor virtue is inborn, and both are the result of the way in which freedom is used. Men carry the responsibility of what they freely do. In consequence each man stands by himself, and the Augustinian conception of the solidarity of men and their consequent participation in a communal responsibility and guilt must be abandoned. The relevance of Adam is not a matter of heredity but of example and imitation. By parity of reasoning, the parallelism between Adam and Christ cannot be maintained: as Adam did not involve all men in sin, so neither did Christ restore to men what Adam had lost for them. God has accorded to all the power to reach perfection, and each must work out his own salvation.

Pelagianism cannot be thought of as offering a comfortable relaxing gospel and proposing an optimistic outcome. On the contrary it was bracing and strenuous. Rightly, it is to be judged as "a reforming movement in the corrupt world of the later Roman Empire."[12]

Long after its demise and up to the present day the elements for which it stood are those that appeal not only to the self-reliant and independent among men, but at a certain level even to the evangelically minded who know perfectly well that human response has to be evoked if the Gospel is to do its work. Yet Augustine discerned that its triumph would have been disastrous for Christian devotion and dogma; and he sprang instantly to the defence of the faith, and mounted and launched a resolute attack. The principal fault of Pelagianism was not that it ignored sin, but that it offered a wrong diagnosis of the complaint from which mankind suffered. This of course Augustine realized. But characteristically his major interest throughout the controversy lay not so much in correcting this defect as in vindicating the grace of God. He was again not content to deal only with the matter directly raised; in making the necessary correction he opened out majestically the power and range of divine grace, and this in turn he could not expound without pursuing the argument to its conclusion in predestination. Here too he practised the kind of Apologetics that not only demolishes but learns from an opponent.

Sin and grace are twin aspects of a profound spiritual experience, and in Augustine's theology they are complementary. To say that "man can live without sin, if he pleases", simply does not cover the facts—either the facts of Augustine's experience or those apparent to any candid observer of the human situation. The will is much more complex than Pelagius supposes, and is divided against itself: "it is no strange anomaly partly to will and partly to be unwilling. . . There are two wills" (*Conf.*, 8.9.21). A more profound analysis is necessary. Augustine supposes that human nature as originally made is free from sin though capable of it, and through exercise of the will which is sufficient for evil but not sufficient for good, he falls into sin. This fall destroys entirely man's ability for good. Individual human beings are involved not contingently through infection or contagion, but through a communal corruption which flows from Adam through the whole human family. Hence the very springs of human action and the roots of man's nature are corrupted. It must be from elsewhere that remedy is sought.

The remedy of the disease Augustine proposes is given along with the diagnosis. It is to be found entirely and sufficiently in grace. This free gift of God does more than rehabilitate the life of men that hereditary depravity has ruined; it more radically reconstitutes it from the very beginnings. At one time Augustine considered that man was capable of taking the initial step qualifying him to receive the gift of grace, an act of faith on his own initiative (*de Predestinatione*, 3.7). (This was the central affirmation of the later Semi-Pelagians: to give room and significance to preaching and exhortation, they held that nature unaided could take the first step to its own recovery.) But this he subsequently retracted. In well-known words: "to solve this question we laboured in the cause of freedom of the human will, but the grace of God won the day" (*Retracta-tiones*, 2.1.1). Thus the entire edifice of Pelagianism is overthrown: "it is by grace you are saved . . . it is God's gift" (Eph. 2.8). From beginning to end Christian existence is conditioned by what God does in grace, from first desire in conversion to final perseverence.

It is evident that this represents a genuine alternative to the Pelagian proposals: Augustine's version of the Gospel and Pelagius' cannot both be true. As the controversy pursued its course this became clear to the Church, and the realization came to be embodied in conciliar decisions and enactments. The Church was availing itself of the massive apologetic which Augustine on behalf of the faith was conducting. Augustine on his side was well aware that it was on behalf of the Church that he did battle—the matter was not a private quarrel between individual disputants, but a dispute which concerned the essence of the faith and in which the integrity of the Gospel was involved. Accordingly in his success Augustine rightly saw the triumph of truth over falsehood, and rejoiced that the Church construed it in this way: the Pelagian case was twice pled before the Roman bishop, and twice rejected; and the words he had occasion to use came to be incorporated in the celebrated dictum: *Roma locuta, causa finita* (Rome has spoken, the case is decided) (*Serm*, 131.10.10).

In rejecting Pelagianism Augustine was not guiding the Church to simple affirmation of the contrary view. Pelagian emphasis upon the obligation resting on man's will if his salvation is to be achieved is repudiated by Augustine. But it is not replaced by a bald denial that man's will has any part to play at all. Augustine's reasoning is much more subtle, biblical, and realistic. The gift of grace is not a substitute for man's voluntary action, but the condition upon which the will can begin to choose and follow the good. If the impact of grace upon the will is said to be irresistible, this means not that it is overcome by a force greater than itself, but that it has now, with true freedom restored to it, no wish to resist. Augustine is not to be interpreted in the terms so familiar to us now of mechanical deter-minism and commercial take-over bids.

Perhaps Augustine himself gives some excuse for such mis-interpretation. For this central citadel in which he properly defends the Christian faith is buttressed by certain outworks that are of more dubious strength and less generally accepted validity. On the one side man's incarceration in the *massa damnata* (the mass of condemned humanity) is inescapably secured by the supposition of the hereditary transmission of sin and its effects. A man then is no more able to escape the entail of sin than to be born without parents. On the other side the omnicompetence of God's grace is worked up into a doctrine of predestination. This secures step by step the inexorable progress of individuals towards the end for which they are severally appointed. Predestination is a doctrine that belongs essentially to the Christian faith. But it is often ill-expressed and more often ill-understood. Augustine's statement of it is imperfect at points and carries, among other sombre implications, the ultimate destruction of by far the greater portion of mankind and the consignment of unbaptized infants to a perdition tempered only by some slight mitigation. These additions to Augustine's central thesis have not been generally accepted by the Church and cannot be regarded as elements essential to Christian Apologetics.

The point at which the most basic disagreement manifests itself between Augustine and Pelagius is the different conceptions of freedom which they entertain. Sometimes one has the impression that in the discussion the two protagonists are really shooting past one another. Pelagius works with a straightforward rather banal notion: we are always free, in his view, to do one of two things. Augustine on the other hand has won from bitter experience a much deeper understanding of the situation: the sheer bondage into which "freedom" thus superficially understood had plunged him could be broken only by divine intervention. Freedom of will is enjoyed and exercised by man only as and when it abjures sin and continues in a fixed habit of virtue. Formally freedom is inability to sin, the *beata necessitas non peccandi* (the blessed necessity of not sinning); materially it connotes a grace-initiated pursuit of the good and of the service of God. Compared with this the Pelagian concept of freedom is a jejune arid thing, consisting in freedom of choice rather than freedom of action. Augustine never denies that this paltry freedom belongs to men. But, he maintains, it did them no good. It could be practised and exercised and yet never lift a man's head clear of the prisonhouse of his sin. Freedom, he says in slightly different terms, "is sufficient for evil; for good it is not enough unless it be empowered by the Omnipotent who is good" (*de Corruptione et Gratia*, 11.31). Real freedom had therefore to be sought elsewhere outside man's own nature and natural endowments. And it was this that the grace of God bestowed as a gift and enabled men to exercise responsibly. If his diagnosis of man's situation is realistic, Augustine's estimate of the remedial action of grace sounds the note of triumphant gladness. On both counts it ranks as an apologetic against which Pelagianism for all its plausible attractiveness has little to retort with.

Augustine's great work **de Civitate Dei** divides up naturally into two parts. Written between 412 and 426, it was occasioned by the fall of Rome to Alaric the Goth. The first ten books comprise Augustine's apologetic for Christianity against the charge that the misfortunes of the Roman Empire are attributable to adherence to Christianity and apostasy from the ancient pagan gods. In Books 11–22 he develops what is usually regarded as a philosophy of history, based upon the perpetual struggle between the *civitas Dei* (the city of God) and the *civitas terrena* (the earthly city). This estimate has been questioned on the ground that transcendental principles figure more prominently than empirical historical facts.[13] But to press this criticism would result in Hegel and others being ejected from the ranks of the philosophers of history; and the judgment ought to be allowed to stand. In any case the first part has more to contribute to Christian Apologetics than the second.

Twice before, Alaric had laid siege to Rome, and twice the threat had been repelled. The third attempt, protracted negotiations having come to nothing, was more successful, and the Goths entered the city on August 24, 410. The threat had become reality, and the Empire was forced to live with it. It is difficult to estimate the amount of physical damage that ensued for the subdued city, but the evidence shows that it was less than could have been expected. Alaric's aim was not to sack Rome but to inherit it, not to destroy it but to utilize it and even augment its glory. Hence no doubt the comparative leniency shown by the occupying forces, which Augustine witnesses. But the psychological shock sustained by the Roman Empire was almost unimaginably great, and it is this that determines the situation which Augustine feels obliged apologetically to answer. Yet it is not Augustine who expresses the deepest disquiet. Jerome is much more outspoken: "The city is taken that took captive the whole world; alas, alas, the whole world falls in ruins . . . The famous city, the head of the Roman Empire, is burnt in one holocaust" (*Ep.* 127, 128).[14] By comparison Augustine's reaction is mild. He speaks of "dreadful things" certainly; but from them he draws no grand lesson that an age is moving to an end.[15] Instead he tends to use the circumstances as occasion for preaching at his flock and Christians in general, that now above all is the time to lay up treasure in heaven. Perhaps Augustine was a little sheltered by the breadth of the Mediterranean that lay between him and the imperial capital itself. But if this tempered the anguish he expressed, it may have given him the chance to appraise the situation more accurately. At all events he is not in the least blind to the fact that Christians, stunned by the events through which they had lived, needed both solace and encouragement. Besides, the circumstances had given occasion for bringing into currency again criticisms that Christians had already had to face. At any rate it is at this point that he perceives a need, and for the lasting enrichment of the Christian understanding of the Gospel he assembles the resources at his disposal and deploys them in an apologetic of unrivalled range and power.

The charge which is to be repelled is not well reasoned or systematically expounded. It is rather the unreflective and instinctive reaction of ordinary people shocked out of the customary patterns into which they normally conveniently slot the contingencies that impinge upon them, and blindly looking round for a scapegoat on which to pin a responsibility of which they wish to rid themselves. Tertullian had earlier reckoned with this kind of rabble-rousing cry: "they think the Christians the cause of every public disaster, of every public affliction with which the people are visited. If the Tiber rises as high as the city walls, if the Nile does not send its waters up over the fields, if the heavens give no rain, if there is an earthquake, famine or pestilence, instantly the cry is raised: *Christianos ad leonem*" (the Christians to the lions) (*Apol*, 40). Now again the conditions are present which make a reaction away from Christianity towards paganism understandable. Paganism had only recently been abandoned by many; it was ready to revive; and it linked the greatness of Rome with the favour of the pagan gods and its misfortunes with neglect of the pagan cult. We must no doubt feel today that such charges are unrealistic and perhaps insincere. But we may reflect that they were real enough in Augustine's day, that the apologetic Augustine mounted against them was both sustained and serious, and that it is because he did the work of demolishing this kind of objection so thoroughly that it does not recur to trouble us now.

The first part of the *de Civitate Dei* is designed to "refute those who think that the worship of the many false gods is necessary for the prosperity of human affairs and contend that evils arise and abound because it is prohibited"—so Augustine himself comments in his *Retractationes*. In fact both parts of the *de Civitate Dei* contain a good deal more than this. We may attribute this to Augustine's realization of the basic insincerity of the objections he takes it upon himself to answer. Or perhaps it is due to the natural vivacity of a mind disposed to use the ruins of a demolished enemy position as base for further operations in the interests of the Christian faith. The whole work is discursive: Augustine having raised a theological hare unashamedly pursues it without bothering to ask himself whether it may not be a red herring. Book 1 is an illuminating study in apologetic versatility, and reference to it in some detail is necessary. The case for Christianity he argues on several grounds. First, on the assumptions of the critics themselves, Augustine argues (1.1) that "those bloodthirsty barbarians certainly showed a clemency far beyond the usual custom of war." This clemency was extended, Augustine contends, for the sake of Christ to those who rejected the name of Christ as well as to believers. Rome was not sacked; and the shrines and basilicas of the city proved inviolate sanctuaries for those who sought refuge in them. Alaric seems to have given express orders to this effect. Augustine, more anxious to expound ultimate causes than proximate, ignores this, and never even hints that Alaric and his invading Goths were Christians, though addicted to heretical Arianism. He claims that the brutalities suffered are attributable to the ordinary customs of war, while the clemency evident is due to the power of Christ's name (1.7). In a *tu quoque* type of argument, he ridicules the critics: why should they suppose that the gods that failed to save Troy should be able to help Rome in its hour of need? (1.3 *et. al.*). But more important are two arguments for which evidently Augustine had more taste. He insists upon the contingent character of the fortunes of life. Running through the course of events there is an element of neutrality, even of indifference. We should look to divine providence not for a neat arrangement of prosperity and adversity in accordance with justice, but rather to learn the lesson of gratitude for temporal good and humility in temporal evil. "Virtue and vice are different although subjected to the same lash. In the same fire, gold shines while chaff burns" (1.8 ff.). Besides, Christianity has shown itself abundantly able to fortify, console and counsel. The prisoner is supplied with comfort, the victims of suffering and rape with the will to recover, while suicide is rejected as the resort of the spiritually craven and insecure (1.14 ff.). The final impregnable refuge of the Christian lies in the assurance: "My God is present everywhere in total power; and no place excludes him" (1.29).

In Book 2 Augustine turns from pure defence to attack. Still largely subscribing to the assumptions of the critics of Christianity, he argues that the relevant facts prove the charges invalid. In a sustained counter-attack he points out that historically, evils were also incurred when Rome worshipped the old gods. His characteristic puritanism prompts him to indicate the licentious elements in pagan cultic observance and the corruption which flowed from them into both civic and artistic life. As philosopher he points out that the example of the gods is more powerful in working moral injury than in warding off the evils consequent on corruption. In contrast to this, Augustine holds up the bracing purity and healthfulness of the Christian religion, and in an eloquent peroration calls upon the Romans once and for all to abandon heathen worship.

In Book 3 Augustine puts in service a wider range of historical and literary evidence to show the ineffectiveness of the gods of ancient Greece and Rome in defending the cities and city states to which they offered protection from calamity and ruin. On the contrary, "the gods who preside over imperial Rome bore the spectacle with equanimity, merely looking on, like an audience in a theatre" (3.14).

In Book 4 Augustine deals with more general matters. The particular opponents he engages have slipped into the background, and he broadens his front and advances. Freed from a limited objective, his observations take on a colour that has not faded and a universality that survives the changes of time. Here is an early anticipation of the realization that war has no real victors, and of the cynical view of religion as the device of rulers to keep the ruled in subjection. In often quoted words, Augustine says: "Without justice what are kingdoms but great bands of robbers, and what a band of robbers but such a kingdom in miniature?" (4.4) He realizes too the inability of warring nations to be judges in their own case, and adumbrates the practical basis on which the idea of international justice and the attempts in modern times to implement it must rest. More generally, the evils suffered in his day are more reliably attributed to war as such, as the immediate cause of misery and injustice, than to the hypothetical desertion of the city by neglected and offended gods. He has no doubt at all that to supply the true cause of wretchedness in place of a false one will have genuine apologetic value and be a source of true solace. No doubt pastorally he would realize the need to supplement such theological considerations with a warmer compassion.

More positive observations occupy the remaining books of Part 1. The pagan gods have been discredited and their influence repudiated. To replace them Augustine develops the concept of the universal providence of the one true God, the creator, sustainer and disposer of all things. Hence if men are advised to learn his discipline from the sufferings endured, they are equally to perceive his goodness in the good fortune they enjoy. Here is the source to which may be attributed the beneficial order bestowed by the Roman Empire and the outstanding prosperity conferred upon Constantine. Even the sturdy Roman virtues, their devotion and their fortitude, fall under the providential ordering of God. Augustine would be untrue to himself in designating them as inherently meritorious. But they did in fact pay dividends of success for Rome, while for Christians they provide an analogy and example.[16]

Augustine now supposes that the burden of the charges against Christianity shifts. It is no longer the terrestrial advantages that paganism has secured but the eternal life it offers that is advanced now in its favour. In Book 6 Augustine has little difficulty in showing that the claim is invalidated by the logical contradictoriness of the relevant mythology, as well as by its moral bankruptcy. The obscenity embedded in paganism and the falsity of the spirits, even as defended by Apuleius, and in a modified way by Plato, have been sufficiently exposed by Christianity. Even in the time of darkness, God did not desert us, but sent his Son, the Word being made flesh. Thus our mind is liberated not only to seek after him but also to render him thanks (7.31, and 8, 9).

If the apologetic Augustine constructs issues in a radical criticism of paganism, he none the less expresses a warm regard for Plato. He exemplifies here some of the uneasy tension that characterizes other apologists of earlier times; and on the whole he follows the usual line of drawing a distinction between the cult and the thought of paganism, between its religion and philosophy. He puts Plato in his proper place: he is neither god nor demi-god, and he is not comparable to angel, prophet, martyr, or even the ordinary Christian man (2.14). The retention of polytheism is a standing reproach to paganism, even if Plato himself is less directly implicated by it. He was a genius a long way in front of his fellows (8.4), and Augustine's heart warms to the philosopher who arrives at the conclusion that the best and highest good is God, who identifies the philosopher with the lover of God, and sees that since philosophy aims at a happy life, he who loves God is happy in the enjoyment of God (see 8.8). He will not believe that Plato had ever met Jeremiah, but neither does he discount the possibility that the Hebrew Scriptures were known to him. He is inclined even to credit this, for he finds in the "I am that I am" of Exod. 3.14 the same truth as Plato held and diligently taught, that he who truly is, is unchangeable, while the things that are changeable have no real existence. This view which remained unchallenged for centuries would win little support from modern exegetes. It only goes to show that here, as elsewhere, Augustine was rather too content to look through the eyes of the greatest philosopher of antiquity at matters where Christian theology and classical philosophy had a common interest.

No doubt a work of Apologetics is liable to go out of date,[17] perhaps in proportion to the accuracy with which it responds to the contemporary anti-Christian charges. A good deal of what Augustine says in the more strictly apologetic part of the de Civitate Dei is likely to seem irrelevant to the modern reader. But much that more sophisticated Christians might wish to discard has its value in places where Christianity has been more recently planted than in the Christian West. Where similar circumstances recur men are apt to respond in the same way; and Augustine's thorough and eminently patient treatment of this response still offers guidance. In any case the unfolding pattern of the course of things is splendidly relevant and instructive for all ages.

In the final book of Part 1 he manoeuvres into the position for developing the theme of the latter 12 books. This theme concerns the two cities already referred to in the opening words of the whole work. Augustine finds the distinction in Scripture, and his ordinary reader will recall how the Epistle to the Hebrews distinguishes the "strange country" through which the Christian travels from the "better country" and the "city which has foundations" (Heb. 11.9, 10, 16). The greatness of his contribution consists not in drawing the distinction, but in the delicacy with which he handles the interlocking of the two distinguishable elements in the world as we know it. With supreme confidence he combines realism with hope, and offers to the critical, the perplexed and the doubting a penetrating analysis of the world as it is and a final assurance of God's eventual triumph. Here the various strands of Augustine's experience are woven together. Augustine sufficiently learned the reality of evil from Manichaeism, even if he theoretically expounds it in privative terms.

The Donatists had demonstrated to him the futility of fleeing the world in pursuit of perfection. To those shocked and vexed by the contemporary disorder and misfortune he counsels patience and expectation. What is true of the world is true also of the Church. "The two cities spring from two different kinds of love, the earthly from love of self leading to contempt of God, and the heavenly from love of God leading to contempt of self" (14.28). Augustine offers men the parable of the kingdom, of the wheat and the tares which must be allowed to grow together, until the time of harvest when the reaper will effect the separation (Matt. 13.24 ff.).

It is not possible to regard Augustine's teaching here as a pure exercise in Apologetics. But like the best dogmatic thought it advances the apologetic enterprise. More generally, the contribution of Augustine marks a turning point in apologetic theology. Harnack writes[18] in well-known words: "The Gospel entered into the world, not as a doctrine, but as a joyful message and as a power of the Spirit of God, originally in the forms of Judaism. It stripped off these forms with amazing rapidity, and united and amalgamated itself with Greek science, the Roman Empire and ancient culture, developing, as a counterpoise to this, renunciation of the world and the striving after supernatural life, after deification. All this was summed up in the old dogma and in dogmatic Christianity." This describes a tendency evident in the early formative years of Christianity. Augustine may be said to have clapped on the brakes without bringing it to a full stop. His theology serves a purer, more biblical and more living understanding of religion. He leaves the ground-plan Harnack describes largely intact; but what he builds upon it does not strictly conform to it. Hence the several tensions apparent in his theology. Above all the Augustinian erection has many more windows than the original plan allowed, and these opened both upon the past and the future, to let in light and give a view of the path that lay ahead.

# CHAPTER SIX

# THOMAS AQUINAS, MEDIAEVAL ARGUMENTS
# AND THEIR DEVELOPMENTS

OF the three major aspects of the undertaking to which Apologetics addresses itself, two have been exemplified in what has been said. Christianity has been seen defending itself against enemies from outside and against wreckers from within, against opponents moved by different conviction, ignorance or malice, and against heretics challenging orthodoxy. These two tasks are distinguishable but not entirely separate. For example in the engagement of Christianity with Gnosticism it is often difficult to know who is declared foe and who mistaken friend.

The third task consists in expounding the grounds of Christian belief with the purpose not so much of overwhelming a specific antagonist as of commending the faith to all those willing to listen to what reason has to say. It would be easy to find elements in most of the Christian thinkers already mentioned which have this un-specified apologetic intention and application, from the Logos doctrine of the Fourth Gospel to Augustine's philosophy of history in the second part of the *de Civitate Dei*. But this aspect of the defence of Christianity becomes more self-conscious and articulate as the Middle Ages succeed the Dark Ages and Christianity begins its second thousand years. Perhaps, too, overt opposition to the faith in the form of enemies of Christianity and opponents of orthodoxy diminishes: it is time to fortify the faithful in their faith by showing them and any others who will listen the inherent rationality of what Christians believe.

One matter demanding this kind of attention more than any other is itself more fundamental than any other. In the course of Christian thought many theologians have felt obliged to give reasons for believing that God exists. They are not the first to do so. Plato, for example, tries to show the reasonableness of belief in God;

and even Aristotle in his own way contributes to this line of thought. Christian writers on the subject have often availed themselves of what Plato said. Clearly the need for supplying grounds of this kind is widely felt. There is something curious here. An immense amount of thought and writing has been devoted to the subject of God. Yet apparently it is impossible to take the very existence of the subject simply for granted. Evidently God is deniable in a particularly plausible way. We all sympathize with Samuel Johnson who, talking of Bishop Berkeley's denial of the existence of matter, kicked a stone, and said: "I refute it thus."[1] The denial was so implausible as to require no other comment. Indeed to prove the existence of anything at all is a very odd procedure. As Søren Kierkegaard remarks,[2] "I do not for example prove that a stone exists, but that some existing thing is a stone. The procedure in a court of justice does not prove that a criminal exists, but that the accused, whose existence is given, is a criminal." But the existence of God is apparently not of this class of things, and if a man deny it we must do more than call him merely silly. We must take up the task of providing reasons why it is more intelligent to believe than to disbelieve God's existence.

It is this task that is taken on by the so-called proofs of the existence of God, the "theistic proofs" as they are often called. Much difficulty has infected the whole subject because of the ambiguous or varied meaning that the word proof carries. Robert Flint bluntly says:[3] "The grounds or reasons which we have for our belief must be to us proofs of God's existence." He derides as preposterous the view which he quotes[4] that "a God who can be proved is no God, for the ground of proof is necessarily above the thing proved." More generally we have often heard it said in similar vein that since belief in God is a matter of faith proof is impossible; if it is in fact offered it is not God that is proved. There is a misunderstanding here which is not easy to unravel. Flint certainly does not think the proof he speaks of is identical with the demonstrations offered in the mathematical sciences or with the methods used by the natural sciences to substantiate a hypothesis. If such proof were offered in the case of God, it would certainly not be God that was proved. The fact is that God is not susceptible of proof of these kinds. This must be borne in mind in what follows, and we must ask in every case where proof is offered, what kind of proof it really is. At this point it is enough to state that all proof is based on evidence and that the evidence called must be appropriate to what is being proved. The kind of proof that substantiates one thing may be inappropriate in the case of another; and proofs of God's existence are not inadmissible because they do not conform to the norms observed in proving other things.

The Apologists of the second century had already availed themselves of proofs. The moral effects of Christianity, the fulfilment of the predictions of the prophets and of Christ, the antiquity of Christianity traced back to Moses who lived before the Greek poets and philosophers, and also more sparingly the miracles of Christ—all these were employed to prove the truth of Christianity. The proofs to which we now come are quite different in character and aim. They are addressed to thinking men, and they rely not on the records of scriptural books but on the judgment of reason. They aim not at establishing the respectability of Christianity but at demonstrating that belief in God is reasonable.

It was some time before this became recognized as a distinguishable proper exercise for theology to undertake. But a beginning was made by Augustine. Proofs appear sporadically in his writings and generally no attempt is made to organize them into a systematic demonstration. A good example is supplied in the *Confessions*, Book 11, where Augustine begins an extended meditation upon Genesis 1 which takes the form of a soliloquy directed to God. "Pardon my sins," he says, "and as thou didst grant to thy servant (Moses) to speak those words (Gen.1.1.), grant me to understand them." Then (11.4) he brings forward his proof. "We look upon the heavens and the earth, and they cry aloud that they were made. For they change and vary. (If anything was not made and yet exists, there is nothing in it that was not there before: and it is the essence of change and variation that something should be that was not there before.) They cry aloud too that they did not make themselves. (We exist because we were made; but we did not exist before we existed to be able to give ourselves existence). And their visible presence is itself the voice with which they speak. It was thou, Lord, who madest them." Then, if the question How? is asked, Augustine replies (11.5): not like an artist who is supplied with his material, but, as absolutely Creator: "Thou spakest, and heaven and earth were created; in thy Word thou didst create them." Here two lines of thought are intertwined. The things around us evidently did not bring themselves into existence; and the changeability they manifest makes it plain that they could not do so. Augustine is already familiar with a kind of argument that becomes more precise and formal at a later time.

The best known sentence in the *Confessions* is certainly: "Thou hast made us for thyself and our hearts are restless till they rest in thee" (1.1). This sentiment itself is really an argument for the existence of God, and it displays the basic form of an argument that often recurs. Man, the argument runs, has an unsatisfied desire for light, happiness, and goodness—in a word for beatitude. This inherent need can find satisfaction only in an absolute good and an infinite and eternal beauty. The argument is as old as Plato and forms the principal and staple basis of the *philosophia perennis* (perennial philosophy) throughout the course of philosophical thinking.

The most ambitious attempt at proof appears in the *de Libero Arbitrio* (2.3.7ff.). It is a closely woven argument and merits some attention. Man who has existence, life and intelligence stands at the summit of the scale of being. While living creatures are able by what Augustine calls an interior sense (perhaps our instinct) to co-ordinate the senses, man in addition possesses reason which rules and judges both senses and the interior sense. If there is anything eternal and unchangeable that is superior to reason, it will be God. Augustine goes on to show that this superior entity must exist. For one thing, the science of number is not dependent on the senses but is common to all who can master it. Further, all men seek truth and happiness; and while they seek it in different directions, it is the supreme good that is sought in different things. Further, some truths are self-evident and these are common to all minds; and judgments of value reach beyond the individuals who make them. The rules of wisdom, like the system of numbers, are true, unchangeable and common to all men. So truth is superior to the mind that apprehends it because it is unchangeable and eternal. This truth has nothing that is superior to it. It is in fact God, the Father of wisdom, whose only begotten Son is his equal. So the existence of God is held to be proved. Those familiar with Plato and his philosophy will recognize in the reference to number Augustine's dependence upon Plato; those not so acquainted will find it a little baffling. But the essence of the argument is simple. The human mind entertains truths of logic, mathematics, ethics and aesthetics. These truths are objective, immutable, and universally and eternally valid. As such they cannot be explained simply as the particular possessions of individual minds. They have their real existence in an essential and all-embracing truth. And this is God. (We note in passing that the mention by Augustine of Father and Son in connection with this God is incongruous and hardly justified by the argument itself.)

With **Anselm** (*c.*1033–*c.*1109) the enterprise of commending the Christian faith on the basis of intellectual reasoning enters a new phase. A man of piety, great strength of character, and luminous intellectual powers, he used the method more independently, imparted to it a greater degree of self-consciousness, and contributed one formulation, "not unworthy of standing on the threshold of the second thousand years of Christian thought",[5] which has fascinated, mystified and repelled different Christian thinkers up to the present day. This is the celebrated **Ontological Argument** or proof of God's existence. Taking seriously the words of the Psalmist (Ps. 14.1), Anselm considers the case of the fool who says in his heart: There is no God. In order to deny God in this way the fool must understand what he denies; he must, that is, entertain the idea of God, even if he does not understand that such a being exists. There is, Anselm says, a clear difference "between having a thing in the understanding, and understanding that the thing is in existence." The hinge of the argument is that while to be *in intellectu* (in the mind) and to be *in re* (in reality) are always different and usually separable, in the case of God they go necessarily together. The grand conclusion follows: "Something therefore without doubt exists than which no greater can be conceived, and it is both in the understanding and in reality" (*Proslogion*, 2). God is *id quo maius cogitari non potest*, that than which nothing greater can be conceived. It is, however, impossible that this should be in the understanding alone. Anselm thinks of existence as a perfection alongside other perfections. Hence if that than which nothing greater can be conceived did not exist, two conclusions would follow: first, it would lack a perfection and so would not after all in itself be that than which nothing greater can be conceived; and secondly, it would leave room for the conception of something else greater than it, namely what was not in understanding only but also in existence. The supposition that that than which nothing greater can be conceived does not exist is thus self-contradictory. Its contradictory must then be true. The existence of God has been demonstrated.

It is not entirely clear what Anselm thinks he has accomplished by this remarkable argument, and the question is still actively debated. Beginning as he does with the fool of the Psalmist, it looks as if he was directing a purely apologetic argument at him. If this is so, he must surely have thought the argument left the fool without a leg to stand on. He could only capitulate, abjure his former denial, and admit the existence of God. (Modern exegesis tends to think that the Psalmist has in mind the impious or impudent rather than the merely foolish, and that his denial is of God's presence and active interposition in the affairs of men rather than of his existence. But for the purpose here this is beside the point.) The fool's position, however, is not so hopeless as might appear. Anselm has his own definition of God and this he is really imposing upon the fool: his denial of God as Anselm defines him is on Anselm's argument indeed irrational. His continued denial can only be the product of confused thinking, as when a schoolboy fails to see the truth of a Euclidean proposition. It is true, as Anselm points out, that in denying something one must have some knowledge of what is being denied. But he too easily assumes that that which the fool denies, and of which he accordingly has some knowledge, is God exactly as Anselm defines him. If this is not the case, then it is not Anselm's God that the fool denies, but some other God. He can then evade Anselm's argument and persist in his denial.

Should we then interpret Anselm's intention differently? Perhaps what he is doing is to explore the content of faith and hold it up to intellectual scrutiny. There are some indications that this is so.[6] For one thing, he himself speaks of *fides quaerens intellectum*, that is of faith seeking, not justification or verification from sources outside itself, but rather the rationale of its own contents. Faith, already assured of God's existence, can seek and find a logical pattern in what it affirms. Moreover, like Augustine, Anselm sets this coolly intellectual argument in a framework, indeed an atmosphere, of prayer. Thus he begins the argument with an *excitatio mentis ad contemplandum Deum* (a rousing of the mind to the contemplation of God): "Lord, teach me to seek thee, and show thyself to me as I seek, for I cannot seek thee unless thou teach me, nor find thee unless thou show thyself . . . For indeed I do not seek to understand in order that I may believe, but I believe in order that I may understand. For this I believe, that unless I believe I shall not understand." And in a final exhortation: "Therefore, Lord, thou who givest understanding to faith, grant to me that so far as thou knowest it to be expedient I may understand that thou art as we believe, and that thou art what we believe" (*Proslogion*, 1). From this point he immediately embarks on the exposition of his argument. All this seems to indicate the narrower intention of simply rationally expounding the content of faith. This is indeed in itself of great apologetic importance, but it does not directly apply to anyone who like the fool has already closed his mind against the possibility of there being a God.

But again, Anselm seems to claim more than this for his argument. For in the succeeding chapter (*op. cit.* 3) he offers thanks to God "for granting that what by thy gift I formerly believed I now by thy illumination so understand, that, even if I were to be *unwilling* to believe in thy existence, yet I *could not but know* it by my understanding" (italics mine; what can he mean here by "illumination"?). From this Anselm does not hesitate to draw an apologetic conclusion. The *thought* of God cannot be misapprehended and rejected. What the fool does is to use the *word* without the thought. It looks as though Anselm in this mood believes his argument to be so cogent that theism is defensible on intellectual grounds without the prior operation of faith.

The novelty of Anselm's argument aroused keen interest. In particular Gaunilo of the monastery at Marmoutier near Tours took up the cudgels on behalf of the fool in his *Liber pro Insipiente adversus Anselmi in Proslogio ratiocinationem*. Gaunilo rightly saw that the nerve of the Anselmic argument consists in an inference from an object in thought (*in intellectu*) to an object in reality (*in re*), and denied the possibility of moving out of the sphere of thought into that of existence. The illustration he uses to make the point is famous. "Some say that there is in the ocean an island which . . . is known as the Lost Island. It is fabled to be more amply supplied with riches and all delights in immense abundance than the Fortunate Islands themselves. And although there is no owner or inhabitant, yet in every way it excels all inhabited lands in the abundance of things which might be appropriated as wealth." This, says Gaunilo, is so far entirely understandable. But if the inference is drawn: "You can no longer doubt that this most excellent of islands, which you do not doubt to exist in your understanding, is really in existence somewhere, because it is more excellent to be in reality than in the understanding only, and unless it were in existence any other land which does exist would be more excellent than it, and so that which you have understood to be the best of islands would not be the best." If on these grounds we are asked to assent to the existence of this island, says Gaunilo, we must suppose that someone is trying to make fools of us. "He must first have shown me that its very excellence is the excellence of a thing really and indubitably existing, and not in any degree the excellence of something false or dubious in my understanding."

Anselm nothing daunted, replied to this criticism in his *Liber apologeticus contra Gaunilonem*. He reaffirms his own position: "It is not possible that the *quo maius nihil* (that is, the that than which nothing greater can be conceived) could be thought to be and yet actually not be. If it can at all be conceived as existing, it must exist of necessity." But, he adds, the right of passing from thought to existence is claimed not in the case of contingent things but solely in the case of the *quo maius nihil*. The retort is a sufficient reply to Gaunilo's criticism, but it adds nothing to the credibility of Anselm's argument. Stalemate has been reached. No argument has in such a degree combined impressiveness with inability to produce final conviction.

Despite its equivocal character—perhaps because of it—the Ontological Argument has continued to generate interest if not conviction, and attract respect without acceptance. St. Thomas Aquinas is sufficiently impressed by it to allow that the proposition: God exists, is self-evident in itself; but since we do not know the essence of God, it is not self-evident to us. Hence he thinks that strictly a priori demonstration of God's existence is impossible, and he replaces it, as we shall see, by a system of a posteriori proof (*Summa Theologica*, Part I, Ch. 2, Art. I). **Descartes** (1596–1650), on the other hand, in a complex argument puts forward the argument again. Whether he borrowed from Anselm in doing so is uncertain. In any case the exposition follows different lines and wears a different form. Beginning by discarding all statements that admit of any doubt at all, he arrives at his celebrated *cogito ergo sum* (I think, therefore I am) which he conceives to be bedrock certainty and beyond all doubt. The character that imparts this certainty to the statement is its clarity and distinctness. Accordingly statements that have a similar clarity and distinctness, but only these, have an equal certainty. Now the idea of perfection is conjoined with that of existence with a similar clarity and distinctness. It follows that a perfect being must also be an existing being: God necessarily exists.

From Immanuel **Kant** (1724–1804) the argument received careful scrutiny and also its most damaging blow. Kant recognizes that the argument possesses great weight and authority, and he himself accords respect to it, while thinking it objectively inadequate. He points out two chief defects. The first is applicable to the form which Anselm had given to the argument, in which it appeared self-contradictory to deny the existence of God. Kant illustrates from the case of the triangle. On condition that a triangle exists, there must necessarily exist three angles: to suppose the existence of a triangle and not that of its three angles is self-contradictory. But if there is nothing at all, then no contradiction arises: to suppose the non-existence of both triangle and angles is perfectly admissible. Similarly, no contradiction arises if we stay by simple denial of God.[7] This argument is almost exactly the same as that which St. Thomas puts forward when he says: "Nor can it be argued that (God) actually exists, unless it be admitted that there actually exists something than which nothing greater can be conceived; and this precisely is not admitted by those who hold that God does not exist." It is a package deal: if you admit God, you must go on to affirm his existence; if you decline to accept God, nothing can compel you to admit his existence.

The second objection which Kant makes applies more to the form in which he knew the argument as it came to him from the hands of the philosopher Christian Wolff who antedates Kant by half a century. Wolff conceived existence to be a predicate like other predicates, and thought that to have existence is to have another predicate added to others already possessed; that accordingly anything perfect cannot lack this predicate any more than it can lack any other; and that therefore the *ens realissimum* (most real being) must have existence among the perfections predicable of it. Kant's criticism of this is essentially simple. Existence, he says, is not a predicate. That is, to affirm existence is not to affirm a quality like other qualities and alongside other qualities; it is to "posit" a thing with all its qualities. To say: God is omnipotent, involves two entities, the "is" relating "God" and "omnipotent" as subject and predicate. But to say: "God is" adds no new predicate, but only "posits" the subject with all its predicates. In a famous illustration Kant reiterates his point: "the real contains no more than the possible. A hundred real dollars contain no more than a possible hundred dollars . . . Existence does not in the least degree increase the aforesaid hundred dollars." On the whole it is a pity that Kant hazarded the illustration. Like Gaunilo's argument, it can carry weight as an argument only in the measure in which God can be classed with other things like dollars. Kant more than most thinkers should have been sensitive to the impropriety of such an analogy. As he later shows, the reason why God's existence cannot be proved by what had in his day come to be known as the Cosmological Argument is precisely that, whatever he is, God is not on a level with other things. For any knowledge of the fact of his existence we are dependent on reason not as it is employed among other things but as it affords insight into the moral constitution of the universe. Kant does his argument disservice by his choice of illustration. But even when cleared of this misrepresentation, Anselm's reply to Gaunilo is not inapplicable to Kant's argument. Certainly in the case of ordinary things existence is not a predicate—in Kant's terminology, the affirmation of existence is synthetic and so can always be denied without contradiction; in modern language, existence is contingent. Yet what is true and even obvious of ordinary things is not so evident in the case of what is not an ordinary thing but the ground of all ordinary things. In any case the question in this form has never ceased to agitate both theologians and philosophers: does *is* imply *must be*, does contingency imply necessity, and does after all a perfect being necessarily exist?

So A. S. Pringle-Pattison[8] believes that what the Ontological Argument is really labouring to express is, in Lotze's phrase, "the confidence of reason in itself", or "that necessary implication in thought expresses a similar implication in reality". On the one hand this line of thought moves towards a Hegelian understanding of reality, where the real is rational and the rational is real. But it moves also in a quite different sense, towards the position in which reason is taught by experience, where the a priori intuition that grasps clear and distinct ideas gives way to the humbler plodding activity of inductive and a posteriori reasoning that pinpoints the implications that seem to arise from the facts of life. By a curious turn of thought we have come back to the alternative mode of thought which St. Thomas preferred to the Ontological Argument. It is this alternative that must be now examined.

**St. Thomas Aquinas** (c.1225–c.1274) is one of the most considerable figures in the whole history of Christian theology, and towers gigantically over the Middle Ages. As everyone knows, his genius inclines him not to novel construction but to comprehensive systematic exposition. However, circumstances provided him with at least a tool that was relatively new. Aristotle's writings, unlike those of Plato, aroused more suspicion than admiration in the minds of the early Church. His rejection of Plato's "ideal" existence as such, and his insistence that "forms" exist only as united with matter, were thought to lead to a materialistic understanding of the world, and Christian theologians understandably enough believed they could get on better without him. Boethius (c.480–c.524), best known for his celebrated *de Consolatione Philosophiae*, devoted himself to the study of Aristotelianism and his translations and commentaries were to become useful in the Middle Ages. But his own Christianity was so insubstantial as to give rise to prolonged doubts whether he was a Christian at all. The work of John Scotus Erigena (c.810–c.877) tended to rivet the attention of Christian theology upon Neo-Platonism which he welcomed as an effective apologetic ally for the commendation of the faith. In the twelfth century, however, Arabic translations of Aristotle's works made by Moslem and Jewish scholars, together with Latin translations of them, began to spread acquaintance of "the Philosopher", as he came to be respectfully known. The initial suspicion with which this new knowledge was regarded was mitigated and finally dispersed by the acceptance given to it first by Albertus Magnus (c.1200–c.1280), and then by Aquinas. Thus Western theology came to be indelibly marked by Aristotelian features. The form Aquinas gives to his demonstration of God's existence is unmistakably Aristotelian.

Aquinas is too much of a systematic theologian to be deliberately interested in Apologetics as such. But if natural theology is a species of Apologetics, then an apologetic strand runs through the two major works. The *de Veritate Fidei Catholicae contra Gentiles* (1261–1264) is usually referred to simply as the *Summa contra Gentiles*. It is written as a textbook for missionaries and contains a sustained defence of natural theology against chiefly the Moslem Arabians. The defence offered hinges chiefly upon a distinction between things which reason can of itself come to know and those for knowledge of which it is dependent on revelation. Aquinas does not invent the distinction. It is one that any theologian who wished to make use of Aristotle in expounding the Christian faith could be expected to utilize. This leads us back to Albertus Magnus, Aquinas' predecessor in Aristotelian interest, who sensed the need, while exploiting Aristotle for Christian purposes, to reserve certain Christian doctrines as beyond Aristotle's reach and trace them to another source than was available to Aristotle. The same kind of action had, however, already been taken by others. Two students of Aristotle, the one Maimonides the Jew and the other Averroës the Arab, had found the distinction useful in working out the relation of Aristotle's thought to Judaism and Islam respectively. Revelation provided a repository from which truths could be drawn that were inaccessible to reason by itself.

If Aquinas did not invent the distinction, he at least gave unprecedentedly clear and authoritative expression to it. Thus in the *Summa contra Gentiles* (1.3) he declares that "in those things which we assert of God, the way of truth is twofold. For there are things true of God which surpass every faculty of human reason—that he is triune, for example. But there are others which are within the scope of natural reason, such as that he exists, that he is one, and others of that kind; these have been proved by philosophers, following the light of natural reason." For the immediate apologetic Aquinas is constructing, the distinction enables him to demonstrate the superiority of Christianity. From revelation Christianity had acquired truths to which Aristotle had not aspired. The apologetic effectiveness of the distinction over against Islam and for that matter Judaism was less apparent, since they too laid claim to truths arising out of revelation. But for those truths that depended on reason alone an extensive and lasting sphere of usefulness opened up. They could be effectively commended to men in virtue of no more than the bare possession of reason. This is a principal element that Aquinas uses in the *Summa Theologica* (his second major work, unfinished at his death) for his demonstration of the existence of God. But to understand the argument there, it is necessary to look at one main principle that determines Aquinas' theory of knowledge. Only then can it be seen why his demonstration takes the line it does.

This principle is the Aristotelian axiom that wherever there is knowledge an essential likeness exists between knower and known. In the case of man whose nature is corporeal as well as intellectual knowledge must begin with and build upon sense perception, for *nihil in intellectu quod non prius fuerit in sensu* (there is nothing in the mind that was not first of all in the senses)—the empiricist's formula in every age. If then we will know of God's existence the argument must begin with the facts of the natural world around us. Aquinas is thus committed to an a posteriori proof: we move from the more immediately known facts around us to the lesser known conclusions to which with inescapable rigour they lead us. Accordingly Aquinas outlines five ways—the celebrated *quinque viae*—in which God's existence can be proved by moving out from the effects of his being that are manifest around us.

It will be noted how closely Aquinas follows the procedure of "the Philosopher" here. When Aristotle rejected the independent existence of ideas or forms and allowed them existence only in particular things, he had to suppose a principle of causation to effect the conjunction of form and matter. This supplied him with the First Cause which he required, the efficient, formal and final cause of the whole world, the Unmoved Mover (*proton kinoun, akinetos*) of all things. This First Mover of Aristotle is not personal and has evidently little or nothing in common with the Christian idea of God. In procedure, Aquinas moves in precisely the same way. Whether the conclusion he draws is any different, whether what he reaches is any more like the Christian idea of God, and if not what the implications are for his argument, are matters not easy to decide.

It is at any rate clear that Aquinas comes down wholeheartedly in favour of that kind of commendation of the Christian faith that can apologetically be addressed to rational men. He will not surrender the claim of reason to supply valid knowledge of at least some things concerning God. That is, he refuses to allow faith to take over the whole field. Thus he rejects the tendencies in this direction apparent before his day among the Nominalists (Roscellinus *ob. c.*1125, Peter Abelard 1079–1142), and by anticipation the even more thoroughgoing Nominalism of William of Occam (*c.*1300–*c.*1349). Settling for the native ability of reason to know God in the measure proper to it, Aquinas is none the less aware of reason's limitations. He declines to follow the path that Anselm pioneered, and to find in an intellectual a priori argument alone the sufficient demonstration of God's existence. It is certainly true for Aquinas that God's nature implies his existence; but this can only be known by one who truly knows God's nature. Hence God himself could use the Ontological Argument, or purely intelligent beings such as the angels. But as men lack any such clear idea of God, they are denied the use of it. The fact is that Aquinas is so dominated by Aristotelian empiricism that he can conceivably use only an a posteriori argument.

The existence of God is demonstrable by natural reason unassisted by revelation, even if it yields not *articuli fidei* (articles of faith) but only *praeambula ad articulos* (preamble to such articles). The existence of God can be proved in five ways (*Summa Theol* 1, Q.2, Art. 3). First it can be proved from the motion evident in the world. "Anything which is moved must be moved by something else." But the process cannot be infinite, for then there would be no first source of movement and consequently no moving things. "We must then arrive at some first source of motion which is moved by nothing else: and such a source all men understand to be God." The argument is similar to Aristotle's proof of the First Mover, and for both Aristotle and Aquinas we must remember that motion includes change, and that change in its turn includes not only change of location but also the transition from potentiality to actuality. As here stated by Aquinas it is also less satisfactory. The conclusion can contain no more than an initial first cause, some convulsive heave by which the whole thing is started off, but which dies away when impetus has been imparted. No element of continuance is included here, and the form in which Aquinas presents the argument lacks the permanent character of the operation of motion which Aristotle presupposed.

The second way considers "efficient causes". It is impossible for anything to be the cause of itself. It is equally impossible that efficient causes should go back to infinity; for this would imply the removal of all cause, and so also of the effect. "We must therefore posit some first efficient cause: and all men call this God." This second argument adds nothing to the first.

The first two ways are varieties of what has come to be called the **Cosmological Argument;** and with them may be associated the fourth way to which we shall come in a moment. In the third way this same Cosmological Argument is presented in a fairly sophisticated form. It moves from the possible to the necessary, and runs as follows. Some things at least are capable of existing or not existing; they can either exist or not exist. All such things, however, cannot always exist, for then they would be indistinguishable from things incapable of not existing. If, however, all things were capable of not existing, then at some time just nothing would exist. Then even now there would be just nothing in existence. This is manifestly false. Hence it cannot be that all things are only capable of existing: there must be something that is necessary. Further, this necessary something must have its necessity in its own right, *per se*, and so may be cause of necessity in other things. "And this all men call God." The argument registers an advance over the first two in accommodating permanence within the concluded something: it is not merely a first and contingent cause that is inferred. The reason why this larger content can be included is that the start is made not with particular things requiring an initial particular thing to set them going, but with the logical character of contingency that affects particular things and requires a logical character of necessity in something other than themselves if their existence is to be explicable at all. This logical character reaches beyond the restrictions of time to what always is; and what has permanence in logic can readily be understood as possessing permanence in fact.

Comparative statements form the basis of the fourth way. We speak of "more or less good and true and noble" and so on. But "more or less are spoken of different things according to their different degrees of approach to what is greatest of all." There is, that is to say, a standard of comparison which is itself perfect in the qualities found in particular things in different degrees. "And this we call God." In this argument too Aquinas leans heavily on Aristotle and the concept of all natural things being compounded of form and matter. But the use he makes of it to infer the existence of that in which the degrees reach their perfection is more Platonic than Aristotelian: pure form is affirmed by Plato but denied by

Aristotle. We should beware of interpreting this argument on lines of the much later theory of evolution. Nature for Aquinas is clearly graduated, and this is the ground for our finding the degrees of more and less. But this is different, despite what modern Thomists have wished to make out, from thinking of nature as on the move from lower to higher. Only evolutionism could impart such a fluent character to the understanding of nature. The staircase of St. Thomas should not be identified with the escalator of evolutionism.

With the fifth way Aquinas moves on to fresh ground where both Plato and Aristotle had preceded him, to give his version of the **Teleological Argument.** He notes that some things without the power of knowing none the less "work for ends". Moreover they arrive at their end with a frequency that cannot be explained by chance but only by intention. Since this intention is not their own, it is to be found elsewhere, as the archer is found directing the arrow. "There is therefore some intelligent being by which all natural things are directed towards ends. And this we call God." It is evident that we must not read too much into this argument. Observation of nature cannot be said to have seriously begun. It may indeed be that the Schoolmen practised it even less than Aristotle and his school. Accordingly the remarkable evidence of adaptation, design and purpose to which later natural science, and especially the theory of evolution, has opened modern eyes is a closed book to Aquinas. What he has in mind is, as his initial reference to the *gubernatio* (government) of things indicates, chiefly the intelligent direction of things in orderly and regular ways. It is not so much an end outside themselves to which they are impelled, as the compliant observance of the order of things to which they belong. But at least Aquinas does not use the argument to prove more than is valid. Though it is included in the Article answering to the question: *an Deus sit?* (whether God is?), he is aware that it proves the existence not so much of God as of an *aliquid intelligens* (some intelligent thing), an intelligence sufficient to account for the limited purposiveness he discerns.

The Cosmological Argument, with which Aquinas is concerned though he does not apply this name, is very different in tone from the Ontological. What Kant called "an invention due to the subtlety of the schools" is replaced by an argument that pursues a "natural" direction, making a beginning at least with its feet on the ground. Apologetically its aim is more limited. While the Ontological Argument attempts to show that God's non-existence is unthinkable, the Cosmological wishes simply to demonstrate that God must exist. Such a commendation of God's existence has a less stunning effect and a more persuasive influence. But neither has it escaped criticism. Aquinas presents the argument in two distinguishable forms, based respectively upon the causal principle and logical implication. In its causal form the argument simply is that every being or event must have a cause. By going back along the causal chain far enough a first cause is reached. Yet this is not immediately evident. Why should not the chain of causes be continued indefinitely without ever ending up in a first member of the chain?

This inability of the argument to help us infallibly to reach a first cause is pressed home both by Hume and Kant. **David Hume** (1711–1776) carried to sceptical conclusions the empiricist philosophy associated with the names of Locke (see his *Philosophical Essays concerning Human Understanding*, 1748) and Berkeley. For he rephrased the statement that all knowledge arises from impressions given in experience, and declared rather that knowledge was nothing more than such a succession of impressions together with ideas which are faint copies of impressions. Similarly we may say that A is the cause of B; but all we have the right to say is that in our experience A has invariably been followed by B. On this view causation does not produce in us the expectation of A-followed-by-B. Causation is in fact nothing more than such a mental association. It is not something behind received impressions, but simply the expectation aroused in us by unvarying succession of certain impressions. It follows that causation rightly understood can only be of impressions and certainly cannot lead beyond them. This renders impossible all talk of a first cause of the world. For the world is not an impression arising out of our experience, and certainly we have no experience of a first cause. If then we accept Hume's analysis, the Cosmological Argument seems to break up in our hands.

However, we need not accept uncritically what Hume has to say. Indeed much of it he did not believe himself. As the sceptic *par excellence* he thought it worth while to probe for the weak points in philosophical theory without feeling any obligation to sort out the disorder that ensued. But Kant carried criticism farther.[8a] Unlike

Hume, Kant did not deny the existence of the suprasensible but only that we could have knowledge of it. It is under this principle that Kant evacuates the Cosmological Argument of real virtue. Kant's language is difficult, but in essence his criticism is simple. The principle that everything must have a cause is valid only within the sensible or phenomenal world. It therefore cannot be used to carry us beyond the phenomenal world. Either the first cause of which the argument speaks belongs to the phenomenal world or it exists outside it. If the former is the case, the causal principle will certainly carry us as far as the so-called first cause; but it will also carry us beyond it. The causal series is one we cannot properly prematurely complete: as Kant suggests, we cannot take this cab so far, and having reached a point in the journey which happens to suit us simply dismiss it. If on the other hand the first cause is thought of as something above the range of phenomenal entities, this principle is quite unable to carry us to it. Evidently the apologetic value of the Cosmological Argument for such people as Hume and Kant is nil.

In its other and logical statement, the Cosmological Argument attempts to show that the existence of contingent things implies the existence of a necessary being; or more briefly, because the contingent is the necessary is. The argument thus presented is not different in substance. But it penetrates behind the physically observable to discern the fundamental pattern. The pattern there discovered may rightly be described as contingent. Is it right and proper to infer the necessary? It may appear that there is some linguistic sleight of hand at this point. There sometimes is—as when the term contingency is replaced by dependence. The weakness of this statement of the argument is that a clearly relative term is employed, and this of course demands its complementary correlate: if a thing is dependent, there must obviously be something on which it is dependent. This could be no more than verbal legerdemain. But a more satisfactory statement of the argument is possible. "It is", says A. S. Pringle-Pattison,[9] "in fact, the *contingence* of the finite which is the nerve of the reasoning. As it has been put, the argument is not so much: 'Because the contingent is, therefore necessity is'; it is rather: 'Because the contingent *is not*, the necessary being is' ".[10] That is, it is not the presence of something that requires us to suppose something else. It is rather the evident lack in the world around us that impels us to think of it as not self-contained or self-explanatory, and so to contain within itself evidence of another upon which it depends. In this form we have the argument in exactly the shape which St. Thomas gives to it in the fourth of his ways, and also St. Augustine. The most important question concerning the Cosmological Argument lies here. Can we or can we not from recognition of this lack argue the existence of an appropriate satisfaction?—the fact of lameness does not prove the existence of the necessary crutch. Or is this lack rightly or wrongly interpreted as the sign of something that is, the fingerprints of that which can abundantly satisfy the need? It would be cavalier to answer the question without careful investigation. But the fact that there are apparently at least two plausible answers to it, a positive one and a negative, necessarily reduces the absolute apologetic effectiveness of the Cosmological Argument.

The Teleological Argument will come up for treatment at a later stage in the enquiry, and so may be more briefly dealt with here. Though he does not hesitate to criticize it severely, Kant regards it as "the oldest, the clearest, and that most in conformity with the common reason of humanity", concluding that it will always have authority even if it be stripped of its demonstrative certainty.[11] In the form in which Kant knew it, the argument is clearer than in St. Thomas. The start is made with a selection among natural things, those namely that manifest purposiveness or design. This arrangement is not native to the world of material things as such. It must be ascribed to a sublime, wise and intelligent cause other than the world itself.

The main point of Kant's criticism of the argument is the limited character of the conclusion to which it leads. It can, he says, "demonstrate the existence of an architect of the world, whose efforts are limited by the capabilities of the material with which he works, but not of a creator of the world, to whom all things are subject." Kant draws attention to the discrepancy between this and the existence of an all-sufficient being which alone can assume the role of God. If the Teleological Argument is made to stand alone, and Kant presents it in isolation of this kind, the criticism is penetrating and just. On the other hand it is not usually so presented by those making apologetic use of it. As in the case of Aquinas, the argument is used to signify a characteristic of the God whose existence is on other grounds sufficiently established. Kant notes a further limitation upon the conclusion that may be reached. The argument enables us to infer only a cause proportionate to the evidential effects; and from a limited effect it is possible to infer only a limited cause. But since no one has a knowledge of the world in its infinity, the cause to be inferred from it under this respect cannot be credited with perfection. This may be an oblique way of suggesting not so much that the argument is limited in its application as that it suffers from inherent weakness.

It is in any case this weakness that Hume exposes.[12] The real difficulty lies in the selection of facts which form its initial premise. It is of course possible to draw attention to aspects of the universe that are harmonious, well adapted and beneficent. The trouble is that nature wears also a quite different aspect; and it is just as easy to pick out characteristics which appear just the contrary of those just mentioned: inharmonious, ill-adapted, maleficent or at least indifferent. Hume in his naughty way suggests that the two aspects can be brought in harmony by supposing that the God responsible is either ageing and unable to keep the order he once maintained, or young and immature with powers not yet adequate to the task of running the world. But unerringly he puts his finger on the most vulnerable point of the argument. The existence of evil weakens its force and disfigures its conclusion. As he acutely observes, it is not necessary to show that the amount of evil outweighs the good. The argument sustains a fatal blow by reason of the presence of any evil at all. For then either the goodness or the power of God is instantly called in question, and lacking even one of these perfections he lacks the qualifications of Deity.

Again it cannot be overlooked that the argument rests on facts that are ambivalent, or on a selection of the facts in disregard of other facts that lead to a different conclusion. In these circumstances, whatever value the argument may have for establishing the faith of those who already believe, the existence of another possible variant conclusion damages seriously the apologetic power of the argument.

This ambiguity has to be taken into account in assessing the validity or usefulness of the arguments. Evidently they do not possess the kind of irresistible force that logically compels the thinking person, just because he is a rational being, to acknowledge the existence of God. They do not talk people into believing. But they do talk to people out of faith. This is most obvious in the case of the two a posteriori arguments, the Cosmological and the Teleological. The Christian believer instantly sees that God stands in relation to the world, both to its existence and to its orderliness; and this he formulates in these arguments. This is *fides quaerens intellectum*, faith expounding its own inner content. But this direction of thought cannot be put into reverse. Belief cannot but see God reflected in certain features of the world. But this does not mean that unbelief cannot but take these features as premises that lead to God as conclusion. Much the same can be said of the a priori Ontological Argument. For belief God cannot but exist. But this assurance cannot be converted into an inexorable and purely rational necessity flowing from the bare idea of God, even supposing there was such a thing. The conclusion is that apologetically the arguments are useful rather than valid, helpful in explicating the content of belief, rendering it intelligible to itself, and making it intellectually respectable, but unable logically to compel assent.

# CHAPTER SEVEN

# DUSK OF SCHOLASTICISM, DAWN
# OF REFORMATION

THE work of Anselm and Thomas Aquinas represents a resolute attempt in two forms to provide a justification, or to outline a rationale, for the Christian faith. The Apologetics in which they are interested is of this generalized kind. Anselm's other great work, *Cur Deus Homo?* is concerned with the atonement. Its title and the form of dialogue which it uses encourage the expectation of an apologetic treatment. But this literary form has seldom proved a medium for the lively interchange of real debate, as readers of Plato's *Dialogues* (or even of Conan Doyle's Sherlock Holmes stories) will know very well. The work is dogmatic rather than apologetic. Nor does Thomas Aquinas deliberately select an opponent upon whom to press a contrived apologetic. Both were concerned to expound the basis of Christian faith in a rationally convincing manner. Anselm in effect argues: You are a thinking man— your thinking logically compels you to accept the existence of God; and Thomas Aquinas: You have experience of things around you— this experience, when its logic is explicated, really implies that God exists. The aim of the proofs differs slightly. Thomas Aquinas seeks by his proofs to establish the existence of God, while Anselm and those who advocate the Ontological Argument are saying that it is impossible to deny the existence of God. But they are equally rigorous, and their difference in aim is practically and apologetically negligible. One might therefore expect a sweeping success for the form of Apologetics they represent. In the event, however, things turned out differently. Not all the objections to the basic tenet of the Christian faith immediately collapsed, and not all unbelievers were instantly swept into the Christian fold. Nor have things altered in later times with the correction and restatement of the arguments.

The arguments proved unable not only to convince the unbeliever but even to hold the believer.

The reason for this is stated in the form of an objection to proof as such in theological matters. This objection takes two main forms. First of all it is said that we should not attempt to prove God. God is the object of faith, and to prove him would be to do too much, since it would make God an object of knowledge rather than faith. Kant is sometimes cited in support of this view. He says with something like satisfaction that he has succeeded in removing knowledge in order to make room for faith. But the faith for which he makes room is specifically defined as "rational faith". It is in fact very rational indeed. In the end it turns out to be simply knowledge of God reached by a route other than the usual ontological, cosmological and teleological arguments: where they fail, Kant thought his moral argument succeeded. But the objection to proof supposes that God is the object of a faith opposed to knowledge, not of a knowledge otherwise called faith. However, the supposition is not well founded. If faith is not knowledge, it can be regarded as only a kind of uncertainty, at the best a second-rate type of knowledge with which we must make do while we are here on earth. This puts our relation to God and the cognition we have of him on the most precarious footing. It is not the view of the Bible that we do not know God, or are unable to have certain knowledge of him. Clearly there is some confusion here. Of course our cognition of God is by faith, and of course it is different in character, or at least differently acquired, from the knowledge we have of other things. But the difference is not in lower degree of certainty; it is rather of kind. Nor does insisting that God cannot be "proved" alleviate the situation or provide a solution. If God cannot be proved in the way appropriate to what he is, then we have no right even to the relationship to him which is called faith. We must have sufficient, if also appropriate, grounds for belief in God.

The second form in which the general suspicion of proof finds expression is a little different. It is not that the proofs are not applicable to God, but rather that God is not reached by the proofs. Something may be reached, but that something is quite unrecognizable as God. This is the point of the mocking surprise Barth expresses at the solemn reiteration on the part of St. Thomas at the end of each of his five ways: "And this everyone understands to be God". "Everyone" does not—and Barth makes a point of importance. It may be true that Aristotle's God can be identified with the conclusions to which Aquinas' arguments lead; but the God and Father of our Lord Jesus Christ cannot be so identified. At the most what is said in the conclusions can be fitted on to the Christian God already known from other sources. It is not clear what Aquinas' intention is. In his case what is reached by means of his five ways is supplemented by what is supplied by revelation, and this supplement follows immediately in the exposition. It may therefore be unfair to detach the five ways from the context in which the exposition stands. But if so the apologetic value of what Aquinas says is seriously impaired in the manner already noted: it will suffice to establish faith already entertained, but not to arouse it. It is again the package deal kind of thing that is offered: what is known in revelation can be shown as rational and so acceptable to the thinking man. But we cannot break up the package into its elements, and starting with the elements build up knowledge. The distinction Aquinas has made between reason and faith stands in need of re-examination. This was one of the projects undertaken by those who followed him.

It was on the philosophical level that the weaknesses of the Scholastic theological approach and presentation became apparent. But the examination also exposed points at which the strength of the apologetic arguments leaked away. They did not immediately lose all their attractiveness and power; and they were to return to favour in the Age of Rationalism. But in the meantime a sag in confidence developed. Thus the way was prepared for the different assessment of the role of theology, and in particular of Apologetics, which was to mark the thought of the Reformers.

In the latter part of the Middle Ages, the followers of St. Thomas after his death became involved in a prolonged debate with the school of **John Duns Scotus** (1264–1308). Duns Scotus differed from Aquinas in several ways. He is deservedly known as Doctor Subtilis, for he employed the analysis and definition that were the admirable tools of Scholasticism for work altogether so ingenious and elaborate that they began to fall into disrepute. He turned with greater reverence to Augustine, and in some degree to Plato, for inspiration. But above all he conceived the office of the will and its relation to intellect differently from the Thomists. Aquinas himself did not disregard the will: he accorded a place to it in matters that pertained to faith or revelation. Certain Christian verities belong to faith, and in faith he allots a certain primacy to will over intellect. Thus their acceptance is a matter of moral decision. Aquinas is not unaware of what is now called the existentialist element in Christianity. But this recognition is limited in two ways. Besides the truths of revelation there are those that reason can discover by itself; and in their case decision has as much room to operate as in the acceptance of a Euclidean demonstration. Further, Aquinas holds steadily, in obedience to the Greek philosophical heritage, that the will by nature strives for what is regarded as good, and for this knowledge it is again dependent on the intellect. The Scotists saw in this a denial of both responsibility and freedom. For them the intellect has the role of presenting objects to the will, but the will itself exercised choice between them and could opt to act in accordance with the choice made. Duns Scotus held that the will directs the activities of the intellect.

In strictly theological matters, the Scotists maintained that God's omnipotence could only be preserved if his will was sovereign absolutely and not determined by the divine reason. While then the Thomists thought that God willed the good because it was good, the Scotists held that the good is good because God willed it so. Hence reason by itself is incapable of knowing unaided what is good: this can be learned only from revelation. Thus reason emerges in a role much diminished. It can be employed to show that revealed truths are not contradictory, to indicate their possibility or probability, and to refute arguments deployed against them. But its ability to reach truths by its own natural light is denied. One side of the "mediaeval synthesis" as outlined by St. Thomas, reason supplemented by faith, collapses, and Christian truths are retracted within the competence of revelation alone. An alternative way of interpreting the Christian faith is thus opened up.

This way is further pursued by **William** of **Occam** (c.1300–c.1349). A rebel in more ways than one, William of Occam pitted himself not only against the Pope on the question of poverty, but also against the dominant Thomist theology of the day, and became the chief exponent of Nominalism. A phrase which the ordinary reader is likely to know gives a clue to the philosophical position held by the Nominalists. The principle known as "Occam's

Razor" requires that *entia non sunt multiplicanda praeter necessitatem*—things are not to be multiplied beyond what is necessary. Occam thought that universals fell under this eliminative rule: while a long line of philosophical thought from Plato and Aristotle onwards had maintained the importance of universals, Plato holding that they were the objects of true knowledge, and Aristotle that at least they existed in individual things, Occam denied that they had any existence outside the thinking mind. With one sweep of his razor he lopped off the whole apparatus of universals and left only individual things. Hence knowledge for Occam could come not through a process of abstraction, but only through intuition; and such knowledge was not of real things but only of concepts or notions. This eventually led to agnosticism, since scientific knowledge could only be notional, having nothing in reality to which it refers.

The consequences for theology are important. St. Thomas had demonstrated that the existence of God could be known by inference from existing things. Occam could only deny this: our knowledge is not of existing things but strictly of notions only. Hence there can be no inference erected upon knowledge of things. The basis on which St. Thomas had constructed the rational portion of the knowledge we have of God immediately collapses. So by an epistemological route, Occam comes to the same conclusion as Duns Scotus. If St. Thomas had distinguished sharply between reason and faith and so between the diverse kinds of knowledge they yield, Occam saw in faith the only possible source for knowledge of God: God's being and his attributes can be known by faith alone. The Thomist alliance between reason and faith becomes a dead letter. Occam, like Duns Scotus, found in Scripture the textbook of faith, and the Church was at hand to give assurance of what Scripture proclaims. Reason is forced to abdicate, and the whole field is handed over to faith.

For Apologetics too the implications are important. Mediaeval theology as crystallized in Aquinas contained an implicit apologetic. Without designating any particular opponent as object to which it addressed itself, it presented Christian belief as something commanding adherence on the part of reason. This grand strategy, accepted by the Church in so far as Thomist doctrine was regarded as official, could now be sidetracked: on the Scotist and Occamist view it is no longer possible to address apologetically rational man as such in the expectation that conviction will ensue. The field of operation for Apologetics shrinks. Its calculated usefulness is reduced to the case of those by whom revelation is already accepted: to them it can display the Christian faith in its richness and its intellectual strength. Revelation must first commend itself before reason can be allotted a role. As St. Paul said of "God's way of righting wrong", according to the N.E.B. version, "it is based on faith and addressed to faith" (Rom 1.17 marg.). It seems as though faith could only talk about itself with itself.

The theology of the **Reformation** allots a minor role to apologetic activity.[1] In doing so it follows the path already taken by the later mediaeval theologians. Whether this happens in direct dependence upon the Occamist and Nominalist theology or independently is not an immediate concern of the present study, though brief reference will have to be made to the question in the case of Luther. However great the similarity, the notable return of the Reformers to Scripture and its testimony to the central themes of the Christian faith inclines them decisively towards discounting the contribution that reason by itself can make and allotting to faith a more clearly independent role. This in itself provides an adequate reason for the decline in direct interest in the apologetic task of theology.

Certain more practical reasons may also be noted. To the Reformers the Gospel sounded with a new voice that roused them to wonder, joy and action, for all the world like the treasure hidden in the field which the man in the parable found and for sheer joy sold all he had to buy the field (Matt. 13.44). Luther himself expresses this when he exclaims: "O, it is a living, busy, active mighty thing, this faith; and so it is impossible for it not to do good works incessantly" (Preface to the *Epistle to the Romans*). It would be quite untrue to suggest that they fell into the trap of enjoying the Gospel without handing it on. On the contrary they showed themselves always conscious of others to whom they were imperatively obliged to communicate the truth they had rediscovered. To do this two distinguishable tasks imposed themselves with urgency. They had to formulate anew the Gospel they were to communicate; and they had to distinguish it from and to defend it against the corrupt thinking and practice of the unreformed Church from which they were extruded. This in turn determined the specific kind and direction of such apologetic activity as they undertook. They had to address themselves to the elements in the unreformed Church with which they came into conflict; and what they had there to defend was not the Christian faith as such but (so far as it was distinct) the reformed pattern of the Christian faith. To this summary description should be added two other aspects of Reformed apologetic defence. The individual Reformers were frequently obliged to defend their own position and the role they played in the events that precipitated the schism of the hitherto undivided Western Church. Later, and unhappily enough, it became necessary for sides to be taken in controversies, some dividing the Reformed from the Lutheran Church, and others causing division within the Reformed Church itself.

Of defending the Reformed pattern of the faith, Calvin's writing *The Necessity of Reforming the Church* is a typical example. The Introduction to an English translation of this document provided in *Calvin: Theological Treatises*, London, 1954, p. 183, gives a summary exposition of its intention. "Mixed motives impelled the Emperor Charles V to summon the Diet of Spires, and among them was certainly displeasure that religious disputes should continue so long, and that the attention of the Protestant princes should be diverted from the war with France. Bucer thought to prepare the mind of the Emperor by a letter setting forth the case for reformation; but doubt assailed him—whether such a writing would serve any purpose— and accordingly he sought Calvin's advise. Calvin with astonishing energy and speed himself took the matter in hand, and by the end of the year 1542 (the Diet was summoned for February 1544), he had prepared a document which Beza in his *Vita Calvini* judges to be among the most vigorous and weighty writings of the age. The *Corpus Reformatorum* finds the treatise commended by both the importance of its contents and the elegance of the style (*C.R.*, VI. p. xxviii f.)." The writing is subtitled: "a humble exhortation to the most invincible Emperor Charles V, and the most illustrious Princes and other Orders, now holding Diet of the Empire at Spires, that they seriously undertake the task of restoring the Church—presented in the name of all those who wish Christ to reign, by Dr. John Calvin." The case is admirably pleaded: the diseases from which the unreformed Church suffered, the absolute need for remedy, and a justification of the way in which the Reformation had carried out the necessary amendment.

Another work of Calvin will suffice to illustrate the more personal type of apologia which circumstances obliged him to undertake. This work he calls simply *Reply to Sadolet*. Cardinal Jacob Sadolet in 1539 composed a letter to the Senate and people of Geneva in which courteously and paternally he recalled them to the bosom and the ancient sanctities of the Roman Church. In a letter to Farel, Calvin acknowledges receipt of a copy of Sadolet's epistle, mentions the persuasions of his friends that he should undertake to reply to it, and states that he is wholly occupied with its composition. Thus another apologetic document came to be written, ranking conspicuously among Calvin's works for elegance of style, lucidity, and the vigour and veracity of its argument. In it Calvin meets the charge of heresy and of schism preferred by Sadolet against adherents of the Reformed faith. In the most celebrated passage, Calvin replies to the picture the Cardinal had painted of the poor case of such people when called to account "before the awful tribunal of the Supreme Judge." Calvin in his turn portrays two hypothetical converts, a minister of the Gospel and a layman, who before the throne of Final Judgment expound the reasons for the action they have taken. The burden of the address by the minister of the Gospel is that the saving truth is to be found in the Word of God and that this has laid a compulsion upon him to reject the accretions, the superstitions and errors of the unreformed Church in favour of a true knowledge of God and of his will. The layman's defence emphasizes the sufficiency of Christ's work of satisfaction for man's salvation which the tyranny of the Papacy had fatally obscured. In both defences we may read, at least between the lines, some autobiographical references to Calvin's own conversion, and an *apologia pro vita sua*.[2]

In both these works, Apologetics is working within a narrow field and with a limited objective: Calvin apologizes for himself and for the Reformation. This is distinguishable from the task of Christian Apologetics as historically conducted by the Church upon a wider scale. In this task too the Reformers play a role, small but significant.

Whether or not **Luther** (1483–1546) is to be regarded as an Occamist and so a Nominalist, and in any case how far these influences determined his thought, are questions that tend to receive different and conflicting answers. Nor does Luther give much help in his writings, impulsive and unsystematic as they often are. When he affirms: *sum enim Occanicae factionis* (I belong to Occam's party), are we to think he speaks in earnest or in irony?[3] We may accept with assurance that "it would be wrong to say that (Luther) was formally a nominalist"[4]; and we are as certainly right in rejecting the suggestion that "the truth is that Luther, brought up on (Occam's) system, was never able to think outside the framework it imposed."[5] The general area in which a right answer lies is probably defined by two factors: the first, that he formulated his doctrine within a context of Nominalist theology; the second, that his training in Occamist thinking came into violent collision with the powerful and more congenial influence that Augustine began to exercise upon him and also with his own increasing submission to the testimony of Scripture.[6]

Something has already been said to explain the subdued emphasis that Apologetics receives in the theology of the Reformation. In Luther's case a further factor was at work. This consisted in a profound distrust of philosophy and a denunciation of the rationalist and dialectical excesses of contemporary theology.[7] Characteristically he gives robust expression to his distaste: "Those grubs of philosophers", he cries, and refers to the "dregs of philosophy" and to "that rancid philosopher Aristotle"; and in a lapidary thesis against the use of Aristotle in theology he bluntly says: *Error est dicere: sine Aristotele non fit theologus* (the source of error is to think that theology cannot do without Aristotle). What Luther is really contesting here is "the aggression of late mediaeval philosophy into theology"; and his positive aim is the "detachment of theology from the 'envelope' of philosophy."[8] But it is as though the force of his attack on philosophy's illicit incursions into theological matters propelled him into attack on the instrument philosophy employed: his distaste for philosophy carries him on to distrust and suspect reason itself. He can call reason an "evil beast", a bitter and pestilent enemy of God: "Reason, thou art foolish . . . So the godly by faith kill such a beast . . . and thereby do offer to God a most acceptable sacrifice and service" (*Commentary*, *Gal.* 3.6). The spirit of Tertullian walks again.

No doubt as in the case of Tertullian there is rhetorical extravagance here. Yet it is seriously enough intended to have implications upon Luther's view of the apologetic enterprise. "We must take care not so to deface the Gospel (not by its own strength but by our powers) that it is quite lost, to defend it so well that it collapses. Let us not be anxious: the Gospel needs not our help; it is sufficiently strong of itself. God alone commends it, whose it is . . . Therefore it is a small wretched thing that this puny breath should range itself against the sophists: what would this bat accomplish by its flapping?" (*Sermon on Faith and Good Works*). "Thus conclude we that there can be no master or judge of God's Word, or any protector, save God Himself" (*Fastenpostille*).[9] Evidently Luther aligns himself with the tendency of which Occam was exponent to withdraw matters of belief from the sphere of influence of reason and locate them within faith itself. But then again, having so expressed himself, Luther shows signs of resiling from the extreme position: reason corrected by faith has indeed a function to discharge. Thus he says: "The natural wisdom of a human creature in matters of faith, until he be regenerate and born anew, is altogether darkness, knowing nothing in divine cases. But in a man of faith, regenerate and enlightened by the Holy Spirit through the Word, it is a fair and glorious instrument and work of God . . . The understanding, through faith, receives life from faith; that which was dead is made alive again" (*Table Talk* translated by Hazlitt para. 294).

We are in a different atmosphere from that generated by Augustine. As A. Richardson rightly points out,[10] Augustine also emphasizes the primacy of faith: "Faith precedes reason", he declares. But in the same passage (*Ep*, 120.3.4) he supplements the affirmation: "Perish the thought that God hates in us that in which he has created us superior to other living creatures! Perish the notion, I say, that we ought to believe that we need not accept or look for a reason for what we believe, since we could not even believe if we had not rational souls . . . It is seen to be reasonable that faith should precede reason. For if this precept is not reasonable, then it is unreasonable—which God forbid! If therefore it is reasonable that faith should precede reason to bring us to certain great matters which cannot yet be understood, then undoubtedly, in however small a degree, reason, which persuades us to it, is likewise antecedent to faith. Hence the Apostle Peter warns us that we should be prepared to answer everyone who asks us for a reason for our faith and hope (I Pet. 3.15)."

Of course it is possible to ransack the many varied writings of Luther to find passages that are apologetic in tone. In the controversy with Münzer, Luther advises the senate of Mulhouse to enquire from where he received authority to teach and who it was that had called him. If his answer was that God had given him his charge, they were further to demand some evident sign of it—in a word miracles; because to give such guarantee is God's wont, when he himself is the author of any extraordinary calling. Luther is thus not averse to citing miracle as justification of a work truly done in the power and by the authority of God. But the main sense of his thought is different. Reason without divine enlightenment is blind. It can be properly employed only when enlightened by faith; and then only may it be used to deal with the matters that faith itself supplies.

We turn to **Calvin** (1509–1564). At the beginning of his book on *The Teaching of Calvin*, A. Mitchell Hunter quotes[11] the epigram that "the watchword of Luther was war, that of Calvin order." The contrast thus expressed is not inept. The circumstances in which they respectively did their work no less than the temperaments they possessed disposed them to different, in many aspects complementary, approaches to the theological problems that confronted their age. But it is perhaps the different backgrounds out of which each attained maturity that influenced them most strongly in reaching the contrasting apologetic positions they occupied. Calvin was trained in law, exposed to humanistic studies, passionately devoted to the languages, literatures and cultures of antiquity, before ever "a sudden conversion" aroused in him a burning zeal for the Scriptures and Christian doctrine. These earlier studies he never abjured, though his attention to them diminished. Instead he employed the erudition he had acquired in his new-found interest. Above all he never vilified or derided reason, as Luther in his more exuberant moods was prone to do. If Thomas Aquinas could speak of the *debilitas rationis* (feebleness of reason), Calvin thinks rather of reason as *incurvatus in se*, turned in upon itself, effective in mundane ways, but ineffective in dealing with divine things until prised open by the entrance of the Word of God or revelation. The knowledge

of faith is independent of philosophical grounds and the construc-
tions that can be erected upon them. So far he agrees with Luther.
But Calvin retains for reason a minor but significant role. On this
in Book 1 of his *Institutes* (*Institutio Christianae Religionis*, 1536,
final edition 1559) he mounts a considerable apologetic argument.

It is a surprise to many to learn from *Inst.* 1.3.1 that Calvin insists
that "the natural mind is naturally endued with the knowledge of
God." At the outset he declares that wisdom consists in knowledge
of God and knowledge of ourselves, closely connected with each
other. For a survey of ourselves leads to the contemplation of God,
since it is evident that we are dependent on something not ourselves;
and on the other hand true knowledge of ourselves can be acquired
only by contemplating God, for only so are our imperfections made
plain to us. Calvin will have nothing to do with the distinction the
mediaeval synthesis imported into the knowledge of God: he refuses
to separate the knowledge *that* God is from the knowledge *what*
God is. Knowledge of God is always acquaintance with what
conduces to his glory and to our benefit; and where there is knowledge of this kind there is worship. Hence the gap that opened out
in St. Thomas' presentation between the God whom reason can
reach and the God made known in revelation does not recur in
Calvin's exposition. Another distinction at a logically later point
replaces it, that between God known in creation and providence and
God known as the author of reconciliation: there is a "natural" and
a redemptive knowledge of God. Apologetically then it is possible
to address men concerning God without presupposing their acceptance of the Christian revelation: they have a natural knowledge.

The ground of this knowledge is found in evidence of two kinds.
The ordinary course of nature, Calvin holds, manifests God as
both creator and governor. There he "daily presents himself to
public view, in such a manner that (men) cannot open their eyes
without being constrained to behold him" (1.5.1). Without
distinguishing them, Calvin employs both the forms of argument
we have come to know as the Cosmological and the Teleological.
Calvin is even willing to allow that "the expression that nature is
God may be used in a pious sense by a pious mind" (1.5.5). But
there is also evidence "apart from the ordinary course of nature".
God manifests himself also in "clemency to the pious and severity to
the wicked and ungodly" (1.5.7). The disquiet and uneasiness of

the wicked testify in the same sense. At the same time, any apparent inequity, the affliction of the pious and the impunity of the wicked, indicates a future life and a judgment reserved to the future (1.5.10). The conclusion is that the best way of seeking God is "to contemplate him in his works, in which he approaches and familiarizes and in some measure communicates himself to us" (1.5.9).

Calvin's use of this evidence adduced for the proof of God is important. The knowledge of God is not exactly an inference from it. Rather the evidence addresses itself to a more deeply seated consciousness of God already possessed. "The human mind", he says (1.3.1), "even by natural instinct, possesses some sense of Deity." "The idea of a Deity impressed on the mind of man is indelible" (1.3.3). "The seeds of religion are sown by God in every heart" (1.4.1). "It is impossible to eradicate a sense of the existence of Deity . . . an idea of God is naturally engraved on the hearts of men" (1.4.4).

This knowledge, naturally sown in men's hearts and testified to by the evidence of experience, is, however, ineffective. It has in fact been overlaid by ignorance and wickedness. Calvin will not separate the two, for "blindness is always connected with pride, vanity and contumacy" (1.4.1). "All degenerate from the true knowledge of God" (*ib.*). Thence arise superstitions and idolatry. It follows that from the testimony afforded by the world around us "we derive no advantage" (1.5.10). A right interpretation is given to the judgment of the Psalmist's "fool" (Ps. 14.1): the Psalmist is talking of "those who extinguish the light of nature, and wilfully stupefy themselves" (1.4.2). They do not, that is, deny his existence, but they "rob him of his justice and providence, shutting him up as an idler in heaven". The function of this corrupted knowledge of God then becomes clear: "whatever deficiency of natural ability prevents us from attaining the pure and clear knowledge of God, yet, since that deficiency arises from our own fault, we are left without any excuse" (1.5.15). The actual condition of men's natural knowledge of God "has no further effect than to render us inexcusable."

The argument is of apologetic importance in a negative sense; as is evident it follows closely the precedent of St. Paul in Rom. 1, though the exposition is more detailed. So far the rationalistic apologist of all ages shares common ground with a typical and persistent strand in Reformed theology. W. P. Paterson judges that the Reformed Church, unlike the Lutheran, "has held that the light of nature guarantees a knowledge of the fundamental truths of religion and morality."[12] Calvin extracts little positive meaning out of this apologetic tactic. Aquinas contends: reason resolutely followed leads to a true knowledge of God. Calvin argues differently: reason cannot lead to true knowledge of God, but its inability to do so shows that knowledge of God is possible and that men in failing to realize the possibility are culpable. The foothold thus secured within the attention of thinking man as such is not very spacious, but at any rate it is a beginning. Faith can do more than merely talk to faith. Calvin breaks out of the dialogue of the faithful in-group with a decisiveness more apparent than in Luther.

The site has now been cleared, as we may think; and Calvin hastens on to erect upon it his positive doctrine. The construction belongs in the nature of the case rather to the dogmatic field. But the first positive step he takes, he safeguards and commends by means of a clearly apologetic justification. Left to himself, the seeds of religion in man's heart would remain unproductive, and from the light supplied by nature concerning divine things he would wilfully avert his eyes. The knowledge of God as creator would remain beyond his grasp, unless further assistance were offered. This, however, God has contrived to do. "We need another and better assistance properly to direct us to the creator of the world. Therefore he hath not unnecessarily added the light of his Word, to make himself known" (1.6.1). The required auxiliary aid consists in Scripture. Thus, Calvin tells us, just as eyes dimmed with age "by the assistance of spectacles begin to read distinctly, so the Scripture collects the otherwise confused notions of Deity in our minds, dispels the darkness, and gives us a clear view of the true God" (ib.). This additional help leads man to the knowledge of God as creator and governor, before conducting him further to know him as redeemer. Man is thus given a standard by which the fictitious surrogates he tends to set up in place of God are exposed in their false unreality, and at the same time a replacement for them is offered.

If Scripture is to afford this additional aid, it must be credited. Calvin therefore is at pains to show on what grounds the credibility of Scripture rests. For this purpose he expounds his doctrine of the *testimonium Spiritus sancti internum*, the inner testimony of the Holy

Spirit. It is not on the authority of the Church or on the basis of any other external authority that Scripture is believed, but because the Holy Spirit witnesses in our hearts to its truth. "As God alone is a sufficient witness of himself in his own Word, so also the Word would never gain credit in the hearts of men, unless it be confirmed by the internal testimony of the Spirit. The same Spirit, therefore, who spoke by the mouth of the prophets, must penetrate into our hearts, to convince us that they faithfully delivered the message which was divinely entrusted to them" (1.7.4). Scripture then carries in itself its own convincing power. Belief is aroused in the individual by Scripture thus supported by the witness of the Holy Spirit, without resort to external guarantees, whether supplied by Church or reason. It must be regarded as "an undeniable truth that they who have been inwardly taught by the Spirit acquiesce fully in the Scripture, that it is self-authenticating and carries its own evidence with it, and hence ought not to submit to demonstrations and arguments from reason, but obtains the credit with which we ought to receive it from the testimony of the Spirit" (1.7.5). This testimony is said to be "superior to all reason"; it is "such a persuasion as requires no reasons; such a knowledge is as supported by the highest reason, in which the mind rests with greater security and constancy than in any reasons; in a word, a sentiment such as cannot be produced except by revelation" (*ib.*).

Here Calvin seems to sympathize with those who wish to find the grounds for believing faith in supernatural revelation. By this means they contrive security for their belief, or impregnability; but they have to pay the price of breaking off conversation on the common ground of reason with those outside the family of the faithful. Belief has its own reasons, but since these spring from a super-natural source they are credible only to those activated by this supernatural source itself. If this were all that could be said, the gap between reason and faith would open up again so widely as to make dialogue across it impossible. But Calvin is not content to leave the matter there. He proceeds deliberately to add "rational proofs to establish belief in Scripture" (1.8.1). The further arguments he now deploys are chiefly to be used for the confirmation of acceptance already accorded to Scripture. They are insufficient to induce acceptance, he says, but increase our respect for and our assurance in Scripture to which credence has already been given. Yet these "rational proofs" in Calvin's exposition press forward to play a role slightly wider than Calvin initially designs for them.

The witnesses summoned are of various kinds. Calvin cites the beauties of the language and the dignity of the subject matter, but observes that on the whole there is an uncultivated and almost rude simplicity. Yet the impression left upon the reader is more profound than the rhetoric of all the classical writers, and the energetic influence of Scripture outclasses the beauties of rhetoricians and philosophers. This makes it easy to perceive something divine in Scripture surpassing human contrivance. He calls in evidence the preservation of the Scriptures through the hazards and contingencies of history and despite their attempted destruction by tyrants. Above all he makes use of the time-honoured arguments based on miracles and prophecy. The divine character of the law and doctrine of Moses, for example, is confirmed by the miracles with which they are associated, "testimonies from heaven of his being a true prophet". Further, the existence of prophecy itself and the fulfilment granted to it, the countless predictions which duly achieved accomplishment, must be regarded as indicating the divine inspiration of the books that record them.

It is here that the question arises concerning the range of impact Calvin thought could be allotted to the rational proofs, and it is not easily answered. On the one hand, he gives the status of "demonstrations" to fulfilled prophecy. Citing Isa. 45.1 and attributing the prophecy about Cyrus to an Isaiah living a hundred years before the release of the Jews from captivity by him, Calvin observes: "Does not this simple unadorned narrative plainly demonstrate that Isaiah delivered not the conjectures of men but the undoubted oracle of God?" What convincing value has such "demonstration" and for what kind of person? It is, Calvin suggests, in the case of a prophecy of Daniel fulfilled, to be used by pious men "to silence the objections of the wicked; for the demonstration is too clear to be gainsaid." He can further say that such fulfilled predictions are so powerfully indicative of divine inspiration "that all who have the use of reason must perceive that it is God who speaks." Taken *au pied de la letre* this would imply that the argument from prophecy was, in Calvin's view, properly directed as an apologetic to thinking man as such, as a convincing proof of the authority of Scripture. Against this interpretation has to be set another more categorical statement (1.9.13), that "those persons betray great folly who wish it to be demonstrated to infidels that the Scripture is the Word of God; for this cannot be known without faith." In view of this conflicting evidence, it ought probably to be concluded that Calvin believes that reason may be suitably addressed by such terms as the rational proofs provide, in the expectation that the attention of the unbeliever will be stimulated; but that this falls short of the reverent acceptance of Scripture as the Word of God to which he can be roused only by the operation of the inner testimony of the Holy Spirit and the accompaniment of faith. At least, according to Calvin, reason and faith are not at each other's throats.

# CHAPTER EIGHT

# CHRISTIANITY IN AN AGE OF REASON

THE period known as the Age of **Rationalism** is apologetically one of the most lively and interesting in the whole course of Christian thought. In Germany it goes under the name of *Aufklärung* —Enlightenment. Some names associated with it are well known: Reimarus (1694–1768) whose name appears in the title of Albert Schweitzer's celebrated book, *Von Reimarus zu Wrede*, translated into English as *The Quest of the Historical Jesus;* and Lessing (1729–81) who framed the question that still agitates theology, whether "incidental truths of history can furnish the proof of truths of reason."

In Britain and particularly England the Age of Rationalism precipitated **Deism** and the controversy provoked by and round about the issues it raised. It is this that we shall be chiefly concerned with. The period can with some neatness be limited to the hundred years beginning with the last decade of the seventeenth century. The area of controversy is rather narrowly circumscribed but the extreme positions possible within it are occupied with vigour for both defence and attack. The issues are fairly clear, though there is a discernible shift of interest about half way through. For much of the time it is extremely difficult to know from the Christian standpoint who is friend and who foe. The modern student is likely to be struck by a certain aridity in the discussion, rather like the atmosphere of a very old-fashioned museum, and at the same time roused to admiration by the exquisite clarity and the elegance of style with which it is generally conducted. Over the period there broods the spirit of the enigmatic David Hume who regularly says not so much what he thinks as what his mind when given free rein comes up with; and also of the bland Bishop Butler whose contribution ensured that in the conflict no one would win or have a prize. At its end the period is neatly rounded off by the emergence of new questions which made it certain that never again would the old ones arise in just the same form.

The factors involved in the rise of Rationalism are difficult to categorize into causes and effects, and no doubt they intertwined in such a way that any one of them could be present both causally and consequentially. Thus a hundred years of religious strife in Britain evoked a desire for a more liberal measure of toleration; and this received satisfaction in the Act of Toleration that followed upon the accession of William and Mary in 1689. But the satisfied appetite is also whetted, and subsequently a relaxed licensing act on publications gave such liberty to expression of opinion, including religious opinion, as to evoke from Voltaire the admiring ejaculation that "an Englishman goes to heaven by the road he pleases."

Along with the new freedom went a new critical attitude towards authority and tradition. In Germany Roman Catholic priests began to speak out against such things as religious orders, celibacy of the clergy, and veneration of relics, while in Protestant England Locke is found pruning rigorously the traditional notion of Christian and ecclesiastical obligation, till it could all be summarized: "these two, faith and repentance, that is, believing Jesus to be the Messiah, and a good life, are the indispensable concerns of the new covenant to be performed by all those who would obtain eternal life" (*Reasonableness of Christianity*, 1696, p. 202). Besides this, new knowledge was flooding in from many sides. In the sphere of religion, information about religions other than Christianity was being brought by far-travelled voyagers. Beyond the cosy limits of a Christendom coterminous with Western Europe, there stretched wider horizons of diverse and conflicting religious belief and practice, and these promoted the notion of a wider religious tolerance and the idea of a study of comparative religion. New knowledge also of a scientific kind was being amassed and propagated in an elementary way, like the flotsam and jetsam from another civilization found upon the beach by savages. But it was to supply material and ammunition for carrying on the controversy concerning how revelation approves itself in the later stages of the Deist discussion.

The overriding characteristic that dominated the thought of the day and determined the way in which men talked about religion is a fundamental trust in the omnicompetence of reason. It is an age in which there are no insoluble problems and no locked doors through which reason cannot pass. The limitations upon our knowledge are brushed aside, if not in practice at least in principle, and nothing lies essentially beyond the grasp of reason. Evidently such an attitude must affect Christianity and its statement profoundly. That all things even in religion should have to be rendered transparently intelligible, if they are to be accepted, is a maxim which may allow Christianity to be credibly stated. But the supposition is a contentious one, and in fact proved to be an apple of discord for over a hundred years.

The aim appropriate to the circumstances and indicated by the place allotted to reason is predictable. It is to set up a "religion of nature" in place of or at the basis of Christianity as commonly and traditionally conceived. This religion of nature will be something that commends itself to reason and may equally be styled a religion of reason. When set up it may be given the role either of taking over Christianity without remainder or of constituting the essential part of Christianity to which, however, there is a supplement in the form of revelation. The Christianity that emerges will differ in some degree from traditional expositions. This is the recurring apologetic situation, and it recurrently precipitates the enquiry whether the substance has been so altered as to forfeit identity. All those elements are present in the discussion of the Deist thesis. There is an additional complication. Not only is friend difficult to distinguish from foe; it is difficult to know in some cases whether the intention is to be friend or foe. Something is regularly commended with all the persuasiveness of hard clear argument; but whether that something is advocated as a variant form of Christianity or as a substitute for Christianity it is sometimes impossible to say.

**Lord Herbert of Cherbury** (1583–1648) wrote his most important work some seventy years before the controversy on Deism had properly begun. But during its course he was styled (by Halyburton in *Natural Religion Insufficient* [1714], a work hostile to Deism) the father of Deism, and the name was so appropriate that it stuck. The epoch-making work that chiefly earned him a title meant to be opprobrious was called *de Veritate, prout distinguitur a Revelatione, Verisimili, Probabili, et a Falso* (1624). It was conceived with an admirably eirenical intention. If a common religion could be distilled from all the conflicting and contradictory tenets held in its name, harmony could replace the prevalent dissension. Herbert gives a philosophical basis to his thesis by supposing an *instinctus naturalis* and a *consensus universalis* to which appeal can be made. On these rest certain *notitiae communes* or innate principles so axiomatic that they neither need nor admit of proof. They are in fact distinguished by the marks of priority, independence, universality, certainty, practical necessity, and immediate cogency. In the case of religion, five ideas exhibit these marks: that God exists, that it is a duty to worship him, that the practice of virtue is the true way to honour him, that men are obliged to repent of sins, and that rewards and punishments will be accorded after death. These ideas are imprinted upon the human mind by God, and they are to be found in all religions. Here then is the desideratum: a natural religion has been defined common to men everywhere and at all times, and disinfected from the peripheral, extravagant and often foolish beliefs and practices by which the essential truths of religion have been historically obscured.

Already in this prophetic work the characteristic marks of Deism are apparent, and especially these two: the entire competence of reason to attain the essential truths of religion, and the concern for the practical duties of life which religion chiefly promotes. Herbert's proposals may seem unrealistic enough to us—as academically remote from the stuff of life as Esperanto in the sphere of language. Yet there is no reason to think he was not entirely sincere. Religion itself is apt to be tepidly held when religious wars are being waged. Even Herbert's attitude to Royalists and Parliamentarians showed little sign of conviction. It was a tepidly held Christianity that he commended; and his commendation of it was in a form that always wins a hearing especially in England, comprising as it did an appeal to reason together with an ethical concern that rendered the appeal not only strong but respectable.

From this point onwards, the debate unfolds, raging between two extremes that at least can be clearly distinguished. On the one hand there are disputants who attempt to "banish mystery from theology and to replace the God of revelation by the God of mathematical demonstration."[1] Their watchword is found in the phrase attributed by Bolingbroke to Foster, that "where mystery begins, religion ends".[2] At the other extreme are those who realize that Christianity cannot tolerate such a reduction, and are driven to find refuge in an opposite obscurantism. Of these the famous William Law, though of much later date, can stand as representative (his *A Serious Call to a Devout and Holy Life* of 1728 is a standard work in the English language on ascetical devotion). He on the other side bluntly ventures the opinion that "God by reason of his own perfections must be mysterious and incomprehensible" (*The Case of Reason, or Natural Religion, fairly and fully stated &c*, 1731, *Works*, vol. 2, p. 99). One thing is here pretty clear, and one thing doubtful. The issue is clear: whether natural religion, i.e. a religion that can be recommended to and accepted by reason alone, is adequate without resort to the notion of revelation. Various shades of opinion are offered on this clear issue, and, as we shall see, Tindal represents the case of those that hold natural religion to be alone sufficient; Conybeare maintains the need of natural religion to be supplemented by revelation; while William Law defends religion by retracting it into the sphere of the unfathomable where reason can only approve but never discover.

But there is an associated matter that is more difficult. The intentions of those who take part in the great debate remain unclear. Whether they wish to communicate the Christian faith or to displace it by something essentially different is obscure. The question whether the Deists were Christian or fundamentally un-Christian is one to which historically different answers have been given. However, in the course of the debate an increasingly anti-Christian tendency became evident. The course set by Deism, with whatever initial intention, came to be followed by those who move over into plain hostility to Christianity. The impetus already gathered could not, it appears, be arrested by the feeble brakes clapped on by Bishop Butler. But the question of intention and practical consequence remains involved and intricate up to the end.

**John Tillotson** (1630–94) was appointed Archbishop of Canterbury and must presumably be credited with the desire and intention of maintaining and promoting the Christian faith. In him the two chief tenets of Deism find powerful expression: that religion is an affair of reason to be tested, commended, and accepted on rational grounds; and that its chief value is extrinsic to itself and consists in its providing sanctions for morality. Faith is simply persuasion concerning the truth of a proposition, "a persuasion of the mind concerning anything" (*Works*, vol. II, p. 203). It is thus purely intellectual and based on rational grounds alone. Such natural religion embraces the truths that there is a God and that he demands virtuous living from those to whom he is thus known. Tillotson does not entirely deny or discount revealed religion. He allots to it a role in the secondary sphere of religion where it supports morality. For natural religion has encouraged morality but provided ineffective sanctions, and revealed religion makes good the defect. So then, "natural religion is the foundation of all revealed religion, and revelation is designed simply to establish its duties" (*op. cit.* vol. 2 p. 333). The Christian religion contains certain distinctive elements in the revelation it professes; but belief in Christ as Son of God and participation in the sacraments have a value to be assessed in purely moral terms. Christ offers an example and an inspiration; and the sacraments represent powerfully the odious character of sin.

It may be that as a churchman Tillotson was aware of some discrepancy between his representation of Christianity and the place of revelation in it and the thinking and practice of orthodox Christianity. At all events he supplements the meagre and apparently dispensable role he allots to revelation by a carefully constructed explanation and justification. He thereby lays one of the foundation stones of the erection that was later to tower over the controversy, the construction devoted to "Christian evidences". For revelation to be accepted as genuine, it must be authenticated by certain signs. Of course no revelation can contradict the principles of natural religion; and its precepts must be in harmony with natural religion and the nature of man. But a further mark is also to be looked for. For Tillotson, any revelation must be reasonable, but not every reasonable teaching is revelation. He says (*op. cit.* vol. 3, p. 493): "though a doctrine be never so reasonable in itself, this is no certain argument that it is from God." Why indeed should it be? On Tillotson's view revelation fits in so closely to the purely rational that any marks by which it is to be distinguished from natural religion must lie in another field altogether. The necessary distinguishing mark he finds in "testimony from heaven". Belief in Christianity is founded "upon the whole evidence which we are able to produce for it, in which there is nothing wanting that is proper and reasonable to prove any religion to be from God. But yet miracles are the principal external proof and confirmation of the divinity of a doctrine." When prophecy is later added to miracles we have the twin foundations of the rational evidences for Christianity which play so large a part in the later thought of the period.

**Samuel Clarke** (1675–1729) more successfully or at least more warmly commends Christianity than Tillotson. In time he follows both Tillotson and Locke, and in opinion agrees generally with both of them. Natural religion is true enough. But men are by nature corrupt and disabled from taking advantage of it. "There was plainly wanting a divine revelation to recover mankind out of their universal corruption and degeneracy, and without such a revelation it was not possible that the world should ever be effectually reformed" (*A Discourse concerning the Unchangeable Obligations of Natural Religion, or Truth and Obligations of the Christian Revelation,* 1705, Prop. 7.1).

**John Locke** (1632–1704), playing the traditional role of dispassionate philosopher and allying himself with none of the parties in the altercation that was building up, contributed none the less significantly to its development. In some ways his *Reasonableness of the Christian Faith* (1695) stands alongside Lord Herbert's work as the epitome of Deism. He disagreed with any notion of *notitiae communes*: the *tabula rasa* which represented man's mind before experience put its marks upon it tolerated no innate principles. But in a much larger area Locke was in agreement with Lord Herbert and the rationalists of his and later times. He shared a desire for simplification of the traditional faith which can be attributed with equal plausibility to apologetic interest or impatience; the putting of religion without remainder at the service of morality; the appeal to miracles and prophecy as formal evidence of the truth of Christianity. In his *Essay on the Human Understanding* (1690), Locke argues that the role of revelation can be no more than very limited. It can offer nothing that is contrary to reason, and it is dispensable in matters in accordance with reason. Almost grudgingly Locke allows that there are some few pure "matters of faith with which reason has directly nothing to do", such as the angelic rebellion against God and the rising of the dead. These matters belong simply to a past or a future to which our rational knowledge in the nature of the case does not extend. Evidently revelation is being squeezed into such narrow limits that its elimination will hardly be noticed. As it turns out, the place it is given is a kind of barometer for assessing what follows: when the barometer is low, stormy disapproval is aroused from the more orthodox side.

The place kept warm for revelation continued to diminish. This is evidenced by the work of **John Toland** (1670–1722). His best known work bore a title that "contained the whole of Deism in a nutshell: I was about to say that the title should become the Deist's slogan."[3] The full title is "*Christianity not Mysterious*, showing that there is nothing in the Gospel that is contrary to reason nor above it, and that no Christian Doctrine can properly be called a mystery" (1696). That elements in Christianity were regarded and treated as mysteries Toland attributes to the early perversion of Christian doctrine by pagan ideas and the deliberate distortion of priests. Even so, revelation cannot be denied, but its contribution is rated even lower: all it can do is to supply information about things of which, because of our place in time and space, we should not have heard and events that we could not have observed. Its contribution then is simply to enlarge a knowledge already quite sufficient by the supply of additional information.

We may regard the contribution of **William Wollaston** (1660–1724) as an attempt to throw the brakes on a movement gathering momentum. In his *The Religion of Nature Delineated* (1722) he says he must "content myself with that light which nature affords . . . I hope that neither the doing of this nor anything else in this *Delineation*, can be the least prejudice to any other true religion . . . That, therefore, which has been so much insisted on by me, and is as it were the burden of my song, is so far from undermining true revealed religion, that it rather paves the way for its reception" (*op. cit.* p. 211). But this is manifestly a rearguard action, a final flaunting of the colours as the retreat begins. Wollaston's intention may have been heroic, but it was not more than a gesture and it could not reduce the speed of developments.

The process comes to something like a climax with **Matthew Tindal** (1655–1733). By his writings he precipitated considerable commotion and ecclesiastical unease; and his *Christianity as old as Creation, or the Gospel a Republication of the Religion of Nature* (1730) became the "Bible of Deists". It may be thought to represent Deism at a comparatively mature stage, as the conclusions to which its direction led became clear. This notable work represented natural religion as having always existed perfect and complete: "there's a

law of nature or reason, absolutely perfect, eternal, and unchangeable; and the design of the Gospel is not to add to or take from this
law", but to liberate men from superstition. The aim of the work
is so to simplify the Christian religion as to make it agreeable to
those of limited intelligence and supply them with a norm for
distinguishing between religion and superstition. Hence on the
one hand the repudiation of all mystery, and on the other the invitation to every man to find the essence of Christianity in what is
common to all the creeds to which revelation adds nothing.
"Nothing", Tindal observes (*op. cit.* p. 220) in a rather breathless
sentence, "can be requisite to discover true Christianity and to
preserve it in its native purity free from all superstition, but after a
strict scrutiny to admit nothing to belong to it except what our
reasons tells us is worthy of having God for its author. And if it be
evident that we can't discern whether any instituted religion contains everything worthy, and nothing unworthy, of a Divine
original, except we can antecedently by our reason discern what is
and what is not worthy of having God for its author, it necessarily
follows that natural and revealed religion can't differ, because what
reason shows to be worthy of having God for its author must belong
to natural religion, and whatever reason tells us is unworthy of
having God for its author can never belong to true revealed religion."
This is the end to which Deism tended from the start. Revelation
cannot be retained in a merely amplifying role; it can only distort.
One of the last marks of Christianity is removed. Of course Christ
is himself a "noble example". The office of Christianity is to destroy
revelations as imposed upon the credulous by divine oracles, and to
"restore, free from all Idolatry the true primitive, and natural
Religion, implanted in Mankind from the Creation" (*op. cit.* p. 347).

Were the Deists trying to destroy Christianity or to defend it at a
point very *avant garde*? The article on Deism in Hastings' *Encyclopaedia of Religion and Ethics*[4] represents one kind of answer. The
Deists "had begun by defending the pre-eminence of Christianity
on the ground that it and it alone corresponded with the true
religion of nature; but, gradually becoming more conscious of their
divergence from historic Christianity, they transformed themselves
into the champions of natural, as opposed to revealed, religion."
A. C. McGiffert thinks that this does them injustice, when he

suggests[5] that we should "speak at least of some of the Deists as defenders rather than opponents of Christianity." To many, however, it did appear that they had gone too far, and a reaction set in. Different ways of correcting the situation were proposed.

An attempt to restore virtually the *status quo ante* was made by **John Conybeare** (1692–1755) in *A Defense of Revealed Religion* (1732), which is directed specifically against Tindal's position. The work criticizes the concept of a natural religion the same in all places and times, and repudiates the idea that such a religion is in any case sufficient. It needs to be supplemented by the teachings of revealed religion. These add both doctrines and precepts to natural religion, and by them the true end of all religion, i.e. morality and virtue, is promoted. The validity of Christianity rests upon the strongest grounds that can support revelation: prophecy and miracles fully authenticate its claims; and to these usual kinds of evidence Conybeare adds the primitive character of the Christian records. Though thus opposed to Tindal, Conybeare is not disposed to call in question the fundamental rationalist presuppositions of Deism. Tindal errs not in his attempt to render religion thoroughly rational, but in his estimate of the religion he thinks to be thus wholly rational. Only if natural religion is supplemented by revelation can it stand up to the demands of reason.

Opposition of a different kind is offered by **William Law,** already mentioned. Conybeare corrects Tindal, Law flatly repudiates him; Conybeare plays along with Tindal as far as he can, Law makes a decisive break; Conybeare tries to amend Tindal by pressing the claims of reason, Law retreats to a position where reason cannot follow. Law declares that nothing in the nature or condition of man obliges him to repudiate all doctrines that cannot be proved to and by reason; that in fact God's nature is quite unfathomable by man's reason; that he is similarly unable to know by reason alone what is good and what evil, and is dependent on revelation for this knowledge. It is evident that Law is really breaking away from the rationalist tradition. In contrast, he manifests a strong tendency towards obscurantism in theology and voluntaryism in ethics: God's nature is mysterious to us until he reveals it; and God's will is unknown to us until he declares it. Thus the two main props on which the Deist understanding of religion was based are denied:

there is nothing in revelation as such to warrant its acceptance by us. Hence only external signs of authentication remain.

This is the line that Law's argument follows. "A revelation is to be received as coming from God, not because of its internal excellence, or because we judge it to be worthy of God; but because God has declared it to be his, in as plain and undeniable a manner, as he has declared creation and providence to be his. For though no revelation can come from God, but what is truly worthy of him, and full of every internal excellence, yet what is truly worthy of God to be revealed, cannot possibly be known by us, but by a revelation from himself. And as we can only know what is worthy of God in creation, by knowing what he has created; so we can no other way possibly know what is worthy of God to be revealed, but by a revelation" (*The Case of Reason or Natural Religion fairly and fully stated in Answer to a Book entitled Christianity as Old as Creation*, 1731, p. 101). "The credibility therefore of any external divine revelation with reference to human reason, rests wholly upon such external evidence, as is sufficient proof of the divine operation, or interposition" (*op. cit.* 107). Law appeals to the men of the Bible, and continues: "If their posterity will let no messages from heaven, no prophecies and miracles persuade them, that God can call them to any duties, but such as they must enjoin upon themselves; or to the belief of any doctrines, but such as their own minds can suggest . . . it is because they are grown senseless of the mysteries of creation and providence with which they are surrounded, and forget the awful prerogative of infinite wisdom, over the weakest, lowest rank of intelligent beings" (101).

So Law exults in the mystery that is God, in what comes from God in the form of revelation, and in the twin signs that adventitiously or at least externally stamp what comes in the form of revelation as also authentically from God. "A revelation is the highest and utmost evidence of its coming from God, and not to be tried by our judgments about the reasonableness or necessity of its doctrines" (110). We could hardly be further away from Tindal or Conybeare. But an unsettling note is struck in the parallelism Law repeatedly mentions between the mysteries of creation and providence and the divine mysteries which only revelation can illumine and only supernatural evidences authenticate. The argument drawn from this is that, if mystery does not disable us from believing in

the first, there is no reason why it should prevent us having confidence in the second. As McGiffert notes,[6] this represents a fateful
anticipation of the double-edged argument Butler employs, which so
far from establishing securely the credibility of faith over natural
religion really undermines confidence in both. To this further
development we now turn.

**Joseph Butler** (1692–1752) is likely to be long remembered for
his contributions to ethics (especially his *Fifteen Sermons* [1726] with
preface and later additional sermons) and to natural theology
(especially his celebrated *Analogy of Religion, Natural and Revealed,
to the Constitution and Course of Nature* (1736). The former is still a
familiar textbook for students of philosophy. The latter is notable
for its elegance, its close reasoning, and in general for an argument
with much interest and many fallacies. The upshot has been variously
assessed, sometimes as almost entirely successful, sometimes as a
nearly complete failure. The intention is clear enough: to establish
the analogy and correspondence of natural and of revealed religion
with nature. The work falls into two parts, each of which has its
own particular concern and is apparently directed to a particular
audience. Perhaps the two were composed in separation[7] and then
brought together under an introduction. But the idea of analogy runs
through both, and in both is to be found a strong dependence upon
the argument from probability.

At all events Part 1 seems to be directed to those who, admitting
there is a God, have not reckoned with the consequences. Butler
takes for granted the existence of God and assumes that the world is
his creation and by him governed (*Analogy*, Introduction 8). From
this he argues that God really does act in accordance with the
principles formulated in Christian doctrine. "We find by experience . . . that he actually exercises dominion and government over
us at present, by rewarding and punishing us for our actions in a
strict and proper sense of these words" (1.2.7). But "there is an
analogy or likeness between that system of things and dispensation
of Providence, which Revelation assures us of, and that system of
things and dispensation of Providence, which experience together
with reason informs us of, i.e. the known course of nature" (Introduction 6). "Analogy or likeness"—and a little later he uses another
curiously vague phrase that invites comment:[8] "analogous and of a
piece" (Intr. 8). It follows that "there is nothing incredible in the

general doctrine of religion, that God will reward and punish men for their actions hereafter ... for the whole course of Nature is a present instance of his exercising that government over us" (1.2.8).

Butler is aware of the limitations of the argument thus presented, and at the same time quite resolute that it is nonetheless convincing. It does not amount to proof. But two distinguishable considerations point at least to its probability. On the basis of analogy with God's natural government of the world, his moral government is credible and beyond our comprehension. Further, herein lies a general answer to apparent discrepancies in its justice and goodness; and this shows that any objections to it have little force (1.7.2). This "credibility of religion ... though it should be mixed with some doubt", is sufficient to merit attention in all men, and to "engage them to live in the general practice of all virtue and piety" (1 Conclusion 2). Many have regarded an apologetic for religion in such prudential terms as "degrading".[9] This may be so. More incontestably, Butler seriously underestimates the power of passion, or overestimates its amenability to the control of such nice rational calculation.

The pivot of the argument in Part 2 is to be found in Chapter 3. In many ways it is a *tour de force*, at least in the way it wrests advantage out of the very teeth of apparent disability. The modern reader is almost obliged to conclude that this is more an exercise in debater dialectics than a piece of serious Apologetics. But he should remember that in its day it did do something to stem the tide that flowed towards radical Deism. Butler contrives to divert the weight of the Deist attack away from the substance (or "scheme", as he calls it) of Christianity to the external "evidence" by which it is supported. Perhaps dividing is a more apt phrase than diverting. At least to his own satisfaction he immunizes the Christian citadel, and then finds himself in an advantageous position to deal with assaults mounted against the outworks.

His key argument is the inability of human reason to be the judge of religious affairs. "Upon supposition of a revelation, it is highly credible beforehand, we should be incompetent judges of it to a great degree: and that it would contain many things appearing to us liable to great objections" (2.3.1). The objections at this point, then, are to be met not with satisfactory answers but with acknowledgment and agreement. His opponents, if this manoeuvre succeeds, are deflected, and their attack must go in at a less central and, as it appears, more defensible sector. That revelation is irrational is not disadvantageous after all but rather expected, for even natural religion is infected by it. "Now if the natural and the revealed dispensation of things are both from God, if they coincide with each other, and together make up one scheme of Providence; our being incompetent judges of one, must render it credible, that we may be incompetent judges also of the other" (2.3.2). Butler is careful to protect himself from the charge of pure obscurantism—in other words he does not care to align himself with Law. He can say: "I express myself with caution, lest I should be mistaken to vilify reason; which is indeed the only faculty we have wherewith to judge concerning anything, even revelation itself" (*ib.*). In the last resort reason would not tolerate or accept a revelation that was immoral or contradictory. It appears, however, that the substance of Christianity is not open to such charges (2.3.13); and any other objections can be only frivolous. This assessment of the role of reason in religion is important. It arrests both the Deist capitulation to reason as the omnicompetent norm against which religion has to be judged and also the obscurantist reaction to this. Of course the fundamental presupposition of Rationalism remains unchallenged: religion is still regarded as consisting of truths, even of propositional statements.

Butler adds two further supports for his view. In his Chapter 6 he again admits with a great deal of candour that proofs for Christianity fall far short of demonstration, and that many difficulties arise concerning revelation. One principal objection rests on the particularity of revelation and the consequent inequality implied: only some have had a chance to hear the Gospel news. It is with a bland application of the argument from analogy that Butler replies. Inequality, he says, is a feature endemic to nature; if the author is not pleased to remove it from this sphere, why should he be expected to do so in the case of revelation? Then in Chapter 7 he deploys the positive evidence for Christianity. On his estimation, there are no objections to Christianity that can stand up to scrutiny; what then can be said to commend it? The answer is in terms of "several things of great weight", but chiefly "these two are its direct and fundamental proofs", miracles and prophecy (2.7.1). As to miracles, they "are to be accepted until disproved" (2.7.6) and their testimony is considerable" (2.7.10). In the case of prophecy Butler is content to urge a small but for him considerable demonstrative value. On the whole he is content to protect prophecy in advance from all objections. Obscurity of part of a prophecy is unable to diminish the evidential value of the rest; that the prophets themselves did not really intend a messianic fulfilment is no objection; in any case the prophecies have perhaps a meaning other than was intended by the prophet himself.

Finally Butler addresses himself in Chapter 8 to objections that can be urged against the principle of analogy. "It is a poor thing," it is said, "to solve difficulties in revelation, by saying, that there are the same in natural religion: when what is wanted is to clear both of them of these their common, as well as their respective, difficulties" (2.8.2). At least the objection is fairly stated. It is doubtful whether the answer is adequate. Butler takes refuge again in a number of devices which he has made particularly his own. It is neither possible nor necessary to remove all difficulties; they do not amount to an impossibility; where they persist we can always retreat into mystery; and in any case when all is said, sufficient credibility remains to constitute a probability which is rather greater than what can be summoned against religion. But the more direct conclusion is simply that Butler's concept of analogy, so far from winning assurance for the Christian faith, only infects it with the same uncertainty as characterizes knowledge of mundane things. The argument from analogy is fatally double-edged.

It is not possible to absolve Butler from certain rather elementary faults in his use of this most characteristic argument from probability. In general Butler repeatedly seems to think that to answer objections to a statement constitutes a positive argument in its favour, even a proof. In particular many critics have pointed out the rather gross error in the argument concerning miracles. "There is," he says, (2.2.3) "a presumption of millions to one against the story of Caesar, or of any other man," and this he seems to think removes any ultimate objection that can be taken to the credibility of miracles. The error is one that Mill identified and defined as confusion of improbability before the fact and improbability after the fact. The analogy between nature and religion upon which the argument so fundamentally rests is really too remote. His reliance on cumulative proof to constitute probability and hence adequate credibility is too uncritical. Leslie Stephen[10] speaks of Butler thus "transmuting blank ignorance into some semblance of positive knowledge". It may be that the modern reader finds it difficult to swallow the urbane smoothness with which he seems to gloss over difficulties and advance undeterred to his conclusion. But it should at least be remembered that J. H. Newman records the debt of gratitude he owed Butler, and specially mentions the assistance he had from his thought about the sacramentalism of nature and the nature of probability.

To commend Christianity as through and through intelligible, and as therefore acceptable to and even already present in reason, was an attempt to base Christianity on the widest possible grounds. It appealed to rational man as such. Alongside this apologetic and often interwoven with it was a commendation of a rather different order. Appeal was made, not to the inherent substance of the Christian faith and what it declares, but to certain external features with which it was associated and which were commonly regarded as evidence authenticating the truth of what Christianity had to say. These features are prophecy and miracle. When revealed religion is accepted and distinguished from natural religion, the latter is thought to include all that can be known from nature and the spiritual constitution of man, while to the former belong the supernatural teaching contained in Scripture together with prophecy and miracle as divinely impressing that teaching upon the mind.

We have already noticed that the New Testament does not give support to the idea of the demonstrative power of miracle: the "signs" of the Gospels are not cited as the ground for believing in Christ. Yet a strand of thought, as we have also seen, began quite early that regarded prophecy and miracle as such external evidences of revelation.[11] The purpose of the appeal to prophecy and miracle is normally not to prove God, but rather to prove that something, manifesting certain ambiguous features not otherwise explicable, is from God. Certainly the argument is used in the eighteenth century in this way. Prophecy and miracle are both miraculous in character, and their miraculousness points to a supernatural agent as responsible for that in connection with which they occur. It too is supernatural in character: we are obliged to refer what comes equipped with these evidential signs to God as its author. Their testimony as such is not to be taken necessarily to deny the rationality of what they are associated with. Augustine was accustomed to declare that "miracles are not contrary to nature, but only to what is known of nature" (*de Civ Dei*, 21.8); and again: "We do not say that God does something contrary to nature because he acts in a way contrary to our knowledge of nature" (*contra Faustum Manichaeum*, 26.3). Their evidence could quite well be integrated into a fully rational scheme for those who believed in the supernatural. Rational men could accept for true what lay beyond the competency of their reason on these grounds. It is in this way that Law, for example, and even more clearly Locke, understand them to be external proofs.

In the great Deist debate the course of things is complex but not too difficult to follow. The Deists, impelled by a strong ethical interest, considered that it was possible to find by reason alone without recourse to revelation what is required of men, and that in any case Christianity should not claim to be a revelation. Hence their interest in the miraculous as evidential sign was extinguished.[12] But it became clear to some in the course of the debate that, bereft of revelation, the only representation of Christianity that could be formulated was inadequate. Hence there is a renewed interest in revelation, and attention fastened again on those evidences by which revelation had been traditionally supported. Hence the rise to prominence once more of prophecy and miracle. When their presence was detected—the argument ran—revealed religion was to be recognized. The miraculous is the sign of that which lies beyond our knowledge. Then restraint could be thrown off: if this were so, the more remarkable the better, and the more dumb-founding a miracle was, the more evidential value it possessed. Miracle then becomes indistinguishable from portent or theophany. Since there is that in God which is beyond reason, there is no ground for supposing that God need keep within the bounds of what reason can know in what he does, and no reason why he should not authenticate his revelation by signs far beyond the limits of reason.

At this point in the debate occurs the intervention of **David Hume**. His "Essay upon Miracles" contained in *Philosophical Essays concerning Human Understanding* (1748) plays a decisive role, though discussion went on long after it had appeared. The "Essay" is a product of the profoundly sceptical philosophy Hume expounded. All perceptions are either impressions of experience or the faded replicas of these impressions, called ideas. The impressions pass in an endless stream, and what is called the soul is simply the sum of perceptions which are connected with one another only by association. In the last resort nothing but single perceptions occur: there is no integrating mind or soul to hold them together. Causality is nothing between things, but merely a psychological association which we turn into a habit of expectancy. These principles he now brings to bear upon miracle. As experience has already been atomized into discrete perceptions, Hume has no difficulty in accepting the idea of miracles. Like any other event they are isolated, and only different for others in being less usual in character. But this is different from saying that such unusual events are provable. Hume takes as his paradigm for reviewing the whole matter the supposition of a dead man being raised to life. He finds that though such a supposition, or any other supposed miracle, is by no means impossible in itself, there is no human testimony that will suffice to prove it. For any that can be assembled cannot manifestly be stronger than the possibility that a fraud has been perpetrated by those who claim to have witnessed it or who report it. The subsequent question can then be answered only in the negative. Can miracle be used to provide evidential proof? The answer is no. No isolated impression could in any case be the bearer of such significance as to act as evidence of anything beyond itself; and this particular kind of impression, the unusual and miraculous, cannot itself supply evidence when it cannot itself be sufficiently evidenced. This means that miracle as a supernatural sign demonstrating the existence of a divine agency must be absolutely discounted. Hume states this conclusion thus: "We may establish it as a maxim that no human testimony can have such force as to prove a miracle . . . I say that a miracle can never be proved so as to be the foundation of a system of religion" ("Essay" conclusion).

Hume's criticism was of course itself immediately subjected to retort and rejoinder. It was only slowly that its devastating character became clear. The end result is to be detected in two significant changes in apologetic emphasis and strategy. There is a movement away from presenting prophecy and miracle as external proofs, like flying buttresses, sufficient in themselves to prop up the Christian edifice. The miraculous comes to be joined more integrally to the substance it is used to demonstrate. Thus William Paley can ask the question: "In what way can a revelation be made but by miracles?

Consequently, in whatever degree it is probable, or not very probable, that a revelation should be communicated to mankind at all; in the same degree is it probable or not very probable that miracles should be wrought" (see below). Soame Jenyns, an earlier and lesser known writer, goes further. In his *A View of the Internal Evidences of the Christian Religion* (1776), the miraculous is not so much conjoined with the revelation it formerly was thought to support, but represented rather as itself in need of the support of revelation. Thus: "to prove, therefore, the truth of the Christian religion, we should begin by showing the internal marks of divinity which are stamped upon it: because on this the credibility of the prophecies and miracles in a great measure depends." With this we come within sight of a view of the miraculous more widely accepted today than the apologetic arguments usual in the eighteenth century.

To **William Paley** (1743–1805) and his *View of the Evidences of Christianity* (1794 et.) is accorded the leading role in another form of evidential argument to which the scepticism of Hume tended to shut up Christian apologists. It should be noted that the argument is used to support belief in the existence of God rather than to demonstrate that revelation has divine origin and therefore authorization. The argument can be summarily stated: "From a watch we infer a watchmaker"[13]. Of course Paley was not the first to employ the illustration, and the argument itself is a form of the Teleological Argument. The important thing to note is that it is to this form of argument that Paley finds himself forced by the collapse of the argument from miracles under the weight of Hume's criticism. The Rationalist at least deployed the demonstration of such beliefs as he possessed on objective grounds. Paley led the way in an opposite direction, and his argument, resting on "supernatural contrivance", really "implies a more or less refined anthropomorphism".[14]

The anthropomorphism strikes us today as being often rather less than more refined. Paley notes, for example, as a curious coincidence that animals require sleep, while night brings about a periodic silence conducive to sleep. He does not apparently realize that the connection is not coincidental but causal, not necessarily due to direct divine contrivance but to natural connection. To an earlier proponent of the same line of argument we owe another striking illustration. John Ray observes: "Here, by the by, I cannot but look upon the strange instinct of this noisome and troublesome creature the louse, of searching out foul and nasty clothes to harbour and breed in, as an effect of divine providence, designed to deter men and women from sluttishness, and to provoke them to cleanliness and neatness" (*The Wisdom of God manifested in the Works of the Creation*, 1717, p. 309). This in turn reminds us of the caricature of this type of argument which Laurence Sterne puts into the mouth of *Tristram Shandy* (1761 ff.) whose grandfather, he alleged, was accustomed to see the hand of providence in his being provided with a nose on which his spectacles could rest. This tendency follows the remarkably acute and prescient observation of Hume himself, when he says that "the savage infers God from the apparent interruptions of order, and the philosopher from order itself".[15] The rise of modern biology was to raise innumerable and unprecedented difficulties for Christian faith; but at least it was to dispel the subjective fog of anthropomorphism with which Apologetics was being affected.

# CHAPTER NINE

# CHRISTIANITY IN AN AGE OF SCIENCE

THE word science has been in use for a long time and its meaning has greatly varied. In the fourteenth century Chaucer could talk about the "science of good works"; in the fifteenth century an entry in the Rolls of Parliament thought of the sciences as "Divinite, Fisyk, and Lawe"; in the sixteenth century Sir Thomas More rendered Paul's Rom. 11.33 as "o the heyght and depenes of the ryches of the wysedome and scyence of god"; in the seventeenth century Archbishop Laud coupled the word in a striking way with conscience, and objected to an author for having written a book "against both his science and his conscience"; in the eighteenth century Cowper spoke of the schoolboy learning "those seeds of science call'd his ABC". This wide general meaning was destined to persist not much longer. During the nineteenth century the word settled down to connote what it mostly means today, becoming synonymous with what is understood more exactly as natural and physical science and having reference to the phenomena of the material universe and its laws.

The development is of more than linguistic interest. It represents a shift of cultural and intellectual emphasis, even a switch of direction of human concern, one of these major upheavals in human history which may rightly be regarded as epochmaking. Science, Charles Singer tells us[1], is not a body of knowledge but an "active process", and even more emphasis might perhaps have been laid on its character as an activity of the human mind. As such the record must be traced back to the early days of civilization.

What we should now call an intellectual breakthrough took place in Ionia and Magna Graecia in the middle of the first millennium B.C., though elementary and as it were involuntary movements can be discerned even earlier. This earliest recorded beginning may well be designated as the "rise of mental coherence". Mankind embarked upon the "task of discerning constancy amidst the diversity and variety of nature".[2] Thales is important not because he suggested that the universe is made of water, but because in his mathematical work, for the first time, something like a natural law is being enunciated, identified and formulated. At this stage there is no clear distinction within mental activity between science and philosophy. In the case of Thales, "his science was a part of his philosophy".[3] Nor is theology distinguished as a discipline separate from either. But it is at least evident that a distinction of interests, even of pre-occupations, is setting in: the scientific tendency of philosophical thought is taking the bit between its teeth and making off on a life of its own. This sudden emergence of scientific interest was not to be paralleled in the history of mankind until the Renaissance nearly 2000 years later.

The voice of Socrates is indeed raised against this preoccuption. According to Xenophon he thought that astronomy was practically beneficial in enabling time to be calculated, but interest in the stars for their own sake he considered "a waste of time". However, Socrates' work in the end contributed to the establishment of a study of human conduct or ethics, and did not seriously deflect the scientific path on which human thought had set out. It was other considerations that put the brake on this movement. Perhaps it should be candidly remembered that if the age of the Roman Empire did nothing to promote science for its own sake as distinct from the practical use to which it could be put, that of the Holy Roman Empire and the Christian Church of the first twelve centuries did little more. The Middle Ages were to come and go before science resumed the voyage on which it had set out from the shores of Ionia and Greece.

To take up again an apparently abandoned expedition is no easy matter in any field. Modern science is the child of what may more generally be identified as the movement of Humanism. Few people in the earliest stages of this new intellectual and cultural development[4] could have predicted that it would go so far, or even promised that it would get into motion at all. It was an impulse from the past that lent impetus to the movement, and the attention that was thus attracted to the past might, one supposes, have remained archae-ological rather than futuristic. The beginning is made with a retrospective gaze *ad fontes*. But between the present and the past there lay what Singer graphically calls the barrier of "that terrible erudition, which, in the absence of general ideas, has been and is one of the enemies of science."[5]

Yet from this unpromising beginning there did arise a vision that looked to the present and the here and now, and took steps that were determinative of and for the future. It was a movement that was to precipitate conflict with Christianity. Yet it was motivated not by deliberate hostility towards religion. In the main, two factors impelled it forward. Interest in man, his situation and the things around him laid a compelling hand upon the attention, and so far there was a diversion of interest from the affairs of the speculative world, whether philosophical or religious. Then too it was found that in order to follow this interest the restraining hands that traditional modes of thought both philosophical and religious attempted to lay upon those who were bent on going forward had to be thrown off, and this was done not only firmly but sometimes with violence.

No advance intimation was given that a clash of major proportions was imminent in the nineteenth century. Or if there were signs of approaching storm they were ignored. In 1858 Mr. Mansel (later Waynflete Professor in Philosophy at Oxford and later still Dean of St. Paul's) delivered the Bampton Lectures.[6] Here was Bishop Butler *redivivus* after nearly a century and a half. While refusing to make his start with knowledge of the divine nature, he deliberately declined to ask "what are the facts and laws in the constitution of the universe",[7] and plunged instead into consideration of the constitution of the human mind and commended the Christian faith by a "sum total of Evidences" of a kind provided by the whole course of Apologetics from Irenaeus to Butler.[8] This was in 1858. In 1859 Ruskin[9] wrote "How strange it seems that physical science should ever have been thought adverse to religion!" In the same year Darwin published his celebrated *On the Origin of Species by Means of Natural Selection*. Instantly the appearance of religious tranquillity was torn to ribbons.

Moltke is credited with the sentiment that more important than the opponent that starts a war is the one who makes it inevitable. Darwin's work triggered off the conflict in which religion and science were engulfed in the last quarter of the nineteenth century and occupied attention through much of the twentieth. But many earlier antecedent events and persons were making it inevitable. To change the metaphor, the fuse smouldered a long time before the explosion occurred. The story covers two centuries if the beginning is made with Newton, two and a half if with Galileo, and three if the starting point is Copernicus. It is a story that has had many recorders[10] and reference here must be brief. "Copernican revolution" is a phrase that, since Kant misused it,[11] has come to mean no more than a radical change of standpoint. However, the change that Copernicus himself introduced is more significant: it meant the deposition (the demotion, as we now say) of man from the centre of things to the periphery. Ptolemy's scheme that had more or less dominated cosmological thought for 1400 years had become top heavy with the supplementary amendments required to make it fit the ascertained facts. It was no match for the simplicity of the Copernican model, according to which the earth is no more the centre of the universe but only one of the bodies which with the planets move round the sun. With this the dismantling of the anthropomorphic view of the universe was begun. Man's retreat from the centre of the cosmological stage to the wings had started. Kepler's contribution only thrust home this new conception with greater vigour, as he added further precision to the observations made, and found it necessary to think in terms of elliptical rather than of circular orbits. From the scientific point of view man was never more to be allowed to wrest back his unassailed priority on the terms hitherto current.

The scientific enterprise takes on two further characteristics with the advent of Galileo. His title to the name of "father of modern science" rests securely on the method of experimentation which he developed with a deliberate resolve lacking, for example, in the case of Archimedes, who in any case stands almost alone. When Galileo sets the ball rolling down the inclined plane, he is combining theory with experiment in order to register a result in terms of mathematical measurements. Sometimes it appears that even he hardly realized how important a chapter he was opening up. For he is found justifying experiment simply as a method of convincing his sceptical critics of the truth of his theories. But his own practice belies this underestimate of what he is engaged on. Manipulation in the case of Galileo intertwines with imagination in a creative role.

But the indirect implication of the new method of experimentation is theoretically even more important than the practical consequences. Interest is being transferred from description in terms of ends to description in terms of concomitant and especially antecedent facts. This means that teleology of the old fashioned kind is on the way out: causal explanation moves in and takes over. "Galileo asked not *why* objects fall, but *how* they fall."[12] In a sense the change is no more than a reduction of the area of interest. Aristotle had imparted to the ages succeeding him the fourfold classification of causes by which things happen, stones fall, oak trees grow, houses are made, and planets move. The future goal represents the final cause; the innate tendency the formal cause; connected events in the past the efficient cause; and the constitution of the matter the material cause. But attention was chiefly directed to the final causes, not to the series of steps by which the end is reached. Hence a purposeful pattern occupied and preoccupied the mind of the ancients and the generations that were dominated by them. The pattern lent itself readily to interpretation by for example Plato in terms of a Deity, and, in the case of the Christian religion, of an absolute God. Suddenly the area of interest contracts. The hitherto neglected efficient causes pre-empt attention. What takes place in space and time, the phenomenal present rather than the supposed future, is now of first importance. In this field too it is possible and important not only to observe but to experiment. The new activity that thus arises has no need to move out beyond the phenomenal sphere for the conduct of its operations; and the sphere in which it operated comes increasingly to look like a self-contained whole.

Some time elapsed before it was realized that science in its advances was posing an issue of critical importance to Christianity as traditionally conceived and formulated. The *de Revolutionibus Orbium* in which Copernicus shifted the centre of the solar system from earth to sun, he dedicated to Pope Paul III. On the whole the theologians on the Roman side of the now dividing Church received the work favourably. It was left to the Reformed side to spring to arms against it. Luther denounced Copernicus as an arrogant fool who contradicted Scripture; and Melanchthon advocated setting in motion the secular arm to suppress such dangerous doctrines. Between these extremes there is detectable a more general apprehension. Copernicus completed his epoch-making work in 1530, but he deliberately postponed its publication, apparently because of nervousness about the expected reactions to it, until 1543, when his dying hand touched the first copy to come from the press. Moreover, Osiander, who saw the work through the press, appended to it a *Praefatiuncula*. The intention was evidently to anticipate or conciliate the prejudices of orthodoxy. For the "little preface" deliberately misrepresented Copernicus' intentions and falsely construed the doctrines of the sun's centrality and the earth's rotation as mere hypotheses not to be attributed reliably to Copernicus.

But hostile feeling was mounting. In 1613 Galileo made clear his adherence to the Copernican view, addressing himself aggressively to the proponents of orthodox belief, and recklessly challenging the astronomical views apparent in Scripture. This provoked the ecclesiastical authorities to censure and warning; and Galileo undertook thereafter to obey the demand of Pope Paul V not to "hold, teach, or defend, the proscribed doctrines." The undertaking was soon breached. Galileo published his famous *Dialogue concerning the two Chief World Systems*, and was instantly summoned to appear before the Inquisition. At 70 years of age he was subjected to imprisonment together with the *examen rigorosum* which in his case may or may not have culminated in physical torture. In the end on his knees he abjured the scientific views he had propounded. Legend has it that after his recantation he added under his breath the celebrated words: *e pur si muove* (all the same it does move). Whether true or false, the legend no doubt exposes a want of moral fibre in Galileo. Even more certainly it reveals the utter ineptitude of the Church in appreciating and dealing with a situation that imposed on orthodox modes of thought strains and challenges that were without precedent.

The course of events in which Galileo was involved, if it caused something less than a wave of panic throughout the intellectual world, had at least one identifiable side-effect of historic importance. Resident in Amsterdam was the man who was to become distinguished as the author of *Discourses on the Method of Rightly Conducting the Reason* and of *Meditations on the First Philosophy*. He had already finished another treatise *de Mundo* and was about to complete the arrangements for its publication, when in 1633 the news of Galileo's censure and condemnation broke. Descartes in consequence not only postponed publication of the book but apparently in part destroyed it. Evidently the ecclesiastical hostility that had kindled the fires in which Giordano Bruno had perished in 1600 and Lucilio Vanini in 1619, that had inflicted upon Tommaso Campanella thirty years of dungeon imprisonment in Naples and Rome (1599–1629), was not subsiding. In the event, Descartes published his *Discourse on Method* anonymously in 1636, while *de Mundo* had to wait until 1677 when it appeared posthumously.

The encounters just mentioned must, in the light of later events, be regarded as more than skirmishes. This tension within the religio-intellectual world bears a striking if also regrettable resemblance to affairs civil and political. Evidently a massive movement is getting under way, heading in a direction which will sooner or later bring it into violent collision with traditionalism not only intellectually entrenched but also religiously absolutized. So far it is no more than individuals that ventured to make raids. Such assaults it was not difficult for established traditionalism with the powers with which it was equipped to contain and destroy. But the time was near when the situation was to get out of hand.

The contributions of **Isaac Newton** (1642–1727) to science are too many and vast to be recounted here (chief of his many notable works is the *Philosophiae Naturalis Principia Mathematica*, 1687). In any case it is the implications of his work that are the primary concern. His unique achievement consists in the extension to planetary movement of the pattern already discovered as regulative of earthly phenomena. "It was Newton who moved men's minds to see that the force that causes a stone to fall is that which keeps the planets in their path. It was Newton who first enunciated a law the writ of which ran no less in the heavens than on earth."[13] The universe was still conceived as a single harmonious order. But the idea of it as a hierarchy of purposes which the Middle Ages, and in large measure also the age of the finest flowering of classical Greece, had entertained, was under notice to quit. It was being elbowed out by a structure of forces and masses. But the new view of the constitution of the universe carried with it profoundly important implications. The physical universe could now be conceived independently without reference to a spiritual order outside it. While Galileo diverted attention away from final to efficient causes, the consequences of Newton's thought was to render it dubious whether there remained any place at all for final causes. The whole thing could be quite well construed simply as an intelligently devised machine.

Yet Newton himself did not push on to the ultimate conclusion that there is in fact no more than a mechanical world operating by scientific determinism. His system did not dispense with God, and even at two points made specific use of him. God was still regarded as first cause. Even when his activity could not be scientifically discerned in the particular thing or event and its relations with other particulars, he still retained a general ordinative role. Newton's statements amount in fact "to an implicit renunciation of particular providence, together with a strong reaffirmation of general providence. They asserted that the world is not an autonomous machine; they affirmed the predominance of spirit over matter in creation."[14] Further Newton was not averse to according God a "continuing function in adjusting the solar system."[15] He was frank enough to take note of data for which his system could not account; and he was naive enough to think that God could be called in at such points. Thus certain irregularities of planetary motion would build up to disorder, he thought, unless God corrected them from time to time.

Barbour sees in this an early instance of what Bonhoeffer more recently was calling "the God of the gaps".[16] If so it eventually met the unavoidable fate of all such manipulation of deity. As Kepler had earlier made sense of the irregularities Copernicus' theory could not account for, by amending a circular orbit to an elliptical, so Laplace in his turn rendered the detritus of irregularity left by Newton's theory explicable by expounding a nebular hypothesis.[17] The residual role arranged for God to play was at an end: no one was required to take up the part; there was in fact no part for anyone to take up. This explains the confidence Laplace displayed in the well known encounter with the Emperor Napoleon. He was thus addressed: "M. Laplace, they tell me you have written this large book on the system of the universe and have never even mentioned its Creator"; to which Laplace replied: "Sire, I had no need of any such hypothesis."

But this is to anticipate. Deism, as we have seen, was active. It overlapped the century in which Newton chiefly lived and worked, and spanned most of the succeeding century. The religious atmosphere in which the Deistic controversy was fought out must seem to us singularly accommodating to the vigorous growth of science. Perhaps a more robust religion giving rise to a more vigorous theology would have appreciated the signs of the times more clearly and been ready to challenge earlier if not the facts at least the pretensions of the new scientific spirit. But if the Newtonian physics virtually extruded God from the phenomenal known world, a religious mood more hospitable than Deism to such ideas can hardly be imagined. Whether related causally or consequentially to the scientific pattern as Newton's work unfolded it, Deism has no wish to find God in the phenomenal mundane world of everyday existence. It held out only for God being in at the beginning to set the whole in motion, and again at the end to wind it up and apportion the prizes. As both these points were opaque to scientific observation, God and his activity could be lodged there quite comfortably, and no one trod on anyone else's toes. Then the later Deists excluded themselves from the company of the orthodox, and the orthodox became immersed in the affair of evidences. What more natural than that the flood of scientific observation that yielded so much evidence of pattern and contrivance in nature should be construed into a demonstration that, in the general way which Newton himself allowed, the universe had indeed a Divine Designer whose name was God?

Then in 1859 there appeared *On the Origin of Species by Means of Natural Selection* by **Charles Robert Darwin** (1809–1892). It was a trumpet call which, if it did not demolish all the walls of security, at least tore great rents in them, and the winds of the new scientific age swept through disconcertingly. In a fragmentary and partial way much of what Darwin was to give the world had already been discovered, recorded, and made public. Of many forerunners, Linnaeus should be mentioned and credited with working out the first comprehensive system of botanical classification. However, the contribution served to harden the general supposition of permanent differentiation of species. Until this notion was overthrown progress was impossible. Buffon had identified the "struggle for survival" and thought of it as a factor in the elimination of some extinct types. Lamarck discerned the connection between the use and the development of organs. But the suggestion was limited in its usefulness because it was tied to the supposition that modifications thus acquired were immediately transmissible by heredity. Darwin himself acknowledged a debt of gratitude to Charles Lyell. In the field of geology Lyell moved significantly towards the idea that the phenomena of, for example, fossils could be explained by means of the operation of laws operating within the order of nature and over vast spans of time.

The genius of Darwin was able to comprehend this significant work, to synthesize it, give it shape, and extort from it a new conclusion which provided an answer applicable to many puzzles. As he himself puts it, he combined the idea of struggle for existence with that of great variation: "being well prepared to appreciate the struggle for existence which everywhere goes on, from long-continued observation of the habits of animals and plants, it at once struck me that under these circumstances favourable variations would tend to be preserved and unfavourable ones to be destroyed. The result of this would be the formation of new species."[18] The pattern of ideas is simple. There are incessant and random variations; there is a struggle for existence; and the net result is the survival of the fittest.

The more immediate implications affected the hitherto accepted scientific views and the general outlook in which they tended to find their place and justification. As Newton had virtually eliminated the concept of deliberate design from the inanimate universe, so Darwin's work ejected it from the field of biology. Here the almost contemporary comment of T. H. Huxley[19] made in 1864 is apposite. "For the notion that every organism has been created as it is and launched straight at a purpose, Mr. Darwin substitutes the conception of something which may fairly be termed a method of trial and error. Organisms vary incessantly; of these variations the few meet with surrounding conditions which suit them and thrive; the many are unsuited and become extinguished. According to Teleology, each organism is like a rifle bullet fired straight at a mark; according to Darwin, organisms are like grapeshot of which one hits something and the rest fall wide. For the teleologist an organism exists because it was made for the conditions in which it is found; for the Darwinian an organism exists because, out of many of its kind, it is the only one which has been able to persist in the conditions in which it is found." The really crucial and decisive factor can be more narrowly defined. There is the random element of variation which in the whole affair plays an indispensable role. But chance is not allowed out on its own. It is itself meshed into the mechanism of selectivity. The adaptation that results is then the consequence neither of purpose nor of chance, but rather of an automatism built into the constitution of nature. Entirely impersonal forces operate mechanically to produce species, order and progress. Reference to a purposive and designing God is superfluous, irrelevant, and almost indecent. Dynamic progressive process operates entirely without him and can effect all the things he had hitherto been thought to do. It is no wonder that men began to look with some apprehension at the citadel of their faith.

But these more immediate consequences had repercussions far-reaching and profound that touched more closely the Christian faith. C. E. Raven appears[20] to have suggested that the controversy over the Darwinian thesis might have remained no more than an altercation between biologists, with Wallace and Huxley and Darwin all engaged, if only Samuel Wilberforce the Bishop of Oxford had not sprung to arms in the name of Christendom against the scientific infidels. It is not easy to accept this judgment. Without Wilberforce the controversy might have occurred at another time, followed another course, and been conducted with less bitterness. But that thinking Christians should for ever have remained so blind to the implications of Darwin's teaching as not at some time to engage with it, or should have been so instantly perceptive as to see that no conflict was necessary, is hardly credible. The more nearly contemporary judgment of Sir William Huggins in his 1905 presidential address to the Royal Society is nearer the truth. He said:[21] "The accumulated tension of scientific progress burst upon the mind, not only of the nation, but of the whole intelligent world, with a suddenness and an overwhelming force for which the strongest material metaphors are poor and inadequate. Twice the bolt fell" (the reference is to Lyell's extension of geological time and Darwin's concept of evolution), "and twice, in a way to which history furnishes no parallel, the opinions of mankind may be said to have been changed in a day. Changed, not on some minor points standing alone, but each time on a fundamental position which, like a keystone, brought down with it an arch of connected beliefs resting on long-cherished ideas and prejudices. What took place was not merely the acceptance by mankind of new opinions, but complete inversions of former beliefs, involving the rejection of views which had grown sacred by long inheritance." Nothing on so big a scale could make its way in the intellectual world without remark and without struggle. In the sphere of religion, Renan judged the foundations had been so shaken that the beliefs resting upon them were destined to become extinct.

We may distinguish three major areas of conflict: the nature of the world or universe; the place of man in it; and Scripture. In the first place, on the Darwinian thesis the need to suppose intelligent design as a factor necessary for explaining the universe vanished. The area in which intelligent adaptation and purposive direction were so strikingly present could be accounted for without resort to divine personal intervention or planning of any kind, simply by the automatic operation of mechanical factors which preserved the useful and destroyed the useless. This has already been said. But it may be further noted that the removal of divine personal supervision did not leave the universe in the static inertness that the terms automatic and mechanical might seem to imply. On the contrary these impersonal forces resulted in dynamic movement on the part of living things which could be characterized only as advance. Providence and the concept of God interposing his finger here and there to adjust and rectify things were no longer needed. They were replaced by evolutionary progress for which the course of nature itself was equipped with the necessary factors. Under its own steam, and without the need to seek motive power from elsewhere, either *a fronte* (from in front) as in the case of Aristotle's *theos os eroumenos*, a god such as can be loved, or *a tergo* (from behind) as proposed by eighteenth century Christian orthodoxy—nature, the universe and the world could move forward. God seemed entirely dispensable.

A reassessment of the place traditionally allotted to man became necessary. That man enjoyed a special dignity among created things was a commonplace of textbook theology and ordinary belief. Theologically this thesis was affirmed in the special relationship in which man stood to the Creator, who had (in the words of Augustine) made him for himself, and had uniquely endowed him with both gifts and dominion over created things. The place thus theologically accorded to man was supported and guaranteed by the firm belief in the permanence and immutability of species to which science hitherto had adhered. The Darwinian thesis, however, shattered this idea concerning species and replaced it by a more flexible and especially a more continuous understanding. Species had indeed arrived—but they had emerged by roads that could be retraced without interruption into earlier times and forms of life. It was not indeed the status of man that was directly under fire; it was only the way in which he had mounted to that status. There was no longer need to invoke a special act of creation or commission or call from a supernatural sphere. Man was part of nature, and by natural processes could be conceived as rising to the position he holds. Of course though nothing of essential value was removed from man by this novel understanding, much of the shine and dignity with which he had been credited was rubbed off by the rather squalid manner of his rise. Man had no doubt got to the top in nature; but he had also been absorbed by and into nature and was accordingly accessible by the same methods of investigation as other parts. Even man's morality became a pawn (on Darwin's view) in the struggle for existence which represented an advantage.

As radical as the effects just mentioned were, the implications of the Darwinian thesis upon the views traditionally held concerning Scripture were equally disturbing. It was indeed at this point that the bitterest engagements took place. A literalist understanding of the Bible was widely held. On the side of the churches of the Reformation, it was the inheritance of a scholastic rigidity that had settled like hoarfrost on the theology of the Reformation; and Pope Leo's (XIII) Encyclical *Providentissimus Deus* bound the orthodox Roman Catholic with increased rigour to the view that Scripture had been divinely and inerrantly dictated. Between this outlook and the new vistas which Darwin opened up there could be no accommodation. Lyell had suggested that the formation of the world had taken place over untold ages of time—Archbishop Ussher said the Bible affirmed that creation had occurred on October 23, 4004 B.C. Darwin suggested that man had become what he is by a process protracted through long periods of time and covering many intermediate stages—the Bible declared he had been made on the sixth of seven days. Terms could not be arranged between such discrepant points of view. But difficulty was occasioned also for those who did not adhere to a strictly literalist interpretation of Scripture. Grave tension could not but develop between those who proposed that man's unique position of eminence in the scheme of things had been reached by a wholly uniform and terrestrial process of natural selection and those accustomed to believe that his was a status specially conferred on him by the Creator.

Darwin devoted himself unremittingly to the exacting task of consolidating the theory he had outlined and elucidating its further scientific implications. He hardly interested himself in the repercussions it was having upon Christian belief, and he was unfitted to do so by reasons of health and disposition. But it is on record that he regretted the waning influence which religious conviction had upon him as he plunged deeper into the scientific work of corroborating the theory with which he had amazed the world; and his last years were coloured by a reluctant agnosticism. He early confessed the grounds on which a later scepticism founded itself. In 1856 he wrote: "What a book a devil's chaplain might write on the clumsy, wasteful, blundering, low and horribly cruel works of nature!" And in 1870 his words were: "My theology is a simple muddle, I cannot look at the universe as the result of blind chance, yet I can see no evidence of beneficent design, or indeed of design of any kind, in details."

Hence it was left to others to follow up and develop the striking and evidently threatening consequences in which Darwinism involved Christian faith. By 1880 those consequences were becoming plain and from about this time **T. H. Huxley** (1825–1895) moved over into attack. In 1885 he enunciated "the perfect ideal of religion" in words that praised the achievement of the eighth century prophets and abruptly reduced their message to a moralistic interpretation of Mic. 6.8, "And what doth the Lord thy God require of thee, but to do justly, and to love mercy" (*Essays*, vol. 4, p. 161). But in 1887 he is found declaring: "That there is no evidence of the existence of such a being as the God of the theologians is true enough" (*Life*, vol. 2, p. 162). It is impossible, he declares, to have or to acquire knowledge such as orthodoxy lays claim to possess. We must content ourselves with something much less, with "the passionless impersonality of the unknown and the unknowable which science shows everywhere underlying the thin veil of phenomena" (*loc. cit.*). This exiguous credo seems to be further reduced as Huxley went on to outline some kind of "agnosticism" in which evidence and reason were invoked as the sole grounds of belief and knowledge, manifestly, however, understood in phenomenal and scientific terms (*op. cit.* vol. 2, p. 221). From this position he plunges into gloom, declaring that "moral purpose is an article of exclusively human manufacture" (*op. cit.* vol. 3, p. 268), and that as the cosmic process gives rise to what is evil in man's moral life, so in the end it will "resume its sway" as evolution passes into its degenerate period (*Essays*, vol. 9, p. 45).

Doubt and hostility having its roots in the new scientific outlook finds expression also in the works of **H. Spencer** (1820–1903). He is perhaps best known for his *Principles of Ethics* (1892–1893) in which he propounded with rather too great simplicity a theory that held moral conduct to be that which conduced to the maintenance of life, and this end is furthered by happiness which is a kind of bonus granted to behaviour and habits which promote life. In his thought disregard of God hardens into disbelief, and the mechanical operation of selectivity is elevated into the position of dominant and sole factor in the promotion of ends wholly inherent within the natural order. On the one hand Spencer is disposed to think there is some profound mystery at the back of the universe "from which all things proceed". But this remains and can remain for him no more than a great unknowable, and "inscrutable existence" incapable of sustaining personal or moral atrtibutes. On the other hand he is inclined to hypostatize the actual consequences of the evolutionary process into a principle in itself, and progress is exalted and in a sense absolutized. "Progress is not an accident," he says, "but a necessity. What we call evil and immorality must disappear. It is certain that man must become perfect." A confidently optimistic note is thus imparted to the prognosis ventured by the evolutionists, which can compete on not unfavourable terms with the expectation available in religious faith. The age of progress unlimited has started its career.

In **Ernst Haeckel** (1834–1919) Evolutionism found an exponent of much talent, wide interests, and remarkable lucidity. His *Die Weltträtzel* of 1899 was translated into many languages and exercised a considerable influence. As a philosopher Haeckel has no place among the immortals. But his works are popularly and brilliantly written. With remorseless thoroughness he swept away any vestiges of teleology that remained and impatiently attacked the dogmas of theology in the interests of what amounted to an uncompromising materialism. As the century turned, the attack upon orthodox Christianity had become formidable.

No West End theatre producer could have wished for a more spectacular first night than the start given to the controversy on June 30, 1860 at a meeting of the British Association in Oxford. **Bishop Wilberforce** engaged with Huxley in open debate.[22]

Wilberforce was a formidable protagonist of any cause, provided the audience was sufficiently undiscriminating or ill-instructed. Jovial rather than knowledgeable, and perhaps a little carried away by the apparently favourable reception accorded to what he was saying, he finally turned to Huxley in a magnificent gesture, and "begged to know, was it through his grandfather or his grandmother that he claimed his descent from a monkey?" Then followed the moment of Huxley's triumph. Invited by popular shouts and the chairman's ruling to speak, he promoted the case for Darwinism with both knowledge and skill, and declared that he would not be ashamed to have a monkey for ancestor, but would be "ashamed to be connected with a man who used great gifts to obscure the truth." The occasion provided a complete forensic triumph for the new doctrines. In some ways it was more than a mere occasion. It proved to be a pattern for much of the struggle that was to follow. Orthodoxy, unable or unwilling to make the effort to appreciate the new situation, was slowly pinned down under an accumulating weight of factual evidence in favour of the side which it too precipitately believed it must oppose. It is sad to reflect that the resemblance between this situation and that of two hundred years earlier is strong. Christianity is again seen rushing out to destroy what it would have done better first to try to appreciate. But there is the notable difference that the Church now is no longer armed with the authority and the instruments of power to make it capable of smothering or even containing the new knowledge.

However, the chips were down and the die cast. While the accredited proponents of each side prepared their respective positions, the plight of the ordinary Christian believer merits sympathy. Bewildered by loyalties that apparently conflicted, poised between a mounting accumulation of evidence that seemed to substantiate a Darwinian hypothesis and a Bible which, without a more sophisticated interpretation than he was always able to employ, seemed in flat contradiction, his position was indeed unenviable. It continued to be so until the first fury of the conflict had exhausted itself and the antagonists disengaged to consider whether terms of some kind could be arranged.

The small-scale map of the terrain reveals three salient features or basic attitudes. Fundamentalism denies the facts science affirms. Modernism surrenders some of the essentials of the Christian faith.

Pietism and Existentialism limit God's work to the inner life and personal decision, and deny or ignore his relation to the visible realities of nature and history. But this merits a closer look in greater detail.

The attitude of traditionalism is easiest to describe. Of its exponents **Charles Hodge** (1797–1878, *Systematic Theology*, 3 vols., London and Edinburgh, 1871–1873), associated with Princeton and one of the greatest American theologians, may be mentioned. Hodge classes "the new theory . . . proposed by Mr. Charles Darwin" along with the heathen doctrine of spontaneous generation under the title of anti-scriptural theories (2.1.2). Hodge speaks for the unsophisticated man just mentioned when he laments the shock, surprise and indignation experienced by common sense on being offered a theory which, "with its scientific feathers plucked off", suggests that "the whale and the hummingbird, man and the mosquito are derived from the same source." Apart from this there are difficulties general and particular. The theory is "impossible" because it assumes that matter does the work of mind; untenable because it is "thoroughly atheistic" and "effectively banishes God from his works"; insubstantial because it is a "mere hypothesis", "from its nature incapable of proof", and only one of other equally plausible hypotheses. With considerable skill and understanding Hodge notes the difficulties Darwin himself with great "candour" asknowledges, especially the absence of "connecting links", magnifies them, and scathingly refers to Darwin's general answer to most of them: let him be given a "sufficient number of millions of years, and fortuitous complications may accomplish anything." Hodge exemplifies the tendency to appreciate more carefully the things that science was really saying, but combines it with an inflexibility of mind that seems incapable of conceiving that the existence of God and the relation of God to his works can be preserved on any terms other than those already worked out by orthodoxy. This type of view continues to be held. L. Berkhof (*Systematic Theology*, London 1939 and later editions) stands in the same succession. He ties rejection of Darwinism even more closely to its contradiction of "the explicit teachings of the Word of God", and quotes with approval that "Darwinism is a compound of astonishing presumption and incomparable ignorance" and "has not a single fact to support it"! (*op. cit.* pp. 184, 187).

But a more accommodating attitude was also reaching expression. Admitting the facts Darwin had brought to light and allowing the theory he had erected upon them to stand for a moment's examination, were the very foundations of the Christian faith so seriously undermined as at first glance had been supposed? What did acceptance of the new knowledge entail? Two types of view are distinguishable. One inclined to think in terms of an identity between God and the newly detected dynamic and progressive process inherent in the universe. The creative activity in which on the orthodox view God engaged was not to be denied; it had to be understood rather differently. It was not a once for all spurt of energy succeeded by inertia: it could be understood as continuing and perpetual. Moreover, the action could be conceived as taking place not from outside but from inside the universe. On these terms an alliance could be arranged, and God who seemed at first to be extruded from his creation brought back again in an immanent and continuously active role. Along those lines **Henry Drummond** (1851–1897) contrived to assimilate the new knowledge with the traditional faith. In his *Natural Law in the Spiritual World* (1883), Drummond accepted the evidence that showed the principle of continuity present and potent in the natural order, and he interpreted the spiritual order in parallel terms. In a later work, *The Ascent of Man* (1894), he attempted to top off his theory by tracing back the story of man's spiritual evolution and speaking confidently of his further rise. Obviously the line of thought Drummond exemplifies lent itself to different emphases. God could be thought of as an impersonal cosmic force, and perhaps Matthew Arnold's view of God as a "force making for righteousness" is to be regarded as a moralistic version of it. There was room also for a return to the originally Gnostic idea that man possesses a spark of the divine, and thus in himself unites a principle of self-motivated advance and of deity. Evidently the Christian faith was not incapable of adaptation to the changing situation.

On the other hand the distinction between God and the newly identified automatism of progress could be preserved. Then the automatism in question will not be identified with God nor God become immanent in the world. Rather it will be regarded as the means or instrument by which God achieves the ends he has in view. As will be recalled, Darwin himself was not averse to seeking relief to the dilemma with which his discoveries had faced him along such lines: teleology on the level of particular phenomena was out, but this did not eliminate its continuance on a macrocosmic scale. Thus, quoting from a work of a later generation,[23] "the whole evolutionary process is seen to be the means by which God is both communicating with us and making us capable of communion with him." This expresses the earlier sentiments of for example Henry Ward Beecher (1813-1887), who is not at all dismayed by the vast stretches of time that Darwinism interposes while man achieves the status he now enjoys. This is no more than "the long-hidden record of God's revelation in the material world", and the narrative of how God contrives the ends he has conceived.[24]

By the beginning of the new century and even amid expressions of the scientific and the religious standpoints which nothing could harmonize, the contestants were disengaging. It was possible to begin to take a longer cooler look at the issue that lay between them. Further matters arose that complicated the situation and placed the Darwinian issue in a wider context. On the one hand the advent of what was unhappily called Biblical Criticism (when what was meant was not uncritical methodical and scientific study of the Bible), itself an area of conflict within the Christian Church, seemed to call in question the authority of the Bible as evolutionism had questioned its veracity.[25] Here views that had at first seemed disruptive of the foundations of Christian faith were proving impossible to reject, and at the same time not only less deleterious for the faith than expected but positively helpful and enlarging. On the other hand, while the precise issue raised by Darwinism was settling, there was no relaxation of effort and activity on the part of science as such. Rather as though stimulated by the extraordinary success that had attended this boldest of all scientific hypotheses, research and study went on with increasing rapidity and undiminished eagerness. The age of "scientism" was beginning, an age marked supremely by "faith in science" which, according to C. F. von Weizsäcker,[26] has replaced faith in religion.

Up to the present day it is this relation between scientism and religion that colours the contemporary scene and characterizes the apologetic task of Christianity. Naked opposition between science and religion has subsided; but the war is not over. There remains a more or less acute tension. "I believe in science," says A. J. Ayer.[27] "That is, I believe that a theory about the way the world works is not acceptable unless it is confirmed by the facts, and I believe that the only way to discover what the facts are is by empirical observation. It seems to me that theists of all kinds have very largely failed to make their concept of a deity intelligible; and to the extent they have made it intelligible they have given us no reason to think that anything answers to it." Scientism has its exponents among the philosophers (note the phrase "empirical observation" above). Besides, the varying suggestions for terms between the two sides indicate that there is still a deep-seated unresolved difference between them.

We content ourselves here with a brief mention of the distinguishable types. In defining the relationship, some incline to emphasize the similarity existing between the two activities. Amid much that obviously differentiates them sharply, at a profound level there is a distinct similarity of outlook. This similarity is located in the attitude of faith. Thus C. F. von Weizsäcker says[28] that "faith in science plays the role of the dominating religion of our time." He goes on to point out that the principal element in faith is not belief but trust, and he finds a "quality of reliance" in the average man who practises science and the believing adherent of a revealed faith. Both science and religion have access to some knowledge, but much more remains invisible and mysterious. In view of this similarity the fact that the object is in the one case personal and in the other impersonal is not so deeply divisive.

Next there is the view that the only proper thing to do is to distinguish sharply, perhaps ultimately, between science and religion. A simple exposition of this view is found in what William James writes:[29] "I can, of course, put myself into the sectarian scientist's attitude, and imagine vividly that the world of sensation and scientific laws may be all. But whenever I do this, I hear that inward monitor, of which W. K. Clifford once wrote, whispering the word 'bosh!' Humbug is humbug even though it bear the scientific name, and the total expression of human experience, as I view it objectively, invincibly urges me beyond the narrow 'scientific' bounds." The distinction is sometimes, as noted by von Weiszäcker,[30] represented as a contrast between reason and faith; and though this is no doubt generally thought to be a pretty exact statement of the case it can hardly stand on its own. Schleiermacher in the eighteenth century attempted a distinction of this kind. In contrast to the dessicated rational propositions into which religion had been broken down, he proposed to seat religion in the region of feeling where it would be able to enjoy an impregnable area over which it had unassailable control.

But in the end the distinction outlawing reason from religion did not work. Neither is it more successful in this more modern dress. Existentialism represents a widespread and quasi-popular attempt to read religion and science as though they came out of different books. "A proposition or a truth is said to be existential when I cannot apprehend it or assent to it from the standpoint of a mere spectator, but only on the ground of my total existence."[31] This concept, emerging from Søren Kierkegaard and fruitfully employed in the 1930s by Martin Buber, has coloured much modern theological thought. It certainly has much to commend it. But in the end it appears either to prove too much or concede too little. It proves too much if the disjunction between the two realms is made absolute: in the end we cannot remain content with a truth that splits from top to bottom up the middle and to which there are two unrelated methods of approach. Or it concedes too little—for in fact the day when we could think of science being clinically aseptic from all taint of the subject and when detachment was the keynote of scientific utterance is over. The frontiers between religion and science are not proof against infiltration from either side.

A third view pursues a path between assimilation and disengagement. Religion and science, it is said, do not speak of different areas; rather they take note of and study different aspects of the same reality. So O. C. Quick criticizes[32] the assertion of a well-known modern writer: "Darwin's *Origin of Species* is today a good deal more profitable as theology than the first chapter of Genesis." He points out that the saying rests on a misunderstanding as though the two were alternatives of which one only could be accepted, whereas they are really complementary. "As to the nature and succession of those events, it is doubtless true that the authority of such experts as Darwin is to be preferred to that of the author of Genesis. But theology is not interested primarily or chiefly in the question of temporal origins, even when it is stating its doctrine of creation. It is interested primarily and chiefly in the end or value of what has been created." Thus an aetiological aspect is carved out for religion to which science is deemed to be entirely indifferent. So C. A. Coulson, addressing the British Association in Edinburgh in 1951: "Theologians have nothing to fear from science. Scientific truth and religious truth are different ways of apprehending the same reality which we call God." Similarly too L. Charles Birch[33] thinks that "the universe has both an outer mechanical aspect and an inner aspect which is akin to mind." In such a universe there is room for the acknowledgment that different interests may wish to pursue different concerns without collision and indeed with mutual benefit. This view is further elaborated to show a strong similarity to the much earlier representation of St. Thomas and the Middle Ages—the view that "the activity of God in the world had to do not with 'mechanical causes', but with 'final causes'." Thus we are right in saying that God is cause, and at the same time right too in emphasizing carefully that "God is not every cause".[34]

Finally we should take note of yet another pattern in terms of which some kind of relationship between science and religion is being defined. This is the "process" view, and it can lay claim to such exponents as Whitehead, Hartshorne and Teilhard de Chardin. Widely different though they of course are these three thinkers hold in common some important fundamental convictions that combine sympathy and understanding towards the scientific outlook with imaginative theological constructiveness. Science and Christianity are not in principle in conflict. It was John Macmurray who said:[35] "The one creative achievement of the Reformation was science and the scientific spirit. Science is thus the legitimate child of a great religious movement, and its genealogy goes back to Jesus." Whitehead himself falls back upon the different aspect understanding of the relationship, reiterating that science is abstractive and symbolic, and that to think that it gives an exhaustive account of reality is to fall into "the fallacy of misplaced concreteness".

The most positive overture towards reconciliation with science made by those in this class can be thought of as falling into three stages. First, a certain primacy is accorded to *time*. Thus at a stroke all ties are severed with the classical ages of philosophy that are dominated by depreciation of the phenomenal and temporal in favour of the real and eternal. By this means, *event* moves into a place of first importance, to become the component out of which, in interfusion with other events, reality is made. Thus a break is made with the agelong representation of reality in terms of substance and attribute. Consequently reality is infused with a dynamism—what characterizes it chiefly is organic *process* which inspires the name of Whitehead's chief work, *Process and Reality*, Cambridge, 1929. At this point roads of differing emphasis diverge. Whitehead is sensitive to the danger of slipping into unitary monism, and he emphasizes the novelty and independence of each event, while holding that each reacts on others. Hartshorne affirms that an event is constituted by order which sets it in context, and by spontaneity which frees it from the monotony of repetition, and in the last analysis also by the influence of God. Teilhard de Chardin is more closely tied to the results of particular scientific observation. Hence his emphasis is on the "thresholds" and "crises" that mark off different levels within the emerging whole without disrupting it. Things are "warm with consciousness" long before at the summit the glow burns up into "a point of incandescence. We must not lose sight of that line crimsoned by the dawn. After thousands of years rising below the horizon, a flame bursts forth at a strictly localized point. Thought is born."[36] Then each moves on in characteristic style to talk of God.

For Whitehead God is the primordial ground of order and novelty. So closely is he involved in the dynamic process that he must be conceived as influenced by events, so that we must reckon with a "consequent nature of God". Hartshorne moves to a similar conclusion and makes what he can of the resultant antinomy by saying that "God is the most irresistible of influences precisely because he is in himself really most open to influence."[37] Yet God is not submerged in the world, but, rather like mind remaining distinct from body, he retains a certain transcendence. Teilhard de Chardin affirms the need to suppose or intuit a "principle" "to explain the persistent march of things towards greater consciousness".[38] This he calls Omega and credits it with attributes identical with those the Christian applies to God.

It is by no means clear that this "process" theology will be able to defend its view of God successfully against the evident perils of pantheism, reductionism, impersonality, and even of a rather crude evolutionary growth. But at least there is a genuine attempt to draw the map of reality in terms that both scientist and Christian can recognize.

F. C. S. Schiller[39] regards **Humanism** as a method rather than a system, and this makes it difficult to assess the case which in some phases it brings against Christianity. In two points it resembles Deism: for while it is scarcely a creed and ought rather to be regarded as a recurrent tendency of thought, it nevertheless crystallizes at one period into an identifiable historical movement.

Those known as Humanists stand at the intellectual centre of the Renaissance. It is helpful to think of this hard core as normative or at least explanatory of the character and intentions of Humanism in general. The Humanists who led the way out of mediaevalism into the modern age pioneered principally emancipation from restrictions of various kinds which traditionalism took for granted. They protested against the bloodless dehumanizing of logic, insisting that in considering the cognitive content of judgments the personal antecedents, context and purpose could not be left out of the reckoning. They protested against the mediaeval metaphysics with its accepted absolutisms, its innate principles, its exclusively deductive method, and the appearance it presented of being a system closed and final. They protested against religion in so far as it had been devitalized by a too close association with a scholastic metaphysics. But they did not protest against religion as such. Some harsh things have been said about Desiderius Erasmus (1466 or 1467–1536), the greatest of all the Humanists: "half-hearted Reformer he may have been, but he was neither half-hearted Humanist nor half-hearted Christian."[40] The Humanists stood as such rather for the insertion of human affairs among the legitimate interests and concerns of men than for the wholesale transfer of attention to this area alone. They did not initially find it too difficult to commend this extension of interest: *studia humaniora* are moved up from the *trivium* or lower division of the seven liberal arts to an independent and first-class place of attention.

This same spirit of protest in favour of emancipation is evident in the much earlier period of classical Greece, from where Humanism is wont to derive inspiration. Indeed a recurrent impetus within Humanism has regularly been the impulse *ad fontes*, back to the origins of things, that is, before putative sophistication fouls or adulterates the springs. In Greece too there occurred what may be identified as a humanist revolt against contamination by sterile sophistry. But here again the object contended against was not religion as such.

Humanism takes on a scientific and more frankly atheistic colour in more modern times. "The essence of Humanism is that it is non-supernatural. It is concerned with man rather than God and with this life rather than the next."[41] The principal charge levelled against religion is monotonously the same: religion is otherworldly and non-temporal in character and interest, and aims to prepare men for the next world while breeding in them a massive indifference to the opportunities and needs of this one. It is equally impossible to accept and to reject this charge in its entirety. No religion perfectly lives out even such ideals as it proposes to itself, and Christianity, though certainly in better case than other religions, is not absolutely different. As Christopher Dawson says:[42] "There is hardly a social abuse or an intellectual fallacy that has not found its stoutest defenders in the ranks of Christian orthodoxy." Humanists tend to reiterate this charge with a zeal as uncritical as it is unremitting.

One of the difficulties in trying to reply to Humanism is to be found in that long lineage to which Humanists tend to lay claim. The *Humanist Anthology*[43] is an impressive collection of little excerpts. It begins with sixth century B. C. Lao-tse and carries on to include writers who were born when Bertrand Russell had passed his half-century. One must ask whether such a collection can be more than a literary curiosity. It is not really possible to accept that "Humanism derives from a far longer tradition than Christianity"[44] either as pure statement[45] or as premise for its superiority to Christianity. The fact rather is that it derives from no historical source at all but from a permanent and certainly useful attitude of mind, sympathetic to human values and intolerant of unjustified impediments to their realization. So too when under the chairmanship of Julian Huxley the International Humanist and Ethical Union[46] drafts a declaration stating that "Humanism unites all those who cannot any longer believe the various creeds and are willing to base their convictions on respect for man as a spiritual and moral being", it is not clear that the unitive force is very strong. It is even less clear why those who can continue to believe should not be eligible for membership along with those who entertain respect for man. It is impossible to avoid the conclusion that Humanist writers have never read an up to date book on Christianity, and that they go around with a lot of ideas that are terribly old hat. They hardly realize that Christians have gone to some trouble to show that there is some difference between

Christianity and the magic and superstition that Frazer's *Golden Bough* expounds; that they do not think that Jesus was a good man who was carried off to heaven; and that they too recognize the acute difficulty of the so-called problem of evil and have done something to put it in a context in which it becomes less than sheer mystery.

However, modern Humanism has given evidence of moving beyond the forms in which it expressed itself in the earlier part of this century; and the direction in which it moves carries it sensibly nearer religion. A. J. Ayer writes:[47] "The Humanist movement is gradually changing its character. Until quite recently its energies were mainly absorbed in a kind of religious war against the Churches. This war, in which only the Humanists themselves took any great interest, was waged on two fronts. They set out, on the one hand, to expose the absurdities of Christian theology and, on the other, to demonstrate historically that religious belief had been a source of more misery than happiness, and especially that the Churches, as political and social forces, were an obstacle to human enlightenment and progress." Ayer thinks that these negative aims are no longer so important to Humanism, though the reasons he gives are chiefly the diminished interest in theological questions any way and the declining importance of the Churches in modern life. Positively, however, there is more to be said. In a Milan meeting of the same Union[47a] an Italian Humanist is reported to have sought alternatives to the vacuum created by "the end of all transcendence", to have said that man "transcends himself continually", and to have hazarded the judgment that Humanism should be regarded as "more than a mental attitude and a moral conviction: it can be the upholding of a new knowledge and a new reality of man, maturing slowly and reaching its roots in the whole history of mankind"—not so far from Teilhard de Chardin, and certainly offering a ground on which dialogue with Christianity is possible.

The word dialogue is determinative of the recent response Christianity has made. The reasons why it has taken this form are various. Christianity and the Church have no longer at their disposal the power with which to contain or destroy a rival system of thought. It is just as well. But neither have they in this case the desire to do so. Humanism, though its sources are diverse, is obviously a kind of truncated Christianity, a Christianity with the transcendent dimension lopped off. While therefore the principles on which it rests are in conflict with the Christian faith, wide areas remain which lend themselves to practical co-operation and intellectual dialogue. Jacques Maritain opened up the possibility of *rapprochement* in his *Humanisme intégral* of 1936.[48] The book penetratingly analysed the failure (as it seemed to the author) of secular humanism, and outlined the possibility of a new Christian order in which Humanists might be able to recognize the aims they themselves advocated. Immediately after World War II in great assemblies at Oxford and Amsterdam (the organization from Amsterdam onwards came to be known as the World Council of Churches), the Church displayed a new and vivid interest in the world and the different forms of belief that attract and hold men away from Christianity. "Most of the secular faiths are in one way or another, humanistic", says one of the preparatory reports.[49] The interest thus alerted has found expression in many ways and at different levels. More recently the Roman Church has exemplified a conciliatory type of response towards Humanism. Following Vatican Council II a Secretariat for Non-Believers has been set up, and some physical contacts and consultative conferences have taken place with organized Humanism.

On the other hand a more cautious response is also apparent. For example Karl Barth reminds the Roman Church that, while of course conciliation is to be welcomed, the Christian Church should not fall over backwards to make concessions to "other faiths" and "non-believers". It must be willing to speak with them, but it may not relinquish the Gospel with which it is charged and in virtue of which alone it has any right to speak to them. With particular reference to the Pastoral Constitution on the Church in the Modern World (*Gaudium et Spes*), he asks:"Is it all so certain that dialogue with the world is to be placed ahead of proclamation?"[50] An early work gives the clue to this attitude. In his "The Humanity of God"[51] Barth insists that true humanity (including all Humanist values) is to be found in God, and that accordingly man's hope of achieving Humanist ideals is based upon what God has done for him in the incarnation of Jesus Christ.

Without some reference to **Communism** the record of this chapter would be incomplete. After all, Communism or Marxism constitutes the most organized and militant attack upon Christianity during the last hundred years. Communism may be regarded as a politico-economic variant of Humanism, though neither Communist nor Humanist may feel entirely comfortable in such an association. The Communist tells us that his doctrine is opposed both to theism of all kinds and to Humanism, because their theses are based on dogmas, but his own premises can be tested in experience.[52] The Humanist on the other hand declares that Humanism is opposed to both Christianity and Communism in that they both rest on dogma and not on the scientific outlook.[53] Perhaps we should just boldly refuse to be terrorized by the bogey of dogma, reflect that for Christianity at least it means nothing but the orderly expression of the Christian faith and its development in face of changing circumstances; and decide to come to a judgment on the merits of the case without depending on a pejorative interpretation of a concept.

We may use the terms Marxism and Communism to denote respectively the doctrinal statement and the practical expression of a creed that may properly be called Historical Materialism.[54] Negatively Marxism denies that religion has any connection with truth. It arises rather from a condition of "self-estrangement".[55] Men think they discover the god which in fact they have themselves constructed as personification of the community. When class levels exist, the gods represent the interest of the "ruling classes", and the morality and law that derive from them keep the "exploited class" in subjection. Positively, the real motive force in history is the class struggle, not ideas. "The history of all human society, past and present, has been the history of class struggle", says the Communist Manifesto. Consequently religion is nothing but epiphenomenal, a superstructure determined by the real factors that are dynamically at work; and the same is true of other intellectual activities such as politics and philosophy. The movement of history is inevitable and irresistible, and it cannot be affected by anything connected with thought process. Here Hegelianism is transposed into the key of materialism. "For Hegel, the thought process is the creator of the real. In my view, on the other hand, the ideal is nothing other than the material when it has been transposed and collected inside the human head".[56] It is not even certain that an optimistic outcome can be expected. On the one hand advance is made as feudalism gives place to capitalism, which is itself replaced by socialism. But Engel at least[57] thought that matter passes through an "eternal cycle" in which organic life itself and consciousness emerge only to be destroyed, and then reappear again. For Marxism at all events mind does not arise from matter: it *is* matter arranged in a particular way. This sheer materialism is challenged not only by the Christian religion but by much of recent science itself.

Circumstances gave Lenin the opportunity to put Marxism into practice and Communism began to take shape. Ideologically the attack on religion continued. "Our propaganda must include the propaganda of atheism", Lenin is quoted as saying[58], "We conduct propaganda and shall conduct propaganda against religious prejudices", echoes Stalin. Religion, Lenin holds, is the creation and instrument of capitalist tyranny: "the bourgeoisie, in order to ensure its domination, needs two functions: the functions of the executioner and the priest. The executioner suppresses the indignation of the oppressed masses by physical means, while the priest does the same by deception and persuasion"—a sentiment not too different from the Rationalist view that nothing will be well until the conspiracy imposed by kings and priests is brought to an end with the last king being strangled by the entrails of the last priest.

Practical effect has been given to the doctrine with varying degrees of rigour. In 1905 Lenin advocated the complete separation of religion and state: "every person should be simply free to profess whatever religion he pleases or to profess no religion at all—to be an atheist, which every sort of socialist ordinarily is." Then ridicule is invoked, and in famous words he states that "religion is opium for the people, a sort of spiritual moonshine or bad home-made liquor, in which the slaves of capital drown their humanity and their demands for even any sort of worthy life." Then in turn this gives way to active discouragement and restriction. In 1932 a Party manifesto declares that "the Party strives for the complete dissolution of the ties between the exploiting classes and the organizations of religious propaganda, facilitates the real emancipation of the working masses from religious prejudices, and organizes the widest possible scientific educational and anti-religious propaganda." Since these earlier days the attitude of the Communist state to religion has fluctuated, but only within a narrow range. The prohibition of religious teaching except privately, and the withdrawal of the right of Churches to hold property are the chief means whereby sanctions and control, whether rigorous or relaxed, can be applied at the will of the authorities.

Communism opposes to Christianity a front much clearer, more militant and better armed than does Humanism. One kind of response made on behalf of Christianity is accordingly deeply hostile. Communism is cast in the role of the twentieth century anti-Christ. This thinking "placed Marxism and Christianity more or less on the same level as life and death antagonists".[59] But this attitude the writer dates as popular 26 years before he writes. As a serious response its day is done, though at unreflective levels it of course receives frequent and often vehement expression. No individual Christians have done more to explode the myth than two who lived and wrote under Communist rule, as indeed they still do. Helmut Gollwitzer (Germany) and Joseph Hromadka (Czechoslovakia)[60] both insist that the sins of the present world cannot be offloaded on to Communism. Both have taught that the source of the difficulties and their cure lie nearer home. And both have shown that it is possible to live with Communism. Gollwitzer says: it is up to Christians not only to enjoy the Gospel but to pass it on; and Hromadka: we need not fear a godless world but only a godless Church. Their testimony is that "the cleavage is no longer final: it can no longer prevent brotherhood".[61]

Thus a basis for possible *rapprochement* has been consolidating itself, and dialogue now takes place. The World Council of Churches plan a World Consultation on Communism which will be attended as a matter of course by leading Communists. The Roman Catholic Church, despite many who think that the quasi-political aims and ambitions which the Vatican has not relinquished impede progress, has already begun setting up conversations, following Vatican Council II. Charles C. West's book is subtitled "Study of an Encounter", and one of its aims is to tell the story of Christianity's discovery of its solidarity with the world pre-eminently in face of the challenge of Communism.[62]

On the intellectual level the contribution of Christianity towards understanding must evidently consist in pressing the need for a right understanding of history. "The difference between Marxism and religion is not mainly a difference over the interpretation of the same facts: it is above all the difference over what are the irreducible data of human experience".[63] Brunner reminds us: "the content of the Christian faith . . . is a genuine external fact which can and must be fixed chronologically, a fact which could very well be the subject of a police report: Jesus of Nazareth 'crucified under Pontius Pilate'."[64] This statement no doubt oversimplifies the issue, but in principle it is entirely right. If event is the basic unit of history, as both the study of history and the understanding of the Christian faith have increasingly come to recognize, then materialism, and with it historical materialism or Marxism with all its anti-religious bias, can hardly claim to be even a possible explanation of the world. It is no more than a highly reductive description of a seriously restricted selection of data. In those circumstances Christianity may commend itself as a more comprehensive appreciation of the total human situation. Both Communists and Christians ought to be very discerning about the facts and also very humble before them.

# CHAPTER TEN

# CHRISTIANITY IN A SECULAR AGE

"WE USED to hear it said, only a decade or two ago, that the day of the old Dogmatic preaching was over. Perhaps there are still some who speak like that. But there are many more who are beginning to wonder whether the day of the new apologetic preaching is not, in its turn, passing away. We are awakening to the weakness of this supposedly improved strategy, and beginning to suspect that the old frontal attack may after all have been better suited to the fundamental realities of the situation." The words were written less than thirty years ago by John Baillie.[1] He is telling us that the day of Apologetics is over, whether in preaching or theology generally. To us who live in the late sixties of the century, the statement can only seem astonishing. No prediction could have been more completely belied by events.[2]

Yet when the words were uttered it is understandable that such a prognosis should have been made. A reading of the signs of the times made it look like sound prophecy. The attention of theology and thinking Christians was being claimed by a call of unwonted urgency and clarity, contrasting strongly with the subdued and uncertain undertones in which Christian thought was usually expressed. Currently "Christianity had ceased to have a message for the mind, and religion was anything one liked to make it"—so said Professor A. A. Bowman in the General Assembly of the Church of Scotland. John McConnachie quotes this as descriptive of the situation about to be invaded by a quite new element. He continues:[3] "The most interesting event in the post-war religious world has been the phenomenal suddenness with which the word of Karl Barth has captured the ear of Europe, and transformed within a few years the whole outlook of Continental theology." By 1939 Barth was having a profound influence in Britain too. What arrested attention was not only what

Barth was saying but the manner in which he said it and the direction in which it moved. "For over a hundred years before the (First World) War, theology had been in covenant with modern thought"[4] —this is the typical apologetic approach. The consequence was to think that the one sure key to the knowledge of God was the knowledge of man at his best. On Barth's view, however, one does not speak of God by speaking of man with a loud voice. It is better to listen to the revelation of God in his Word than be preoccupied with what modern thought is saying. The apologetic tendency is abruptly terminated, and replaced by a declamatory or dogmatic approach. Barth himself says[5] that theology "will spare both the world and itself the pain of a specific apologetic, the more so in view of the fact that good dogmatics is always the best, and basically the only possible, apologetics. Those who are without, or partly without, hear theologians best when they do not speak so ardently at them, but pursue their own way before their eyes and ears." Clearly Barth is not indifferent to Apologetics; but he thinks that faith is best commended by plain statement rather than by special pleading. It is at least a quite sensible view.[6] That this view was being expressed with such massive weight, and advocated by some of the leading figures in the contemporary theology, might well mislead one into thinking it was here to stay. But it was not; and, while it will for all time have a contribution to make, its dominance lasted for no more than a winter's day.

In the event theology took a different turning and struck out in quite another direction. As already said, the tendency of theology before World War I was to present the Gospel to man in terms of his own thought and aspirations, as the reinforcement of his own ideas and the fulfilment of the ideals he cherished. It was the heyday of theological liberalism. After the War severe disenchantment set in. The Gospel was proclaimed in the strong even strident tones of the dialectical theology of Barth, Brunner and others. This proclamation took the form of a divine No to human ideas and ideologies and certainly to our ideals. Today the situation is again quite different and at the same time very complex. The world of today possesses unprecedented prosperity, unevenly distributed, and so accompanied by profound and increasing want and suffering. It is a world unifying under the influence of a common culture raining down upon it through the orifices of countless mass media, and at the same time disintegrating under the impact of resurgent nationalism. Above all it is a world becoming saturated with secularism. In this situation the tendency is to present the Gospel as something vital to men in their humanity; and the corresponding theology is worked out from the situation in which contemporary man finds himself, in which we all find ourselves. The style of recent theology has been predominantly apologetic. Indeed the judgment may be ventured that theology has entered on a phase more emphatically apologetic than any since the early Apologists.

It seems that these are the facts. Is there an explanation of them? Why has recent theology swerved in this direction? An answer may be found by enquiring why the prediction mentioned at the beginning of this chapter missed the mark so widely. It was evidently based on a premise that turned out to be false. "During the last several generations we who preach the gospel have been far too ready to assume that the modern man had developed an immunity against its appeal. We have approached him apologetically . . . And now, it would seem we are beginning to learn our mistake."[7] But the assumption was not in fact a mistake—or if it was, it was so for a time so brief as to be over almost before it began. Where modern theology exhibits growing points, the assumption is taken as true. It is accepted as the key giving entry to the modern world and the mind of modern man, and hence a key of which theology must avail itself if Christianity is to be effectively got across. Hence the impressive resumption of apologetic theology that is so notable a feature of today. Theology has moved in this direction because of a revived interest in the world in which Christianity operates, and because this interest has led to an appreciation of the world that has to admit the truth of the assumption.

Almost suddenly, it seems, thinkers committed to Gospel and Church have become newly aware of the world. It is all very well to sing blithely: "There were ninety and nine that safely lay in the shelter of the fold: But one was out on the hills away, Far off from the gates of gold." But it is a gross misappreciation of the situation. As someone reminds us,[8] "ninety five are already outside and giving precious little sign that they feel even chilly. And of the other five, four are peering over the top wondering what it is like outside." It is a commonplace to say that the Church is once again everywhere in a missionary situation. The practical theologians and ecclesiastical strategists have been saying this for quite a long time. Now it seems that the theoretical theologians have caught up.

Christianity does not easily understand the world, nor can it readily prescribe what the relation of the Christian to the world should be. There is little doubt that an essential part of the difficulty derives from the distinction so facilely made between Church *and* world. No doubt the principle that Scripture supplies is clear enough: in the world, but not of it. But what exactly does this mean in practice? what especially does it mean for today as the Church feels the world breathing down its neck? Certainly we no longer live in an Age of Constantine; the day of the dream of a *corpus Christianum* is over. So what do we do now? Some face the situation with apprehension. Christians feel nervous about the proximity of the world and are tempted to retire into a Christian ghetto. From there no doubt timorous little apologetic sorties may be made to bring Christ to a world from which he has been shut out. But no one's heart will really be in such ventures. The *journées des barricades* are with us again. At best, interest will swing towards improving the domestic defences; at worst in the direction of interior decoration. Then the apologetic task goes by default—it cannot be undertaken seriously with averted eyes. But another typical attitude to the new situation is marked rather by elation. J. A. T. Robinson, with his usual flair for striking quotations, cites[9] the testimony of Monica Furlong: "The best thing about being a Christian at the moment is that organized religion has collapsed . . . I cannot imagine a more enjoyable time to be a Christian, except possibly the first few centuries of the Church. For while the great holocaust is sweeping away much that is beautiful and all that is safe and comfortable and unquestioned, it is relieving us of mounds of *bric-à-brac* as well, and the liberation is unspeakable. Stripped of our nonsense, we may almost live like the early Christians painting their primitive symbols on the walls of the catacombs—the fish, the grapes, the loaves of bread, the cross, the monogram of Christ—confident that in having done so they had described the necessities of life."

So the world has moved up into very close quarters with the Church. It is a situation that is equally full of threat and of promise—a situation exhibiting the classic features of apologetic opportunity. How have the theologians tackled it? The answer seems to be that some have worked at explaining it and others at devising tactics to confront it. We ought to look at each of these responses in turn.

Like the skyscrapers of Fifth Avenue and now elsewhere, a new kind of age has arisen around the Church, towering over it and dwarfing what were once prominent landmarks. But the change is not the result of explicit hostility to the Christian faith. It has not even taken place in separation from it. It is rather to be seen as a consequence flowing from Christian faith. The revolution has been triggered off by science—but by science in its modern guise, not the science practised in classical or mediaeval times. How does modern science differ from its older counterparts? The differentia seems to be the emergence of the experimental method. Experimental method in this context means the manipulation of the things of nature: the investigation of them under "lab" conditions in which they are isolated from their natural context and obliged under, as it were, cross-examination to answer questions directed to them. No doubt many discoveries of first-class importance have been made by accident—an apple falling at Newton's feet, a boiling kettle disturbing George Stephenson's drowsiness. But it is the application of systematic experimental method that has made the advance of science so swift and sure-footed.

The experimental method can be employed only where men feel at home in the world and on a familiar footing with it. Serious investigation will never be undertaken so long as taboos, superstitions and fears impede men in their handling of natural things. The investigator must feel secure about his place in the world, and not be handicapped by nervousness that the world may in some unforeseeable way answer back. This feeling of security the Greeks, for example, never had: "the Greeks were always afraid", says Gilbert Murray. To illustrate, if the Englishman's home is his castle, his playground is his garden. But the Greeks never had gardens. The nearest thing they had were the groves surrounding the temples, and these were specifically the domain of Pan, and hence areas if not of terror at least of profound uneasiness. Yet from say the time of the Renaissance the experimental method was put into operation, and the conditions making it possible must have been fulfilled. How were the inhibiting nervousness and fears overcome? They can conceivably be overcome by a reliable intimation that the world around is in the hands of a power well-disposed towards men. This assurance the Christian faith is clearly well able to give. In the light of the Gospel the fears not only disappear but are destroyed. But if this is true, then it is no longer war to the knife between faith and science, between the Christian religion and the modern world. Christian faith has been largely instrumental in bringing to birth the world as today we know it. The launching pad is thus prepared for a positive apologetic commendation of faith to the modern world.

This line of thought has had distinguished advocates. John Baillie was accustomed to accept it largely in the terms in which it has been stated. John Macmurray writes:[10] "The one creative achievement of the Reformation was science and the scientific spirit. Science is thus the legitimate child of a great religious movement, and its genealogy goes back to Jesus." "Christian faith frees man from the world"—in these words R. G. Smith[11] rightly sums up the message of Gogarten; and in the preceding pages he supplies a note on the development of this line of thought by recent advocates. Similarly C. F. von Weizsäcker[12] holds that the rise of science and scientism is unintelligible unless it is referred to the seedbed of Christian thought from which it has arisen.

The same kind of argument is developed in greater detail and at greater depth by **Arend Th. van Leeuwen** in his important work called *Christianity in World History*.[13] It is not so much the scientific or technical aspect of the modern world that arrests his attention, but rather its secularity. When secularization is traced to its source, it is discovered to take its rise from the understanding to which the Old Testament gives expression and of which the New Testament and Christianity are the heirs. Van Leeuwen starts by comparing the people of Israel with the surrounding primitive cultures. Where these saw all existence as an unbroken whole of sacred power, Israel saw the world as the arena of its ethical covenant with God. It knew itself called to historicity instead of myth, to responsibility instead of mysticism. In contrast with the static cultus of that world, its culture was a spirit of dynamic secularity. Secularization takes its rise from Israel. Here is raised the protest against the unitariness of the cosmic totality, against the sacralizing of all being, against the supremacy of fate, against the divinizing of kings and kingdoms. Here a break is made with the everlasting cycle of nature and the timeless presentness of myth. Here history is discovered at the point where covenant is made by the Creator with his creation, by the Lord with his people, and this bursts wide open the solid oneness of the universe. So man is given the taste of freedom and room in which to practise it. The world is secularized; it is made the arena of history; and it moves forward towards regeneration through pain and travail, as it awaits the redemption and consummation of all things.[14]

Van Leeuwen supplies the terms in which this can be expressed when he suggests that the pagan understood the world as an ontocracy, whereas Israel conceived it as a theocracy. That is, the pagan regarded all things as ontologically one, God and the world making one single totality; but Israel perceived that God was God and the world was the world, and that a line of distinction ran between the two, the rift which God has bridged from his side by his making covenant with Israel. This is the starting point of the process whose latest products we today witness. The secular spirit is the result of what God has revealed to man through Israel, through the coming of his Son, and through the proclamation of the Gospel. If this is so, then mankind is being led into secularization by the Lord of history himself. There are no doubt dangers, but God is prepared to risk them; and those he leads forward he arms with promises.

Secularization is thus explained not as the inexorable foe of Christianity, but rather as a continuation of Christianization.[15] The view that the process of Christianization ground to a halt at the time of the Renaissance and was replaced by a fundamentally different process, that of secularism, may cheerfully be abandoned. It is also clear that this explanation of the modern world involves a certain practical attitude on the part of Christians: explanation spills over into the theology that is more concerned with the tactics demanded by the situation. So far from abandoning the world and letting it go to the devil in its own way, Christians should rather be infinitely concerned for the world, and also deeply interested in what the secularizing world has to say to and for the faith. Secularization is potential ally rather than irreconcilable foe. The defence of the faith consists not in running away, but in instituting conversation between the biblical, theological, orthodox heritage, and the contemporary human situation.

One proviso has to be made. Secularization is the Christian ferment in history; it is Christ incognito at work. But a simple identification of the two is not possible. Secularization is not only a remarkably hidden work of God; some of what goes on under its name is not Christ at work at all. Van Leeuwen distinguishes[16] between secularization and secularism. Secularization is a process, continuing and dynamic, describable as "the withdrawal of life and thought from religious, and finally also from metaphysical, control, and the attempt to understand and live in these areas in the terms which alone they offer." This imparts a sense of freedom, as the fetters of traditional thought are thrown aside. But this new-found freedom may fall into the wrong hands: secularism may take charge. Secularism in distinction from secularization is an ideology which thinks of a concrete world without God, but forgets that this can be rightly said only because God has told men in this modern age to live this way. Hence van Leeuwen's apologetic explanation of the modern world by no means endorses all that goes on in it. The situation to which secularizing tendencies have led is ambivalent. All depends on whose hand grasps the tiller. Secularization is a continuing process in which man is aware of the relativity of his perspectives. Secularism on the other hand is a fixed and absolutized ideology with a tendency towards pagan or nihilistic totalitarianism, in which man's freedom is denied and conformity to human authority substituted for responsibility before God. According to the first God holds himself back in restraint and at some distance, giving men a chance to be freely responsible. According to the other, God is a priori outlawed and denied; and the irons drop on to the wrists and lock themselves fast again. It will be observed that at this point there is close resemblance to Bonhoeffer.[17] But this leads to the second apologetic handling of the modern situation, which proposes the tactics to be adopted.

What **Rudolf Bultmann** has to say is of both theoretical and tactical importance. General attention focused upon him when, in company with Martin Dibelius, he devised a method of biblical study which came to be known as Form Criticism (*Formgeschichte*), based on a recognition that the circumstances in which the Gospels were written affected their composition.[18] Bultmann himself proceeded further along the same road and discovered that it opened out into another distinctive method of biblical study for which in 1941 he first used the forbidding term "demythologizing" (*Entmythologisierung*).[19] The intention lying behind the construction and application of this method is manifestly apologetic in character. He wishes to make the Gospel as intelligible as possible to modern man. However, one major obstacle prevents modern man's acceptance of it: the mythological form in which it is presented in the Scriptures. But this particular difficulty is quite adventitious: the mythical form was the natural way in which to present the Gospel in the day when it was first preached. Only since then has it become an embarrassment and a difficulty. For example, it was natural then to think in terms of a three-decker universe, with heaven above, the under-world below, and the world we know in between; and accordingly natural also to think of Jesus coming down from heaven, of a descent into hell, and of an ascension taking him back to heaven. But it is quite alien for men today to think in such terms. Bultmann finds that this mythological element is fortunately dispensable. Since it invests the Gospel today with unnecessary difficulty, it must be stripped off. Hence the demythologizing enterprise.

Bultmann would deny the suggestion that he is simply making the Gospel agreeable to man, and he is justified in doing so. He really does think there is a genuine *skandalon* in the Gospel; and this stumbling block he will not attempt to remove. His intention is to cut it down to Gospel size and shape, and this means paring away the accretion of adventitious difficulty associated with it. In his own words,[20] we must "eliminate a false stumbling block and bring into sharp focus the real stumbling block, the word of the cross." Hence Bultmann's proposal has nothing to do with the liberalizing tendencies observable at the beginning of the century. His apologetic approach is really quite different.

But the mythological form did in the first and biblical presentation of the Gospel have a real function to perform. It sharpened the Gospel into the form of a challenge for the men to whom it was addressed. If Bultmann is not by discarding the mythology of the original Gospel to lose an important element, he must look around for something to perform for modern man the function it discharged. He finds it in the existentialist philosophy of Heidegger and others. The dominant principle of this philosophy is that man is to be understood not as something that is but rather as something that is in the making or becomes; and he becomes by the decisions he makes. To cut a long story very short indeed, authentic existence can only be reached by way of the right decisions being taken. Jesus

Christ comes to man as the one who makes the right decisions possible for him.[21] In him God offers us a really live option which, if we decide upon it in faith, leads to the achievement of this end. In this way God can be made meaningful to modern man.

Taking stock for a moment before pressing on, we may note that it is very doubtful whether Bultmann is right in thinking that biblical mythology is a difficulty for modern man of the dimensions he makes out. But this objection even if true is not of first-class importance for the present purpose. What is of greater relevance is the direction in which Bultmann is evidently turning. He invites us to focus attention upon man himself, his present being, his potential authentic being, and the means whereby he can attain that authenticity. In his desire to commend the Gospel to man, Bultmann takes up position beside him and argues the Christian case from that standpoint.

On the other side of the Atlantic the most considerable figure in theology has for quite a long time been **Paul Tillich**.[22] From start to finish Tillich is similarly by intention a purveyor of the Gospel and deliberately adopts an apologetic approach. Theology must make contact with man, for only so does it discharge its responsibilities. In principle Tillich turns in the same direction as Bultmann: he takes a long hard look at man in himself. Theology, he says,[23] "must answer the questions implied in the general human and the special historical situation." Already the special object of his attention has disclosed itself. The examination discovers three elements. There is concern. "Man, like every living thing, is concerned about many things, above all about those which condition his very existence, such as food and shelter."[24] But "man, in contrast to other living beings, has spiritual concerns—cognitive, aesthetic, social, political." In particular he is possessed by an "ultimate concern"; and while all the spiritual concerns mentioned compete for ultimacy, none of them is identical with it. Faith according to Tillich "is the state of being ultimately concerned", and accordingly can find satisfaction in none of them. In the second place Tillich accepts in his own way the idea of revelation. "God," he says,[25] "is manifest only through God." Hence man himself is not the source of knowledge of God. Such knowledge must be given to him. Then the third point follows. This giving takes place in terms of the principle of "correlation". There is, he says,[26] a "correlation between existentialist questions and theological answers"—the first we ask, the second God supplies. We must accept "the inability of man to reach God under his own power". Tillich does not think we can "derive the divine self-manifestation from an analysis of the human predicament". But he does believe that analysis of the human predicament reveals a situation upon which the content of the Gospel can apparently be exactly superimposed for its relief. And he does think that man knows God at least under the form of a question: "Man as man knows the question of God." When it is discovered that the answer given fits the questions asked and the concern felt, then a man has existential awareness of God, and faith and belief follow. Under the principle of correlation, the Gospel slots neatly home into a position whose shape is determined by human concern.

Clearly this raises a serious question. Is the correlation of "existential question" and "theological answer" really so exact? Does superimposition take place neatly edge to edge? Is such a close fit possible without any remoulding of the situation? An element evident in the Gospel has apparently been allowed to slip out: the Gospel must itself arouse in man the questions to which it is the answer. In the New Testament Jesus asked questions that had never occurred to anyone: is healing lawful on the sabbath? why do you call me good? who do you say I am? and countless others. Moreover the answers he gives do not at all fit the questions already in men's minds, e.g. what would the Messiah do and be like when he came? In other words, correlation is not the whole story: the Gospel answers to the situation only by first of all profoundly disturbing it.

Fundamentally Bultmann and Tillich employ the same apologetic approach. The one diagnoses *Angst* as characteristic of the human situation, and the Gospel delivers him from this disagreeable condition. The other diagnoses questions asked in advance of God's revelation, which receive their reply in the revelation given. The approach is expounded in startling simplicity by John Macquarrie.[27] "The first principle of hermeneutics", that is of interpretation, and this means of Apologetics, is that there should be "some basis of common ground between an interpreter and his audience". Language about God is not such a starting point today. Where then shall we begin? The answer is that, whether we are Christians or secularists, we share in humanity. Let us therefore begin there. It is true that throughout the course of Christian thought the Gospel has been represented as being applicable to the human situation: it is *pro me* (for me), and in Christ *mea res agitur* (my business is being done). So Athanasius:[28] "It is then proper for us to begin by speaking of the creation of the universe, and of God its artificer, so that it may be duly perceived that the renewal of creation has been the work of the self-same Word that made it at the beginning." So St. Thomas: *gratia non tollit naturam sed perficit*[29] (grace does not destroy nature but perfects it). So Anselm: when he raises the question *Cur Deus Homo?* (why the God-man?) he answers in terms that show excellently how the work of salvation fits the human condition. But so far as I know never in the course of Christian thought has so resolute an attempt been made not merely to fit salvation to human need, but to discover in human need the very contours of the salvation the Gospel offers. It cannot be assumed that communicability is a reliable test of truth. If it be said in defence of the modern way of thought that a desperate situation needs desperate apologetic measures, one may sympathize, but at the same time doubt whether the remedy advocated contains the fulness of the Gospel, and if not whether the remedial measures will meet the case.

**Dietrich Bonhoeffer** has something in common with the thinkers just dealt with and much not in common.[30] He shares with them the great seriousness with which they regard the modern world. He agrees that this modern world manifests a striking godlessness which has to be taken into account. But from this point on there is more disagreement than agreement. Bonhoeffer is in fact much more radical in his diagnosis than Bultmann and Tillich. They work with the idea of an *Angst* in men that is met by the Gospel, or questions already being asked to which the Gospel replies. Hence they think it is the job of Apologetics to bring back God in a form congruent with the situation as they have diagnosed it. But Bonhoeffer will have nothing to do with *Angst* and already formed questions; and hence he cannot bring back a God to comply with these terms. Rather, he says, we have to make up our minds that God really has withdrawn and to fortify ourselves with the knowledge that it is really God intact and unreduced that has withdrawn.

Bonhoeffer's theology, fragmentary as it is, bears the print of nails. In his experience of evil incarnate in the totalitarian system and the concentration camp, the world suddenly disclosed itself to him in its shameless godlessness. There is no awareness of God, no inclination for God. It is a world that cannot even conceive that God can have any intelligible meaning.[31] You say "God" in this situation—and there is not a ghost of an echo. How then do you communicate God and the things of God where resonance is entirely absent? Bonhoeffer's answer is not to patch up a Gospel measured by the needs disclosed by analysis of the human situation. God is not thus to be measured, and such a measured God cannot be commended to the world. Rather Bonhoeffer asks how the world got like this. Reflecting that much of what has come from his pen was written in the prison camp at Flossenburg, we might suppose that he would identify the cause of this modern malaise as sheer badness, a badness that makes modern man turn away from God, a badness so monstrous that the old argument from the goodness of the world to the existence of the good God is farcical. But this is not at all Bonhoeffer's diagnosis. It is not from man's sinful weakness that the modern inability to take God seriously arises, but rather from his strength; not because he is unsuccessful in the business of living, but because he has been so successful. Secular man gets on very well without God. The secularized world has no room for him. In his famous phrase, man has come of age.

The fact is that the traditional way of looking for God has proved a failure. Here theology as a whole and Apologetics in particular come in for strong criticism. They have been accustomed to put up defences for God and fight rearguard actions to protect him. They have fitted him into the gaps where human knowledge had not yet penetrated—only to find, however, that one by one these gaps yielded before the advance of modern knowledge. Slowly and surely the spheres in which God was supposed to be active contracted as modern knowledge expanded; and its advance necessitated God's ignominious retreat. Miracles are an obvious example. Finally God had to be confined to the areas on the limits of secular existence—the so-called ultimate questions concerning guilt, death, and so on. But, asks Bonhoeffer, what if these too should yield to the assaults of secular knowledge? What if they too were capable of being answered without recourse to God?[32] If you try to fit God into gaps of human knowledge and experience, you are forced into a continual retreat taking your God with you. The number of places where God can hole up is diminishing; and from this diminished number he is being steadily smoked out. The God of the gaps is being "killed by inches"; he has "died the death of a thousand qualifications".

If then we look around the world, we are unable to find convincing evidence for God. But, Bonhoeffer tells us, this is not a situation to be regretted, but rather to be accepted and welcomed. This is precisely what we have to mean in speaking of man as come of age. He has come to the realization that God is not to be found where traditionally it was thought he could be. As the secular world is the consequence of the growth of man's knowledge, it is not to be resented but accepted, and regarded as in fact a direct though rather surprising consequence of the place which God has accorded to man in his universe. This means that God is himself leading men into this new age:[33] he is calling on them to live as fully responsible persons, *etsi deus non daretur* (even if God is not given), not simply as though there were no evidence of him in the world, but even if in fact there is none. God will mollycoddle us no longer: we have to be up and doing in this world from which he has withdrawn himself. This is the essence of "religionless Christianity" which is all that is now left to us. Bonhoeffer's plea is that we cease to defend God before the world by trying to find God in that world. We have rather to defend him as the God who really has withdrawn, just as when he came to the world he was sent to the cross. God in great humility holds himself aloof to make room for the world to exercise a new-won independence. But at the same time we have to "stand by God"[34] since we are still those "to whom God has spoken"[35]. Bonhoeffer meets the unbeliever in partial agreement: God *has* withdrawn; and also in fundamental disagreement: *God* has withdrawn.

If Bonhoeffer is put into context with Bultmann and Tillich, it appears that he halts the movement of thought and diverts it in a new direction. God is not simply an explanation of human existence, but is plainly more and other than that. This is indeed stated in terms strikingly different from those used in orthodox Dogmatics or Apologetics. But they are terms that at least are intelligible to modern man. The outcome of what he has to say can be thought of under two aspects. Christians have to abandon the morose and suspicious attitude they have so often taken up over against the world. This secular world is not to be disapproved but approved, not to be shunned and avoided but entered with discrimination and without fear. It is God's world, and the very shape it now assumes is not atheist in essence but fundamentally theistic, though in an indirect and concealed way. Even the unbeliever is not out of touch with God. It would indeed be a gross injury to his responsible existence to say that he is a concealed theist after all. But it is true to say that God has not broken off contact with him. The other aspect then becomes clearer. The difference between believer and unbeliever is that the one is aware and the other unaware that this is the case. Quoting Yves Congar approximately, we may say that "the world is in God like a wounded man recovering consciousness". You do not run for refuge behind barred doors from a wounded man: you run out to him with all the medicaments on which you can lay hands. Who will not say that the finest medicaments are not in the hands of those who have the Gospel? In this sense then the finest and in the end the only right defence of Christianity is to move out into the world, stricken with its own coming of age, and by saying and doing the Gospel in its fulness make the Gospel evident and available. Bonhoeffer's is an apologetic that summons to action.

It is not yet clear whether the **'Death of God' Theology** is going to last very long or make a very deep impact on theological thinking. The answer is probably not. But it merits attention here because of its evidently apologetic character. It is idle to talk of success or lack of success—some who called themselves Christian apologists have been reckoned to have done more harm than good to the understanding of Christian faith; and it may be that some who do not so call themselves will do more good than harm in commending it. The lines dividing friend from foe at the present time are even less clear than usual, and in the no man's land between a good many skirmishers are operating who do not evidently wear the badges of one side or the other.

But apologetic work is being carried out by those that can be assembled under the intriguing appellation of the "death of God" theology. This is made clear by the cool and unsentimental look they have directed upon the modern world and the appreciation to which this leads them. They wish at all costs to talk to and about the real situation, not to shut themselves up in ivory towers and broadcast communiques which, however true, are not listened to. Thomas J. J. Altizer for example is foremost in demanding that the modern world be scrutinized, understood and assessed: only then can theology really speak to it, for "only a contemporary theology can be a Christian theology".[36] This scrutiny leads them to the conclusion that, so far from being a help in explaining the world, the idea of God is a positive hindrance to modern man. According to Paul van Buren[37] the term God is meaningless; and hence his theology is developed without reference to God. According to Altizer God is not only a meaningless idea in the culture of today but a total absentee. The doubt inspired by linguistic analysis whether the term God has any real referent is developed into a denial that there is anything in the direction indicated by the term. It takes little skill to see that here a process reaches its terminus. Bonhoeffer tells us that we must live *etsi deus non daretur*—not that God is not, but that he is not given. J. A. T. Robinson thinks that God conceals himself in a strange anonymity in the depths of all experience and especially in the relationships we have with others. Van Buren believes the existence of God to be so doubtful that he prefers to construct a reductionist theology in which there is no place for God. In Altizer the line runs out to its end in the assertion that what does not discernibly figure in experience, life or world, neither is there nor even is, and the death of God is announced.

This is heady stuff. What does it amount to? Beneath the eye-catching headlines an apologetic aspect is detectable. It is not being alleged that God simply ceases to exist, or that he is non-existent. The meaning rather is that what we say about God, i.e. his relevance to the world, cannot be expressed in the terms traditionally used, such as supernatural, transcendent, miracles, or even inner experience. Modern man is simply not aware of any sphere over and above and beyond the absorbing world around him; and characteristically he has no longer an experience or feeling of God to which appeal can be made. Certainly in his actions he takes less account of God than ever before. Even the man of faith today is put off praying and reading the Bible by the character and atmosphere of the world around him. What then is said about God must be said within the general awareness of the absence of God, or within the general absence of awareness of God. The "death of God" theology is an attempt to answer the question: how does one do that? The intention is not fundamentally atheistic. Rather it tries to present God to an atheistic generation.

The attempt has some similarity to Bonhoeffer's work. But it is also deeply dissimilar. In Bonhoeffer there is a tension: God is of course real; but the secular world is also real. God's presence there can only be as the crucified, the one that has to be got rid of, the one who is pushed to the wall. But the new radical theology relinquishes this solid unambiguous affirmation and conviction concerning God. It follows then that the tension Bonhoeffer saw characterizing the relation of Christianity and the world is relaxed. The relationship of God to the world is nothing like so drastic or shocking as a cross. Not at all—if there is a God he is quietly there, somewhere anonymously present, not calling attention to himself. Man therefore has only one reality to bother about: the secular world. Then, relieved of the tension, man may live in the world secularized as it is, with abandon and joy: it is to be accepted exultantly. The question of God is not a different question from the world itself. It is somehow part of the world and so does not give rise to the uneasiness that a genuinely other factor must occasion. So the world becomes the grave of God. It is true that in some form God may be thought of as there—buried, his remains really remaining; and over them the epitaph: God is dead.

When we assess this radical theology we are really commenting upon the whole course of this rather strange modern theology of which it is the end product. The first thing that strikes the observer is the very uncritical view taken of the secular world. William Hamilton[38] talks of it as "the new optimism". No doubt Christianity has too often been morose and grudging in its assessment of the world, far too slow to acknowledge the advantages that secular activity has achieved without help from Christianity or Church. But the unrestricted endorsement of the modern world recommended by the radical theology rings hollow—a kind of ghastly frenzy of praise trying to drown the disturbing sounds made by a world in which not only are more people more affluent than ever before but also more people are more distressed than since the dawn of history. There is an earnest endeavour to be "with it", but not much to be discerningly prophetic.

The new appraisal of the world leads to a presentation of the Gospel which disregards a central contention of that Gospel, that the world is a place in which a cross stands. Here is a sign of inexhaustible significance. It is rightly taken as the sign of forgiving love. But this by itself can easily slip into acceptance of Heine's blasphemy: *Le dieu pardonnera naturellement—c'est son métier* (of course God will pardon—it is his job). The fact is that it is equally the sign of man's utter need of forgiveness. So we must rather say that God makes it his *métier* to forgive—he allows himself to be constrained by our need. In order then to effect reconciliation between himself and man, God lets himself be pushed out—on to a cross. That was real and visible enough. As Bonhoeffer reminds us: God's weakness is plain for all to see. Of course he does again assert his strength (though this is an element to which Bonhoeffer hardly does justice). But when he does so, it is in a quite hidden manner, by means of a resurrection which is not a purely historical event.

To take the cross with this Gospel seriousness has consequences which the radical theology fails to observe. As said, it tries to present God in terms understandable to a godless world. In order to do so, it goes out into the world and takes up position in it alongside of the modern man to whom it is commending the Gospel. As real compassion in action, this is from any point of view admirable. But the action goes farther. The man beside whom position is taken up is pushed into the centre of things, into a place where he becomes not so much the beneficiary of the Gospel but the measure of it. The revelation is regarded as authentic in so far as it ministers to his needs. The measured mile on which the Gospel shows its paces is man himself. The norm of validity is man. Here new theology shows itself as old anthropology.[39] From the heart of the Gospel there sounds a note of warning and correction. When Jesus entered upon his public career, the first word is: Repent (Mark 1.15). When the Church embarked upon the discharge of its commission in public ministry to the world, its first word also is: Repent (Acts 2.38). It is difficult to think that this is a dispensable element in the Gospel. If it is not dispensable, the anthropocentric standpoint of the new theology is undermined. It is changed man that is member of the Kingdom. An apologetic that is preoccupied with analysis of man as he is, denies or obscures this; and then the Gospel is not conveyed and commended in its fulness.

We are obliged now to turn back the pages to a theologian whose birthday 200 years ago was remembered in 1968. **Friedrich D. E. Schleiermacher** said of someone: "He did not found a school but an era"; and Karl Barth applies the words to him.[40] Barth continues: "The first place in a history of the theology of the most recent times belongs and will always belong to Schleiermacher, and he has no rival." Though he lived a long time ago, Schleiermacher struck out on the path which in one of its sidetracks has led to the new radical theology.[41] Schleiermacher's first notable work is the *Reden über die Religion*[42] of 1799, which is unmistakably apologetic in intention. Schleiermacher's objective is to carve out for religion and so for Christianity a warmer place in the sun than the chilly intellectualism of the eighteenth century allowed it. Religion, he says, is more than knowing (as Wolff, Kant's predecessor made out) and more than doing (to which Kant inclined to reduce it). Beyond these, religion is a function in its own right, a function of feeling, and may be defined as the feeling of absolute dependence or pious self-awareness.

It might seem that in making this proposal Schleiermacher was doing little to commend Christianity. But this is not so. Both in the work named and in the famous Introduction to *The Christian Faith*[43] he plunges into the contemporary modern world which he regarded as inadequately analysed into science and ethics alone, and shows that its culture is incomplete without religion, its cultural awareness a headless torso without the feeling of absolute dependence. Schleiermacher is the apologist *par excellence*, sympathetically absorbing the culture of his day, incisively analysing it, passionately affirming it, anxiously proclaiming that religion brings to completion the unfolding and exaltation of human life that culture too desires. "He wanted in all circumstances to be a modern man as well as a Christian theologian."[44]

The formal similarity with recent radical theology is evident. But there is substantial similarity as well. Schleiermacher deliberately makes religion anthropocentric. The essence of religion is feeling; the object of theology is pious self-awareness; the statements of theology, he even suggests, are descriptions of human states of mind: "Christian doctrines are accounts of the Christian religious affections set forth in speech"[45]; their only value that thereby "the utterances of the religious consciousness come into circulation more surely and with a wider range than is possible through direct expression."[46] Schleiermacher thus deflects theological thought into a new and uncharted channel. The presentation of Christianity from which he dissents had reduced Christianity to reasonable propositions about God, and Christian faith to assent to them. Schleiermacher is certain this view is wrong, and accordingly stokes the fires that smoulder in religion itself behind this cold intellectual facade until they glow hot again. Thereby he switches attention to man's response to God and locates religion in feeling. He still believes that this procedure can yield something genuinely objective. He can speak of "descriptions of human states, or conceptions of divine attributes and modes of action, or utterances regarding the constitution of the world." But clearly we are near the edge. A strong head is needed to withstand the currents sweeping towards pure subjectivism. It is all too easy to strip these reports arising from examination of human states of their outward reference, and reduce them to private statements without real referent or public validity. There is no doubt that Schleiermacher genuinely tried to conceive of religion as an ellipse with twin foci: there is God's revelation and there is man's experience of it. But his attempt to hold the two foci separate and to give them equal value is not wholly successful. Slowly and ineluctably they move towards one another towards the point of coincidence. Schleiermacher leaves theology with the possibility that the two may come to coincide.

Barth recalls[47] words Schleiermacher used. "I rejoice in the conviction that I have seen at least from afar the form of a freer and livelier way of treating the teaching of faith." He was justified in saying so, for he prepared the trail leading into a new land that no one had mapped before. The modern radical theologians are well within this Canaan. With them the two foci which Schleiermacher declined to unite move increasingly close to one another, until in the end we have served up to us an anthropology in which there is room only for a dead God. The reasons why Schleiermacher's reluctance has been overcome are no doubt various. Each age has its characteristic intellectual difficulties which it is the task of Apologetics to try to remove. A technical age knows itself the beneficiary of extraordinarily successful thinking activity and is liable to be slightly intoxicated by its own success. Man's creatureliness comes to be thought of as consisting not in agreement with nature but in protesting against it. In upsetting and revolutionizing nature he makes history. This is one of the important growing points of thought today. It is also the point at which it is not simply unintelligible to hold that the concept of man in his full powers ought simply to displace the idea of God. Bonhoeffer declares that modern man has ceased to need God. So man and his activities are great and obvious, and God and the things of God look small and elusive. God is there, but not evidently there. This delicate balance the radical theologians are unable to maintain. The two foci man and God slide towards one another and the world begins to eclipse God. For Bultmann God is known functionally. He is *pro me*; but it is a new and authentic self-understanding that is evoked. J. A. T. Robinson discards the symbols used to make reference to a transcendent God. We must find him in the depths of personal relations. Van Buren speaks for the most recent radical theology when he asks whether "Christianity is fundamentally about God or about man", and replies: "it is fundamentally about man".[48] The submergence of God in the "spiritual" activities of man is almost complete. But not quite. The "death of God" theologians convert the submergence into a drowning and announce that God is dead. Altizer believes that theology has only two options before it: either to withdraw from the present age into the security of orthodox ecclesiastical tradition, or to affirm the death of God. Only one of these options is acceptable: the key to the twentieth century is "the collapse of any meaning or reality lying beyond the newly discovered radical immanence of modern man, an immanence dissolving even the memory of the shadow of transcendence."[49] Schleiermacher's two foci have come to coincide; in their identity the eclipse of God is complete.

"Are you related to the great Dr. Haldane?" Professor J. B. S. Haldane was once asked. He replied: "It depends on whether identity can be called a relationship." If the reply leaves the question just the slightest degree open, so at the end of this trail we may think that perhaps the transcendent God who appears in the Bible is not quite so dead as has been reported.

The apologetic enterprise on which the radical theologians have embarked is at least bold. It is by no means clear that they have managed to transmit the Gospel intact. But their endeavour has one great value. They have undertaken the most serious engagement with the modern world, have made a perceptive appreciation of it, and have genuinely entered into it with at least their version of the Gospel in their hands. It has been said that this is a case of fools entering in where angels fear to tread. This may be so. But why are the angels so afraid?

# SOME BOOKS FOR FURTHER READING

*Chapter One:*
C. H. Dodd: *The Apostolic Preaching and its Developments*—Hodder & Stoughton, 1936.
G. B. Caird: *The Apostolic Age*—Duckworth, 1955.

*Chapter Two:*
F. L. Cross: *The Early Church Fathers*—Duckworth, 1960.
A. C. McGiffert: *A History of Christian Thought*, Vols. 1 & 2—Scribners, 1932–3.

*Chapter Three:*
F. L. Cross, see above.
A. C. McGiffert, see above.
Hans von Campenhausen: *The Fathers of the Greek Church*—Lutterworth Press, 1963.
Hans von Campenhausen: *The Fathers of the Latin Church*—Lutterworth Press, 1964.

*Chapter Four:*
A. C. McGiffert: Vol. 1, see above.
Hans von Campenhausen: *The Fathers of the Greek Church*—see above.

*Chapter Five:*
Gerald Bonner: *St. Augustine of Hippo*—S.C.M. Press, 1963.
J. H. S. Burleigh: *The City of God*—Nisbet, 1949.

*Chapter Six:*
Etienne Gilson: *The Spirit of Mediaeval Philosophy*—Sheed & Ward, 1936.
F. C. Coplestone: *Aquinas*—Pelican, 1955.
A. MacIntyre: *Difficulties in Christian Belief*—S.C.M. Press, 1959.

*Chapter Seven:*

E. G. Rupp: *The Righteousness of God*—Hodder & Stoughton, 1953.

Thomas M. McDonough: *The Law and the Gospel in Luther*—Oxford University Press, 1954.

François Wendel: *Calvin*—Fontana, 1965.

J. T. McNeill: *The History and Character of Calvinism*—Oxford University Press, 1954.


*Chapter Eight:*

L. Stephen: *History of English Thought in the 18th Century*—London, 1876.

A. C. McGiffert: *Protestant Thought before Kant*—Duckworth, 1911.


*Chapter Nine:*

I. G. Barbour: *Issues in Science and Religion*—S.C.M. Press, 1966.

C. F. von Weizsäcker: *The Relevance of Science*—Collins, 1964.

Charles C. West: *Communism and the Theologians*—S. C. M. Press, 1958.


*Chapter Ten:*

David Jenkins: *Guide to the Debate about God*—Lutterworth Press, 1966.

Lesslie Newbigin: *Honest Religion for Secular Man*—S.C.M. Press, 1966.

Thomas W. Ogletree: *The 'Death of God' Controversy*—S.C.M. Press, 1966.

Dean Peerman: *Frontier Theology*—S.C.M. Press, 1967.

Leslie Paul: *Alternatives to Christian Belief*—Hodder & Stoughton, 1967.

# NOTES

*Introduction*

[1] See A. B. Bruce, *op. cit.*, p. 42.

[2] See A. B. Bruce, *op. cit.*, p. 37.

[3] As A. Richardson, *op. cit.*, p. 20.

[4] *Church Dogmatics*, Vol. 1, Part 1, Edinburgh, 1936, p. 31.

[5] *Op. cit.*, Vol. 2, Part 1, Edinburgh, 1957, p. 95.

[6] *Op. cit.*, p. 93.

[7] *Dogmatik*, Band 1, Zürich, 1946, p. 110 (the English translation does not convey the meaning with the same sharpness).

[8] *Principles of Christian Theology*, London, 1966, p. 35.

[9] So also C. F. D. Moule, *The Phenomenon of the New Testament*, London, 1967, p. 6.


*Chapter One*

[1] See especially his *The Apostolic Teaching and its Developments*, London, 1936, and his *History and the Gospel*, London, 1938.

[2] *History and the Gospel*, p. 51.

[3] *Ibid.*, p. 53.

[4] E. Evans, *Corinthians* (The Clarendon Bible), Oxford, 1930, p. 73.

[5] *Op. cit.*, p. 74.

[6] A. Nygren, *Romans*, London, 1952, pp. 102–7; cf. C. H. Dodd, *The Epistle to the Romans*, London, 1932, pp. 18–30.

[7] See Hastings, *Dictionary of the Bible*, 2nd edition, 1963, article "Hebrews" by H. Chadwick.

[8] *The Epistle to the Hebrews*, Edinburgh, 1922, pp. 199 f.

[9] *History and the Gospel*, London, 1938, p. 123.

[10] *Revelation and Reason*, London, 1947, p. 289.

[11] *Apologetics*, Edinburgh, 1892, p. 376.

[12] See my own *The Authority of Holy Scripture*, London, 1957, pp. 260 ff., for a longer treatment of the subject.

[13] *Heil als Geschichte*, Tübingen, 1965, p. 300.

[14] *The Gospel Tradition and its Beginnings*, a study in the limits of *Form—geschichte*, London, 1957.

[15] *Introduction to the New Testament*, London, 1966, p. 99.

[16] *Luke the Historian in Recent Study*, London, 1961, p. 63; cf. p. 43.

[17] C. E. B. Cranfield, *The Teachers' Commentary*, London, 1955, p. 44.

[18] Each of the two options receives the support of modern scholarship: C. E. B. Cranfield supports the A. V. view, *op. cit.*, p. 440; the N.E.B. view is supported by A. J. B. Higgins in an unpublished essay on "The Fourth Gospel".

[19] *Op. cit.*, p. 162.

[20] *Op. cit.*, p. 163.

[21] *Loc. cit.*

[22] For a useful brief account see "The Relevance of the Logos Christianity" by David Hill, *Expository Times*, February, 1967; and also J. Jeremias, *The Central Message of the New Testament*, London, 1965, Ch. 4.

[23] C. H. Dodd, *The Interpretation of the Fourth Gospel*, London, 1953, p. 277.

[24] *Expository Times*, *loc. cit.*, p. 183.

[25] *New Horizons in Biblical Research*, London, 1966, p. 45.

*Chapter Two*

[1] *The Spirit in the Ancient Church*, London, 1912, p. 3.

[2] See J. N. D. Kelly, *Early Christian Doctrines*, London, 1958, pp. 22–8, for a longer account of Gnosticism.

[3] So called by Henry Chadwick, *Early Christian Thought and the Classical Tradition*, London, 1966, p. 14.

[4] *Op. cit.*, p. 31.

[5] See Henry Chadwick, *op. cit.*, p. 46.

*Chapter Three*

[1a] Ambrose was a convert friend and wealthy patron of Ovigen.

[1] *The Early Christian Fathers*, London, 1960, p. 137.

[2] *Patrology*, Freiburg, Edinburgh and London, 1960, p. 167.

[3] Altaner, *loc. cit.*, Cf. Charles Péguy: "Absence of God, presence of God—it is always God." See Daniel Halévy, *Péguy*, London 1946, p. 69.

*Chapter Four*

[1] Hooker has an English version of this phrase: "The whole world against Athanasius, and Athanasius against it" (*Laws of Ecclesiastical Polity*, 5.42.5).

*Chapter Five*

[1] *Dictionnaire de Theologie Catholique*, 1903, article "Augustin".

[2] See Gerald Bonner, *St. Augustine of Hippo*, London, 1963, p. 54, n. 2.

[3] *Op. cit.*, p. 157.

[4] *Oxford Dictionary of the Christian Church*, *ad loc.*

[5] Bonner, *loc. cit.*

[6] Bonner, *loc. cit.*

[7] Quoted Bonner, *op. cit.*, p. 161.

[8] See Bonner, *op. cit.*, p. 205, who offers the alternative descriptive names "whole picture" and "longterm view".

[9] *De Natura Boni*, 38; see J. H. S. Burleigh, *The City of God*, London, 1949, p. 338.

[10] See Bonner, *op. cit.*, for references, p. 218.

[11] In his "wager essay" (*Pensées*, Lafuma edn., p. 343), Pascal writes: "Heads God exists—if you win, you win everything; if you lose, you lose nothing . . . Take a bet that he exists."

[12] Bonner, *op. cit.*, p. 353.

[13] See e.g. M. C. D'Arcy, *Saint Augustine*, Cleveland, Ohio, 1957.

[14] See also Burleigh, *op. cit.*, p. 17

[15] *Op. cit.*, 10 *et al.*

[16] So. J. H. S. Burleigh, *op. cit.*, quoting *utcumque sunt similes* (5.18).

[17] So. J. H. S. Burleigh, *op. cit.*, p. 217.

[18] *The History of Dogma*, Vol. 7, p. 272.

*Chapter Six*

[1] Boswell, *Life of Johnson*, Hill-Powell edn., Vol. 1, p. 471.

[2] *Philosophical Fragments*, Princeton, 1936, p. 31.

[3] *Theism*, 1877, p. 59.

[4] *Op. cit.*, p. 425.

[5] Caldecott and Mackintosh, *Selections from the Literature of Theism*, 1924, p. 2.

[6] On this, see Karl Barth, *Anselm—fides quaerens intellectum*, London, 1960, and *Church Dogmatics*, Vol. 2, Part 1, Edinburgh 1957, p. 185.

[7] This and the following references from Kant are taken from the section "The Impossibility of an Ontological Proof of the Existence of God" in *Critique of Pure Reason*, N. Kemp Smith's edition, London, 1929, pp. 500-7.

[8] *The Idea of God*, London, 1920, p. 240.

[8a] See the section "The impossibility of a Cosmological Proof of the Existance of God", *op. cit.*, p. 507-514

[9] *The Idea of God*, p. 250.

[10] Quoting from E. Caird, Critical Philosophy of Kant, Vol. 2, p. 125.

[11] See the section "The Impossibility of the Physico-theological Proof", *op. cit.*, pp. 518-24.

[12] See especially his *Dialogues concerning Natural Religion*, 1779.

*Chapter Seven*

[1] Such a standard work as A. B. Bruce, *Apologetics*, Edinburgh, 1892, contains no mention of either Luther or Calvin in the index.

[2] See John T. McNeill, *The History and Character of Calvinism*, New York, 1954, pp. 116 f.

[3] R. H. Fife, *The Revolt of Martin Luther*, New York, 1957, p. 60, believes the first; Gordon Rupp, *The Righteousness of God*, London, 1953, p. 88, n. 2. the second.

[4] Thomas M. McDonough, *The Law and the Gospel in Luther*, Oxford, 1963, p. 162.

[5] Louis Bouyer, *The Spirit and Forms of Protestantism*, London, 1956, p. 153.

[6] So Rupp, *op. cit.*, p. 92.

[7] So McDonough, *op. cit.*, p. 43.

[8] So Rupp, *op. cit.*, p. 93.

[9] Both quoted by K. Barth, *Church Dogmatics*, Vol. 1, Part 1, Edinburgh, 1936, p. 33.

[10] *Christian Apologetics*, p. 24, n. 3.

[11] London, 1950, 2nd edn., p. 7.

[12] See J. K. Mozley, *Some Tendencies in British Theology*, London, 1951, p. 143.

*Chapter Eight*

[1] Leslie Stephen, *History of English Thought in the Eighteenth Century*, 1876, Vol. 1, p. 420.

[2] Lord Bolingbroke, *Works*, 1793 edn.

[3] E. Gilson, *God and Philosophy*, New Haven and Oxford, 1941, p. 106.

[4] By G. C. Joyce, 1911.

[5] *Protestant Thought before Kant*, London, 1919, p. 228.

[6] *Op. cit.*, p. 233.

[7] So McGiffert, *op. cit.*, p. 234.

[8] For example, by Anders Jeffner, *Butler and Hume on Religion*, Stockholm, 1966, pp. 71 *et al.*

[9] So McGiffert, *op. cit.*, p. 234.

[10] *Op. cit.*, Vol. 1, p. 287.

[11] A. Richardson, *Christian Apologetics*, p. 154, generalizes inaccurately when he says: "Until the nineteenth century it was generally agreed by Christian theologians, Catholic and Protestant alike, that the divine revelation given in the Scriptures was divinely guaranteed by the supernatural evidences of miracle and prophecy."

[12] A. Richardson (*op. cit.*, pp. 157 f.) seems to think that with the Deists belief in the miraculous was the first thing to be surrendered. But the order of things is rather different. As Deism passed over to denial of supernatural revelation and so parted company with orthodox Christian belief, it also relinquished belief in the miraculous for which it had no further use.

[13] L. Stephen, *op. cit.*, p. 409.

[14] L. Stephen, *op. cit.*, p. 410.

[15] Quoted by L. Stephen, *op. cit.*, p. 410.

*Chapter Nine*

[1] *A Short History of Science*, Oxford, 1941, pp. 1 f.

[2] *Op. cit.*, title of Ch. 1 and p. 10.

[3] *Loc. cit.*

[4] C. Singer, *op. cit.*, begins his account of the "revival of learning" with the heretical Peter of Abano, late thirteenth and early fourteenth centuries.

[5] *Op. cit.*, p. 164.

[6] *The Limits of Religious Thought Examined*, Oxford, 1858.

[7] Lecture 2, p. 66.

[8] Lecture, 7, pp. 248 f.

[9] *Arrows of Chace*, 1880, 1, 194.

[10] See for example the recent Ian G. Barbour, *Issues in Science and Religion*, London and Englewood Cliffs N.J., 1966.

[11] See N. Kemp Smith, *A Commentary to Kant's Critique of Pure Reason*, pp. 22 ff.

[12] I. G. Barbour, *op. cit.*, p. 26.

[13] C. Singer, *op. cit.*, pp. 251 f.

[14] R. S. Westfall, *Science and Religion in Seventeenth Century England*, p. 206, quoted by I. G. Barbour, *op. cit.*, p. 43, n. 20.

[15] I. G. Barbour, *op. cit.*, p. 42.

[16] *Op. cit.*, p. 43.

[17] In his *Exposition du Système du Monde*, 1796.

[18] Francis Darwin, *Life and Letters of Charles Darwin*, London, 1887. Vol. 1, p. 83.

[19] In *Lay Sermons, Essays and Reviews*.

[20] See G. E. Quinton, *Scientific and Religious Knowledge*, London, 1950, p. 39.

[21] See *Encyclopaedia of Religion and Ethics*, 1911, article "Darwinism", p. 403.

[22] For a racy account of the encounter see William Irvine, *Apes, Angels and Victorians*, London, 1955, pp. 3 ff.

[23] R. H. Strachan, *The Authority of Christian Experience*, London, 1929, p. 178.

[24] Quoted by I. G. Barbour, *op. cit.*, p. 103.

[25] See my *The Authority of Scripture*, London, 1957, pp. 14 ff.

[26] See *The Relevance of Science*, London, 1964, p. 13.

[27] In a *Why I Believe* Collection of Essays.

[28] *Op. cit.*, p. 12.

[29] *The Varieties of Religious Experience*, London, 1902, p. 519.

[30] *Op. cit.*, p. 13.

[31] *Op. cit.*, p. 13.

[31] Karl Heim, *God Transcendent*, London, 1935, p. 75, n,

[32] *Doctrines of the Creed,* London 1938 etc., pp. 35 f.

[33] *Nature and God*, London, 1965, p. 82.

[34] *Op. cit.*, p. 96.

[35] *Reason and Emotion*, London, 1962, p. 172.

[36] *The Phenomenon of Man*, London, 1959, p. 160.

[37] *The Divine Relativity*, Yale, 1948, p. xv; see I. G. Barbour, *op. cit.*, p. 446, n.

[38] *The Phenomenon of Man*, p. 271.

[39] See his article in *Encyclopaedia of Religion and Ethics*, 1913.

[40] Hugh Watt in his article "Humanists" in Hastings' *Encyclopaedia of Religion and Ethics*.

[41] Margaret Knight, *Morals without Religion*, London, 1955, p. 19.

[42] "Christian Freedom", in *The Dublin Review*, July, 1942.

[43] London, 1961, compiled by Margaret Knight.

[44] *Op. cit.*, p. xiii.

[45] At best it can be only man's second oldest faith, as someone has pointed out, based on the serpent's suggestion in the garden of Eden that man usurp God's place for himself.

[46] Amsterdam Conference, 1952.

[47] *Encounter*, London, June, 1966.

[47a] See p. 185.

[48] English translation, *Christian Humanism*, 1938.

[49] *The Church's Witness to God's Design*, in *Man's Disorder and God's Design* Series, London, 1948, p. 38.

[50] *Ad Limina Apostolorum*, Zürich, 1967.

[51] *God, Grace and Gospel, Scottish Journal of Theology* Occasional Papers No. 8, 1959.

[52] See Karl Marx and Friedrich Engels, *The German Ideology*, translated by R. Pascal, 1938, pp. 6, 7.

[53] Margaret Knight, *Morals Without Religion*, p. 35.

[54] See J. M. Cameron, *Scrutiny of Marxism*, London, 1948, p. 83, n., a study to which what is written here owes much.

[55] Marx and Engels, *op. cit.*, pp. 22 ff.

[56] Karl Marx, *Capital*, preface.

[57] *Dialectics of Nature*, translated by C. Dutt, 1941, pp. 24, 25.

[58] *Agitator's Guide*, May, 1937, para. 13.

[59] Charles C. West, *Communism and the Theologians*, London, 1958, p. 12.

[60] Gollwitzer's *Unwilling Journey*, London, 1953, is an extraordinarily moving account of response to Communism, a spiritual classic fitted to stark modern conditions; the works of Hromadka are not readily available to English readers, but copious reference is made to them in C. C. West's book.

[61] Gollwitzer in *Evangelische Theologie*, October, 1950, used as a study document by W.C.C.

[62] A remarkable list ten pages long of books and articles in several languages appears in the periodical *Study Encounter*, No. III, Geneva, March, 1967.

[63] J. M. Cameron, *op. cit.*, p. 78.

[64] *Man in Revolt*, London, 1939, p. 439.

*Chapter Ten*

[1] *Our Knowledge of God*, London, 1939, pp. 14 f.

[2] It did not stand alone. The Editors' General Introduction to the Library of Constructive Theology, London, 1930 and later, suggested that "the time has gone by when 'apologetics' could be of any great value." See A. Richardson, *Christian Apologetics*, London, 1947, p. 24, n. 1.

[3] *The Significance of Karl Barth*, London, 1931, pp. 14, 13.

[4] *Op. cit.*, p. 14.

[5] *Church Dogmatics*, Vol. 4, Part 3, Edinburgh, 1962, p. 882.

[6] I allow myself a comment. It is a great pity that some theologians seize on such simple statements as though they could do duty for the sum total of what Barth has to say. They certainly save themselves a lot of trouble, but their consequent judgment is quite unreliable. See A. Richardson, *Christian Apologetics*, p. 22, n. 1: for Barth "faith is the contradiction of reason; the only true apologetic is the confrontation of unfaith by faith"—a comment that reflects harmfully on its writer rather than on Barth. Cf. too a similar sentiment expressed by Daniel Jenkins, *The Christian Belief in God*, London, 1964, p. 6, about Barth's "summary dismissal of unbelief".

[7] *Op. cit.*, p. 14.

[8] *Breakthrough*, Spring, 1966.

[9] *The New Reformation?* London, 1965, pp. 28 f.

[10] *Reason and Emotion*, p. 172 (quoted in previous chapter).

[11] *Secular Religion*, London, 1965, p. 152.

[12] *The Relevance of Science*, London, 1964.

[13] London, 1964.

[14] See Chs. 2 and 3.

[15] *Op. cit.*, pp. 329, 403.

[16] Pp. 334 *et al.*

[17] See p. 413.

[18] See Martin Dibelius, *The Message of Jesus*, London, 1939, and Rudolf Bultmann, *Jesus and the Word*, London, 1935.

[19] See Charles W. Kegley (editor), *The Theology of Rudolf Bultmann*, London, 1966, p. xxv.

[20] *Jesus Christ and Mythology*, London, 1960, p. 36.

[21] "The figure of Jesus . . . is no more than a kind of signal to men of the

occult truth which to know is life eternal"—so writes C. H. Dodd in *History and the Gospel*, London, 1938, p. 55. Dodd writes here of the Gnostics. Without a change of word, the statement might be applied to Bultmann.

[22] *Systematic Theology*, 3 vols., London, 1951–63; *The Dynamics of Faith*, London, 1957, supplies a reliable and much briefer account of Tillich's theology.

[23] *Systematic Theology*, Vol. 1, p. 35.

[24] *The Dynamics of Faith*, p. 1.

[25] *Systematic Theology*, Vol. 2, p. 75.

[26] *Op. cit.*, pp. 14 f.

[27] *Studies in Christian Existentialism*, London, 1965, p. 3f.

[28] *De Incarnatione*, 1, 4.

[29] *Summa Theologica*, qu. 1, art. 8.

[30] Many people have realized that the relation in which J. A. T. Robinson in his *Honest to God*, London, 1963, tied him up with Bultmann and Tillich does Bonhoeffer great injustice and disservice.

[31] So *Letters and Papers from Prison*, London, 1953, p. 152.

[32] *Op. cit.*, p. 178.

[33] So also van Leeuwen.

[34] *Op. cit.*, p. 200.

[35] H. Gollwitzer, *The Existence of God*, London, 1964, p. 238, n. 1.

[36] Thomas W. Ogletree, *The 'Death of God' Controversy*, London, 1966, p. 19; and for references to Altizer, n. 14.

[37] *The Secular Meaning of the Gospel*, London, 1963.

[38] *The New Essence of Christianity*, London, 1966.

[39] Theology in not alone is being affected by modern man's preoccupation with himself. Among younger people today there is much disenchantment with science, with its terrible objectivity and its inability to say what ought to be done. So the sociological disciplines have the largest classes in the universities. Similarly a different section of modern youth is creating a current vogue for seeking in the mysticism of the Far East a self-fulfilment without responsibility.

[40] From *Rousseau to Ritschl*, London, 1959, p. 306.

[41] David Jenkins in his *Guide to the Debate about God*, London, 1966, offers an appreciation of Schleiermacher's relevance for recent radical theology.

[42] English translation, *Religion Speaks to its Cultured Despisers*, 1893.

[43] German version 1821–2, English translation 1926.

[44] Karl Barth, *op. cit.*, p. 314.

[45] *The Christian Faith*, title to para 15.

[46] *Op. cit.*, para. 15.          [47] *Op. cit.*, p. 338.

[48] Quoted from an article by T. W. Ogletree, *op. cit.*, p. 51.

[49] *The Gospel of Christian Atheism*, Philadelphia, 1966, p. 22.

# INDEX TO SCRIPTURE PASSAGES CITED

# INDEX OF NAMES AND SUBJECTS